Iceland and E

'Thorhallsson's analysis provides the leading explanation for Icelandic resistance to European integration. His contribution significantly enhances our understanding of how and why political elites in Iceland are less likely to advocate EU membership than their neighbours. This book challenges theoretical approaches to the study of European integration from the inside out. It is a must read for scholars interested in diverging patterns of cooperation and resistance as Europe unifies.'
Professor Christine Ingebritsen, University of Washington

Why has Iceland not sought membership of the European Union?

This unique volume uses the case study of Iceland – the only Nordic state never to have applied for EU membership – to explore the complex attitudes of small states to European integration and provide a new theoretical approach for understanding such relationships.

The contributors seek to explain why the Icelandic political elite has been reluctant to participate in European integration. In this context, they analyse the influence that Iceland's special relationship with the USA and the fisheries sector have had on its dealings with the EU. Also considered are 'new' variables, such as national administrative characteristics and particular features of the domestic arena of the political elite, as well as the elite's perception of international relations and its political discourse concerning independence and sovereignty.

Iceland and European Integration will appeal to all those interested in European integration and the international relations of small states.

Baldur Thorhallsson is Associate Professor of Political Science, and Chairman of the Institute of International Affairs and the Centre for Small State Studies, at the University of Iceland.

Europe and the Nation State
Edited by Michael Burgess and Lee Miles
Centre for European Union Studies, University of Hull

This series explores the complex relationship between nation states and European integration and the political, social, economic and policy implications of this interaction. The series examines issues such as:

- the impact of the EU on the politics and policy making of the nation state and vice versa
- the effects of expansion of the EU on individual nation states in Europe
- the relationship between the EU and non-European states

1 **Poland and the European Union**
   Edited by Karl Cordell

2 **Greece in the European Union**
   Edited by Dionyssis G. Dimitrakopoulos and Argyris G. Passas

3 **The European Union and Democratization**
   Edited by Paul J. Kubicek

4 **Iceland and European Integration**
   On the edge
   Edited by Baldur Thorhallsson

5 **Norway and an Integrating Europe**
   Clive Archer

6 **Turkey and European Integration**
   Prospects and issues in the post-Helsinki era
   Edited by Nergis Canefe and Mehmet Uğur

Iceland and European Integration
On the edge

Edited by Baldur Thorhallsson

Routledge
Taylor & Francis Group
LONDON AND NEW YORK

First published 2004
by Routledge
2 Park Square, Milton Park, Abingdon, Oxon, OX14 4RN

Simultaneously published in the USA and Canada
by Routledge
270 Madison Ave, New York NY 10016

Routledge is an imprint of the Taylor & Francis Group

Transferred to Digital Printing 2006

© 2004 Baldur Thorhallsson for selection and editorial matter;
individual contributors their contributions

Typeset in Times by Wearset Ltd, Boldon, Tyne and Wear

All rights reserved. No part of this book may be reprinted or
reproduced or utilized in any form or by any electronic, mechanical,
or other means, now known or hereafter invented, including
photocopying and recording, or in any information storage or
retrieval system, without permission in writing from the publishers.

British Library Cataloguing in Publication Data
A catalogue record for this book is available from the British Library

Library of Congress Cataloging in Publication Data
Iceland and European integration : on the edge / edited by Baldur
Thorhallsson.
 p. cm.
Includes bibliographical references and index.
1. Iceland—Foreign relations—Europe. 2. Iceland—Politics and
government—20th century. 3. European Union—Iceland. I. Baldur
Thorhallsson.
DL375.I24.2004
327.41704'09'045—dc22

2003020219

ISBN10: 0-415-28252-7 (hbk)
ISBN10: 0-415-40666-8 (pbk)

ISBN13: 978-0-415-28252-9 (hbk)
ISBN13: 978-0-415-40666-6 (pbk)

To my children, Álfrún Perla and Guðmundur, who never stop asking critical questions.

Contents

List of figures	ix
List of tables	x
Notes on contributors	xi
Foreword	xii
Preface	xiv
List of abbreviations	xvi

1 Approaching the question: domestic background and conceptual framework   1
BALDUR THORHALLSSON

PART I

2 The first steps: Iceland's policy on European integration from the foundation of the republic to 1972   21
BALDUR THORHALLSSON
AND HJALTI THOR VIGNISSON

3 A controversial step: membership of the EEA   38
BALDUR THORHALLSSON
AND HJALTI THOR VIGNISSON

4 Deeply involved in the European project: membership of Schengen   50
STEFÁN EIRÍKSSON

PART II

5 Partial engagement: a practical solution   61
BALDUR THORHALLSSON

Contents

6 **Life is first and foremost saltfish**   67
   BALDUR THORHALLSSON
   AND HJALTI THOR VIGNISSON

7 **The special relationship between Iceland and the United States of America**   103
   BALDUR THORHALLSSON
   AND HJALTI THOR VIGNISSON

8 **Discussing Europe: Icelandic nationalism and European integration**   128
   GUÐMUNDUR HÁLFDANARSON

9 **The Euro-sceptical political elite**   145
   GUNNAR HELGI KRISTINSSON
   AND BALDUR THORHALLSSON

10 **Shackled by smallness: a weak administration as a determinant of policy choice**   161
   BALDUR THORHALLSSON

11 **Towards a new theoretical approach**   185
   BALDUR THORHALLSSON

   Index   209

Figures

6.1	Shares of individual market areas in Iceland's goods exports, 1955–99	71
6.2	Percentages of MPs with connections to the fishery sector in seven parliamentary terms, by party	81
6.3	Percentages of MPs with connections to the agricultural sector in seven parliamentary terms, by party	82
6.4	Percentages of MPs with connections to the industrial sector in seven parliamentary terms, by party	83
7.1	Location of the four principal parties in Iceland in terms of Left–Right orientation and their position on NATO membership and the US military base at Keflavík	106
7.2	Merchandise exports to the USA 1940–2000 as a percentage of total merchandise exports	121
10.1	The number of people working in the Icelandic foreign service from 1945 to 2003, all personnel included	168

Tables

6.1	Contribution of the fishing industry to the Icelandic economy, percentages of total	70
6.2	Percentages of MPs with connections to individual occupational sectors in seven parliamentary terms	80
6.3	Percentages of MPs with connections to individual occupational sectors in the Althingi's relevant standing committees	84
7.1	'To what region in the world should Icelanders feel closest?'	105
7.2	Earnings from work done for the Iceland Defense Force	121
9.1	Senior Icelandic officials' education abroad: country of study	153
9.2	Proportions of the electorate living in the regions and the Greater Reykjavík area, and the MPs representing them	156
10.1	Numbers of people working in the foreign services of the EU member states, EFTA states and seven applicant states, excluding locally employed personnel abroad, April 2001	164
10.2	Numbers of people working in the foreign services of the smallest states in Europe, excluding locally employed personnel abroad, April 2001	165
10.3	What have been the overall consequences of EU/EEA membership on the department's area of competence?	169

Contributors

Dr Baldur Thorhallsson is Associate Professor of Political Science at the University of Iceland. He is also Chairman of the Institute for International Affairs and the Centre for Small State Studies at the University of Iceland. His main research focus is small states and European integration. He has published a number of articles on Iceland and the EU. He has also published articles on small states and European integration, and a book, *The Role of Small States in the European Union* (Ashgate 2000). Baldur's homepage: http://www.hi.is/~baldurt/indexenska.htm

Dr Guðmundur Hálfdanarson is Professor of History at the University of Iceland, specializing in European social and intellectual history, with a focus on the history of nationalism and the nation-state. He has written extensively on Icelandic social and political history; his latest book is *Íslenska þjóðríkið – uppruni og endimörk* [The Icelandic Nation-State – Origins and Boundaries] (2001).

Dr Gunnar Helgi Kristinsson is Professor and Head of the Department of Political Science at the University of Iceland. He is also Chairman of the Institute for Public Administration and Politics at the University of Iceland. His recent publications include: *Staðbundinn stjórnmál* [Local politics] (2001), *Úr digrum sjóði* [Budgeting in Iceland] (1999) and *Embættismenn og stjórnmálamenn* [Bureaucrats and politicians] (1994).

Hjalti Thor Vignisson is an MA student at the University of Iceland, Baldur Thorhallsson's assistant and a researcher at the Institute for International Affairs and the Centre for Small State Studies in Iceland.

Stefán Eiríksson is Deputy Permanent Secretary of the Icelandic Ministry of Justice and Ecclesiastical Affairs and Director of its Police and Judicial Affairs Department. He was Counsellor for Justice and Home Affairs in the Icelandic Mission to the EU in Brussels in 1999–2001. He has written articles and given lectures in areas including Justice and Home Affairs, Human Rights, Schengen and the EU.

Foreword

To outside observers, Icelandic relations with the European Union (EU) are something of a conundrum. How can a small state (or perhaps a 'micro-state') like Iceland, that is so reliant upon international trade, buck the trend followed by many others and continue to resist the temptations and attractions of full EU membership? Indeed, Iceland is regarded as somewhat of an icon among EU-sceptics. At the same time as avoiding full membership status, Iceland has tried to find methods of achieving a closer relationship with the Union – most notably through participation in the European Economic Area (EEA).

At the very least, there is much to be gained from a deeper exploration of Icelandic perspectives on European integration precisely because they explain a specific form of 'reluctance' towards the Union. Nevertheless, there have been few comprehensive studies of Icelandic relations with the European Union available in English. This book, edited by Baldur Thorhallsson, seeks to address this notable deficit.

In my view, this book represents a valuable addition to the literature on 'Europe and the Nation-State'. At one level, it examines the Icelandic–EU relationship from numerous directions – providing an historical overview and a survey of the key policy issues affecting the relationship, such as fisheries. The authors also address the nuances of Icelandic domestic debates in terms of nationalism and Euro-scepticism and discuss the challenges for the ruling elite in overcoming these various pressures.

What makes this book also distinct is the discussion of theoretical approaches. In particular, the application of Katzenstein's arguments is of interest. The country's partial engagement in economic aspects of European integration can be accounted for by the existence of greater external economic pressures when compared to those arising from the social or security aspects. Such approaches explaining Iceland also need to 'dig deep' and take account of Icelandic domestic structures to explain its reactions to the EU. Above all, the accommodation of other aspects – the size and characteristics of the national administration and the role and attitudes of particular leaders – may add insights into Icelandic policy towards European integration.

There is merit in this, especially regarding our wider studies of 'Europe and the Nation-State'. As these authors convincingly argue, Iceland can overcome the constraints on a small state by having intelligent and capable leadership. Such studies of national administration and leadership may ascertain how such 'intelligence' is utilized and judge any effectiveness. Thus, this text provides not just a comprehensive analysis of Iceland. It also represents the articulation of a pressing future research agenda for those interested in the study of small states and European integration. Please take heed!

Lee Miles
Deputy Director
Centre for European Union Studies (CEUS)
The University of Hull

Preface

This book is the outcome of a detailed analysis of the responses of political leaders and governments in Iceland to European integration since its early days. The period during which it was written, running from 2000 to just after the general election of May 2003, saw increased discussion in Iceland on whether or not to apply for membership of the European Union. When the study began, not a single political party advocated making an application to join the EU. At present, the Social Democratic Alliance advocates making an application, two parties have adopted what can be called a 'wait and see' approach and two oppose membership of the EU, one of them, the conservative Independence Party, being the country's largest.

The analysis is built on my engagement with small-state studies, which began when I started looking at small states and European integration at the University of Essex ten years ago. Small-state studies are a rapidly growing academic field, and I am grateful to all those who have contributed to the analysis of how small states have responded to the European integration process. Small-state studies have brought states that for a long time were neglected in academic circles into the centre of the research stage. Increased academic focus on small states is particularly important for a small state like Iceland: it brings a tiny country on the edge of Europe into the academic arena and may help us to understand responses of other small states to the European project. To encourage studies in this field, a Centre for Small State Studies has been created at the University of Iceland, with participation by a number of academics from elsewhere in Europe and North America (http://www.hi.is/~smallst/centre_enska.htm). I hope that this book, and also the Centre, will contribute to small-state studies by providing a 'new' theoretical approach to understanding the responses of small states to European integration.

Primary sources were extremely valuable for analysing the approaches of politicians and governments to European integration. These sources were found in the National Archives of Iceland, the National and University Library of Iceland, the Central Bank Library and the Iceland Defense Force Public Affairs Office, and material was also made available by government ministries, political parties and interest groups. Naturally,

Preface xv

data from EFTA and the EU was of primary importance. All discussions in the seven rounds of debates in the Althingi were scrutinized. Moreover, nearly all news and articles in the Icelandic press on European integration from 1957 onwards were analysed with a particular focus on the debates identified. Speeches on European integration by leading politicians were also examined. Interviews with civil servants in the government ministries were taken in the period from November 2000 to May 2003, mainly to seek clarification on questions that other resources raised. Information obtained in these interviews is acknowledged by the reference 'interview with officials' in the text and bibliographies of the relevant chapters. Naturally, books and academic literature on Iceland's involvement in European integration were also valuable sources.

I should like to thank the other contributors to this volume for all the time and effort they have put into their chapters. I am particularly grateful to my assistant, Hjalti Thor Vignisson, who worked on the project for two years. Gratitude is also due to all the people who read over individual chapters and made valuable comments: Professor Gunnar Helgi Kristinsson, Professor Ólafur Th. Hardarson, Assistant Professor Valur Ingimundarson, Professor Christine Ingebritsen, former Ambassador Einar Benediktsson and Counsellor Ragnar Gísli Kristjánsson. I wish to thank Jeffrey Cosser, who translated parts of the book and proofread the entire text. Finally, I wish to acknowledge, with gratitude, the enormous support the project received in the form of grants from the research fund of the University of Iceland, the research fund of the Icelandic Centre for Research and the Innovative Fund for Students in Iceland.

Baldur Thorhallsson
Reykjavík, June 2003

Abbreviations

ASÍ	The Icelandic Federation of Labour (*Alþýðusamband Íslands*)
CFP	Common Fisheries Policy
CFSP	Common Foreign and Security Policy
EAGGF	European Agricultural Guidance and Guarantee Fund
EC	European Community
ECA	Economic Co-operation Administration
ECSC	European Coal and Steel Community
EEA	European Economic Area
EEC	European Economic Community
EFTA	European Free Trade Association
ESDP	European Security and Defence Policy
EU	European Union
FAO	Food and Agricultural Organization
ICC	Iceland Chamber of Commerce (*Verslunarráð Íslands*)
IDF	Iceland Defense Force
IFPC	Icelandic Freezing Plants Corporation (*SH*)
LÍÚ	The Federation of Icelandic Fishing Vessel Owners (*Landsamband islenskra útvegsmanna*)
MEP	Member of the European Parliament
MP	Member of Parliament
NATO	North Atlantic Treaty Organization
OECD	Organization for Economic Co-operation and Development
OEEC	Organization for European Economic Co-operation
OSCE	Organization for Security and Co-operation in Europe
PSE	Producer Subsidy Equivalent
SDA	Social Democratic Alliance (*Samfylkingin*)
SDP	Social Democratic Party (*Alþýðuflokkurinn*)
SÍS	Federation of Icelandic Co-operative Societies (*Samband íslenskra samvinnufélaga*)
UN	United Nations
UNESCO	UN Educational, Scientific and Cultural Organization
WTO	World Trade Organization

1 Approaching the question
Domestic background and conceptual framework

Baldur Thorhallsson

Introduction

The primary aim of this book is to explore the complex relationship between a small state and European integration. There is a shortage of literature on this topic, and this book seeks to fill this gap by adding 'new' variables and broadening others in explaining the approach of a small state to the European integration process.

The book is a case study on Iceland, and seeks to explain why the Icelandic political elite – defined as the members of the Althingi (the national parliament) and the government – has been reluctant to participate in European integration. The primary focus is on the responses of successive governments to developments in the European integration process, and particularly on why they have not sought membership of the European Union (EU). The study covers the period from the early days of European co-operation in the late 1940s to May 2003, just after the general election in Iceland.

The study is based partly on existing theoretical frameworks that seek to explain approaches of small states to European integration. Its aim is to test various hypotheses in order to find out whether or not they help us to understand the approach of governments in Iceland to the European project. It applies Katzenstein's theoretical framework (1997a, 1997b) on how small states have responded to European integration to the case of Iceland. Katzenstein's thesis claims that all small states in Europe seek to minimize the economic and political constraints they experience from the international system and European integration by closer participation in European integration. The study also applies Ingebritsen's sectoral approach to Iceland in order to examine to what extent Iceland's leading economic sector, the fishing industry, influences its approach to European integration (Ingebritsen 1998). Furthermore, it examines the approach of Archer and Sogner, which indicates that security is an important variable in explaining states' approach to European integration (Archer *et al.* 1998).[1] Moreover, the study analyses whether Gstöhl's (2002) national identity variable and Neumann's (March 2001) national identity and political discourse variables must be considered in order to explain Iceland's approach to the European project.

The book provides a new theoretical approach to explain a small state's response to European integration. It argues that 'new' variables, such as the size and characteristics of national administrations and particular features of the political elite, need to be taken into account in explaining Iceland's approach to European integration. It also argues that national identity and political discourse concerning independence and sovereignty need to be examined carefully in order to understand Iceland's approach to Europe. Small states have some important common characteristics that influence their international behaviour (Katzenstein 1984, 1985, 1997a, 1997b; Archer et al. 2002; Thorhallsson 2000), but the special features of each and every state need to be examined in order to explain fully their international approach. The distinctive characteristics of Iceland, as compared to the other Nordic states, will be used to explain the more cautious approach of Icelandic governments to European integration. The case of Iceland is of particular importance, as Iceland is in a special position among the Nordic states, being the only one that has never applied for membership of the EU. An explanation is thus called for.

EU affairs are far from having dominated politics in Iceland. However, developments on the Continent have on a number of occasions forced governments to decide whether or not to take a step towards closer integration. European integration has had a profound influence on the openness of the economy and governments' choices concerning external affairs. Debates on participation in the different aspects of European integration have differered widely. On occasion they have taken place within the closed circle of politicians and interest-group leaders, while at other times they have taken the form of a broad public debate, all depending on the interests at stake at any given time and the political circumstances in the country. The outcomes of the debates have also varied from rejection to acceptance of participation in European integration.

Seven rounds of debates

There have been seven rounds of debates in Iceland on participation in European integration. The first of these took place when Icelandic officials were actively involved in discussions within the Organization for European Economic Co-operation (OEEC) on the establishment of a free trade area in Western Europe in 1957–59. However, various domestic factors, mainly connected with the policy of restrictive controls that was then dominant and had been in place for some time, were seen as preventing Iceland from participating in the free trade area. In the event, nothing came of the proposed free trade area, though it can be argued that these moves led to the foundation by some states of the European Free Trade Association (EFTA) following the discussions. Due to a serious dispute with Britain over fishing rights, Iceland was not invited to participate in the foundation of EFTA.

The second round of the European debate in Iceland took place in 1961–63, when politicians and business leaders gave a considerable amount of attention to the question of whether or not to apply for membership of the European Economic Community (EEC). At this time, nearly all sectoral interest groups pressed for membership of the community, and the government gave serious consideration to the question. Following thorough consultation with government officials in the EEC countries, the government came to the conclusion that it was not appropriate to apply for membership at the time, since completely different circumstances were seen as prevailing in Iceland from those in its neighbouring countries, this being partly due to the smallness of the country; on the other hand, it was seen as desirable to apply for associate membership. However, the refusal by President de Gaulle to admit Britain to the EEC, which effectively excluded Denmark, Norway and Ireland as well, meant that these plans on the part of the Icelandic government came to nothing.

The third round of the debate followed at the end of the 1960s when the issue of membership of EFTA came to the fore. Long and heated discussions took place on the question of membership, and accusations of the assignment of sovereignty and the forfeiture of independence were frequently made in the Althingi. One of the reasons advanced for membership of EFTA was that it would give smoother access for Iceland's fish exports to the markets of the EFTA states, and also that it would open the way to making a free trade agreement with the European Community (EC). Iceland joined EFTA in 1970, following which it made a free trade agreement with the EC, which took effect after the end of one of the 'cod wars' with Britain in 1976.

The fourth round of the debate on European integration took place following the negotiations between the EFTA states and the EC on the establishment of the European Economic Area (EEA), reaching a climax when these negotiations were completed in the early 1990s. Heated debates took place in the Althingi over the agreement, and the electorate took an active part in the discussion by writing to the press, joining a movement against EEA membership and organizing petitions. Leaders of interest groups representing both employers and workers also took part in the discussion by making formal declarations on the pros and cons of membership of the EEA. The government piloted the agreement through to acceptance, and it took effect at the beginning of 1994. Membership of the EEA means that Iceland upholds the 'four freedoms' of the EEA Agreement, though with certain qualifications, and according to an estimate by its ministry for foreign affairs, about 80 per cent of the EU's legislation is now adopted in Iceland.

The fifth round of the European debate in Iceland began when the small Social Democratic Party (SDP) became the first party in Iceland to include the intention to apply to join the EU in its policy statement in 1994. The party leadership sought to harness this policy as a means of gaining support in the general election campaign the following year, but a split in the party made this difficult.[2] For two reasons, Iceland made no move towards an EU application in this round of the European debate. First, the rejection by Norway of the option of applying to join the EU ensured the future of the EEA Agreement and gave the anti-EU movement a boost, and second, Iceland's largest party, the conservative Independence Party, which was in coalition with the SDP from 1991 to 1995, said that EU membership was not on the election agenda. When pressed on the issue, the party followed a 'wait and see' policy, which characterized the position of most parties in the country on the integration issue (Kristinsson 1996). On the other hand, the Conservatives took a clearer position at their national congress in 1996 with a resolution to the effect that Iceland should not apply to join the EU, and have followed this line unswervingly ever since. The unequivocal position adopted by the Independence Party silenced many party members who had up to that time been advocates of EU membership.

Discussion of membership of Schengen can be seen as the sixth round of the European debate in Iceland. The issue was examined by the Althingi from 1999 to 2000, but it never assumed the same proportions in Iceland as it did in Norway, for example, where it featured prominently in public discussion. As a result of Iceland's participation in Schengen, the country has, since 2001, taken an active part in European co-operation in the spheres of policing and justice. In these areas, Iceland has become more closely involved in the co-operative process than have two EU member states, Britain and Ireland, which are not involved in Schengen.

Iceland is currently facing the seventh round of discussion of the issue of how it should respond to the process of integration that is taking place in Europe. The question is now couched in essentially the same terms as it was four decades ago: should Iceland apply to join the EU? It is virtually impossible to predict how long this round of the debate will last, and even more difficult to say what the outcome will be. On the other hand, it is clear that never before have the pros and cons of membership of the EU been subjected to such careful scrutiny. In one of the two main lines of discussion, the minister for foreign affairs and chairman of the Progressive Party has done much to promote debate of the issue since the middle of 2001. In that year the Progressive Party, historically Iceland's agrarian party and champion of the regions, dropped from its policy statement the assertion that the country should not apply to join the EU and replaced it by the 'wait and see' policy. In 2002 the party's internal committee on European affairs came to the conclusion that the EEA Agreement should be strengthened, but if this were not possible, Iceland would have to look for other means to secure its interests in Europe, negotiation on EU membership being one of the options that must be considered (Morgunblaðið 24 June 2001). The party's manifesto for the general election in 2003 stated: 'The Progressive Party wants an informed and unprejudiced discussion of the pros and cons of EU membership to continue, as it is clear that the time to take a decision on the issue may come within a few years' (Progressive Party 19 April 2003). On the other hand, there is within the Progressive Party substantial opposition to Iceland's joining the EU, even though the chairman's statements can scarcely be understood otherwise than as indicating that he is in favour of membership, though he has never actually declared as much. In the other main line of discussion, the recently formed Social Democratic Alliance (SDA), a left-of-centre coalition created in 1999 by the Social Democratic Party (SDP), the People's Alliance and the Women's Alliance, declared its view at the end of 2002 that Iceland ought to define the goals it wished to achieve in negotiations with the EU, apply for membership and submit any terms of entry that might be secured to a referendum.

Political parties and their European policies

One of the striking features of Iceland's policy concerning participation in European integration is the reluctance of Icelandic politicians to adopt a pro-European position. In the general election of May 2003, only the Social Democratic Alliance supported application for EU membership. Two parties, the Independence Party and the Left Green Movement, opposed it, while the Progressive Party advocated a 'wait and see' approach, as did the Liberal Party.

This scepticism towards EU membership is in sharp contrast to the view of most politicians in Norway and Denmark since the early 1960s and politicians in Sweden and Finland since the early 1990s (Svasand et al. 1996). It is also in sharp contrast to the view of politicians in the fifteen EU member states: 92 per cent of them support membership of the EU (EOS Gallup Europe 1996).

Furthermore, in contrast to the position in all the other Nordic states, the electorate in Iceland has not had the opportunity to decide the country's position on EU membership. Thus, the question of accession to European integration has been in the hands of Icelandic politicians. Also, the Icelandic electorate has had a very limited chance of voting indirectly for EU membership in general elections, since only twice have parties advocated membership in general elections: the SDP in 1995 and the SDA in 2003.

It is also apparent that support for EU membership has been greater among Iceland's general population than among its political elite. Roughly one third to over half of the electorate have supported EU membership in the last 10 years (Thorhallsson 2002; Kristinsson 1996). This is contrary to the case in the other Nordic countries, where European integration has had an elitist character, since support for EU membership has been greater among the political elite than among the general populace (Svasand *et al.* 1996).

The Icelandic party system, which was created in the second and third decades of the twentieth century, contains four parties: a conservative party (the Independence Party 1929–), an agrarian party (the Progressive Party 1916–), a social democratic party (the Social Democratic Party 1916–99, the Social Democratic Alliance 1999–), and a left socialist party (the Communist Party 1930–38, the Socialist Party 1938–56, the People's Alliance 1956–99, the Left Green Movement 1999–). This party system is considerably different from those in Scandinavia. First, the conservative Independence Party has been by far the largest party, receiving about 40 per cent of the votes, while in Scandinavia the largest parties are the Social Democrats. Second, the People's Alliance, named the Socialist Party and the Communist Party in the past, was from 1942 to 1987 larger than the Social Democratic Party. The SDP was in fact the smallest of the four parties, the Progressive Party being the second largest. Since the early 1970s, a fifth and on occasions a sixth party has most often been represented in the Althingi. The Women's Alliance was the most successful of these parties and was represented in parliament from 1983 until it joined the Social Democratic Alliance in 1999. The party system changed in 1999 with the formation of the SDA, in order to challenge the dominance of the Conservatives. The SDA became the second largest party, receiving nearly 27 per cent of the votes, leaving the Progressives in the third place with just over 18 per cent. In the general election in 2003 the SDA established itself as the second largest party with 31 per cent of the votes, the Progressive Party receiving less than 18 per cent. The Conservatives received one third of the votes in 2003, 7 per cent less than in the previous election.

The Left Green Movement was created by a split from the People's Alliance, some members of the Women's Alliance and environmentalists who opposed the merger of the three parties in the SDA. It gained about 9 per cent of the votes in 1999 and 2003. It is sceptical of EEA membership and opposes Iceland's membership of NATO and the defence agreement between Iceland and the USA; it is the only party to do so. It also campaigns fiercely against EU membership. The Left Greens would prefer a bilateral treaty with the EU to membership of the EEA. The party's scepticism towards political and economic integration in Europe is well demonstrated in a draft resolution that it submitted to the Althingi in November 2000. This proposed that Iceland should not be a member of any free trade area but should make special trade agreements without membership (Tillaga til þingsályktunar um stefnu Íslands í alþjóðasamskiptum 5 October 2000).

In the election in 1999 the Social Democratic Alliance advocated the policy that Iceland should not apply for membership in the coming election term, i.e. the next four years. This policy was a compromise between the three parties forming the SDA. The People's Alliance and the Women's Alliance had campaigned against membership of the EU, while the SDP advocated membership from 1994, as is described above. In 2001 the SDA published a detailed report on the pros and cons of EU membership but hesitated to take a clear stand on the issue. However, in 2002 a referendum within the party decided with a huge majority to adopt the policy to apply for EU membership, as is stated above.

The Liberal Party, which was formed in 1999 with the main objective of changing the country's fisheries management policy, received just over 4 per cent of the votes that year and over 7 per cent in 2003. It has been willing to consider EU membership if Iceland were able to retain sole control of its fisheries zone (Liberal Party July 2001). The agenda approved by the party's national congress in 2003 states: 'Immediate steps should be taken to find out what position Iceland would be offered in collaboration between the countries of Europe in regard to its natural resources' (Liberal Party March 2003). Regarding closer co-operation, the party stated the proviso that all foreign encroachment into Iceland's business and financial sectors must be prevented and that collaboration with other countries in Europe must be secured on an equal footing, i.e. 'subject to the condition that Iceland's interests regarding control of its fisheries resources must be guaranteed' (Liberal Party March 2003).

Davíð Oddsson, chairman of the Independence Party, prime minister since 1991 and the longest-serving prime minister in the history of Iceland, has been one of the most outspoken critics of applying to join the EU. He has stated time and again that Iceland's fisheries interests would be hugely damaged by joining the EU. He has repeatedly rejected any transfer of sovereignty to the EU. The fact that the right-hand side of the political spectrum in Iceland is united has led to the dominant position of the Independence Party since the end of the Second World War. The Conservatives have been in office for 45 of the 59 years since the creation of the Republic in 1944. Moreover, a small minority of the party's MPs, under the leadership of its vice-chairman, led a government for three of the remaining 14 years when the Independence Party itself was in opposition. By contrast, the Social Democratic Parties have been the most prevalent in the other Nordic states during this time. The Independence Party has had no stable alliance except with the SDP between 1959 and 1971 and the Progressive Party since 1995. Since 1971 the Conservatives have formed six government coalitions with the Progressives over a total of 17 years. Their coalition since 1995 has had a clear policy towards the question of EU membership: application is not on the agenda. However, the opening of the EU debate by the party chairman of the Progressive Party in 2001 seems to have caused a considerable stir between the party leaders. Despite this, the parties formed their third government after the election in 2003.

The theoretical structure

A number of hypotheses will be put forward in order to explain the scepticism of Iceland's political elite towards the question of participation in European integration. The obvious starting point is to look at Katzenstein's theory (1997a, 1997b) on how small states have responded to European integration. It is very interesting to apply Katzenstein's theory to Iceland: it is a small state that is highly dependent on external trade, a member of the EEA and Schengen, yet at the same time a state that has been very reluctant to open up its borders. Katzenstein's framework of analysis (1984, 1985)[3] also helps us to identify the main characteristics of Iceland as a small state and compare it with the other Nordic states. This is particularly the case since Katzenstein's description of the economic and political environment in small states contains many features normally considered Scandinavian (Griffiths *et al.* 1995: 36). Katzenstein links various economic and political characteristics of small states together and argues that a combination of them explains the behaviour of small states in the international system (Katzenstein 1984, 1985). In explaining small states' approaches to European integration, Katzenstein emphasizes their economic vulnerability and political flexibility. He claims that 'all of the smaller European states seek to diffuse and reduce their dependence through closer European integration' (Katzenstein 1997b: 260). Katzenstein argues that small states in Europe experience the effects of European integration according to the duration and depth of their participation in the European project. Small states that are deeply involved in European integration experience these effects as soft constraints. On the other hand, those that play only a limited part in European integration experience the effects of European integration as hard constraints (Katzenstein 1997b: 261). As a result, all the Nordic states, except Iceland, have applied for EU membership. Their intention has been to minimize the international effects which subject them to constraints. The interesting question is why Iceland has not followed the others. Why has the economic vulnerability of Iceland not led to a request by the political elite for full participation in European integration? What makes the case of Iceland unique? Katzenstein's hypothesis will be applied to Iceland in order to answer these questions. This can be formulated as follows: *Participation in European integration eases international and European constraints on Iceland.*

It will be argued that a combination of economic and political features of Iceland explains why the political elite has not sought for full participation in European integration, and support will be adduced for Katzenstein's claim that small states have considerable leeway in their responses to European integration: their domestic politics and policy choices are not forced into 'a uniform mold' (Katzenstein 1997b: 257). Also, the study supports Katzenstein's thesis that small states seek to diffuse and reduce their dependence by closer participation in the European integration process

(Katzenstein 1997b: 260). However, the case of Iceland indicates that full participation in European integration can be seen as hardening international and European constraints on a small state. This is contrary to Katzenstein's claim that these constraints become softer as smaller states participate closer in European integration. The political elite in Iceland does not regard the EU as a multilateral institution that eases international and European constraints on Iceland. Membership of the EEA is seen as alleviating these constraints, while membership of the EU is seen as leading to unbearable constraints for Iceland. Thus, it is necessary to look at other variables in order to explain why the political elite has not opted for EU membership in order to minimise international and European constraints.

Katzenstein seeks to explain responses of small states to European integration by a combination of domestic and international factors (Katzenstein 1997a, 1997b). A number of variables have been identified in the literature as possible explanations of small states' responses to European integration. Some of them focus on responses by states to international changes, while others concentrate on the domestic level and the importance of the characteristics found there. For instance, Wallace argues that different perceptions of interests shape the diverse responses of small states to European integration. He identifies a number of variables that determine these responses: domestic politics, national myth and identity, economic strength or weakness, security constraints and geographical position (Wallace 1999: 14). Bulmer adopts a domestic perspective and argues that different domestic features such as economic structures, domestic institutions and political traditions lead to different integration strategies (Bulmer 1983: 349–63). Others identify the smaller resources of small states (administrative, military and economic) compared to larger states as the main variables in explaining their international behaviour (Papadakis *et al.* 1987: 423; Archer *et al.* 2002). On the other hand, it has also been argued that smallness can be of advantage, as small states can respond more quickly to international challenges (Kautto *et al.* 2001; Archer *et al.* 2002; Geser *et al.* 1975). Notwithstanding all the hypotheses put forward in order to explain small states' approaches to European integration, few attempts have been made to study in detail the reasons for particular policy outcomes in small states concerning involvement in European integration.

One of the most comprehensive frameworks to analyse why some states resist European integration while others are more willing to take an active part is offered by Ingebritsen. Ingebritsen supports Katzenstein's thesis, as she claims that European integration has proved 'to be remarkably resistant to inevitable national pressures against often painful liberalisation measures' (Ingebritsen 1998: 257). She argues that the sectoral approach is an ideal framework of analysis in order to examine the different responses of states to European integration. She declares that this is particularly the

10 Domestic background and conceptual framework

case of the Nordic states because of their dependence on a limited number of exports. She claims that European integration has developed 'according to a sectoral logic' (Ingebritsen 1998: 39) from one economic sector to another and that the strength of the sectoral approach lies in 'the implicit interaction of both the domestic and international polity' (Ingebritsen 1998: 39). She claims that the leading economic sector in each of the Nordic states determines its response to the European project. Sweden and Finland, which depend on manufacturing, felt more pressure to join the EU from related organized interests than did Iceland and Norway, which rely on the export of raw material. Actors from the leading economic sector play a key role in state policy formation of the state on European integration (Ingebritsen 1998).

The fisheries sector is strategically the most important sector for Iceland. For instance, exports of fish and marine products constituted over 40 per cent of total exports of goods and services in 2000. Until 1999, fisheries exports always accounted for more than 70 per cent of total exports of goods, running at over 80 per cent and even up to 96 per cent in the period from 1920 to 1969. The fisheries sector accounted for about 10 per cent of gross domestic product (GDP) in 2000; for further details see Table 6.1. (National Economic Institute 25 July 2002). Ingebritsen argues that fish is at the heart of Iceland's opposition to EU membership and that 'the interests of fishermen are synonymous with government policy goals' (Ingebritsen 1998: 127). Thus, the fisheries sector is seen as playing a significant role in the policy-making process of the government concerning European affairs.

The aim of this study is to examine this claim in detail in order to answer the question whether the fisheries sector is the most important variable in explaining Iceland's opposition to closer participation in European integration. Politicians in Iceland tend to refer to the fishing sector in their opposition to EU membership. Membership of the EU's common fisheries policy (CFP) is seen as entailing unbearable constraints on the fisheries sector and the Icelandic economy. Opponents of EU membership completely reject fishing by foreign vessels in Icelandic waters, foreign investment in the fishing industry and any transfer of power from Iceland to the European level concerning fishing management. This is also the case of most interest groups supporting membership application. On the other hand, no detailed studies have been made in order to explain how interest groups in the fishing sector have influenced the policy-making outcome of governments concerning European integration. The relationship between fishing interests and governments is an unexplored field. For instance, it remains an unanswered question to what extent the fisheries lobby is represented in political parties, the national parliament and employers' and employees' associations and how its representation in these bodies compares with that of other economic sectors. It also remains an unanswered question how the fisheries sector conducts its lobbyism in

Iceland in order to secure a favourable outcome concerning better market access to the European market. The relationship between governments and political parties, on the one hand, and the fisheries lobby, on the other, remains a closed 'black box' which has to be opened in order to explain to what extent the fishing sector determines the policy-making outcome of governments in Iceland concerning European affairs. The second hypothesis to be examined in this study is based on Ingebritsen's thesis, and can be stated as follows: *Priorities of fisheries interest groups have been the controlling factor in the reluctance of Iceland to participate in European integration.*

While emphasizing the sectoral approach in order to examine the different approaches of states to the European project, Ingebritsen acknowledges its limitations. She argues that states' choices are not always defined by economic sectors and that security interests may prevail over the influence of economic sectors. Also, the process of defining the interests of sectors in relation to European integration is political, being based on expected winners and losers in the integration process (Ingebritsen 1998: 44–45). Thus, other variables have to be considered in order to examine why some states resist European integration while others are willing to take part in it.

This leads us to the security policy of Icelandic governments and what influence the special relationship between Iceland and the United States of America has had on the participation of Iceland in European integration. Iceland's security policy has been based on two pillars: membership of NATO and a defence agreement with the USA, which has a military base in Iceland. The defence agreement, signed in 1951, makes Iceland's relations with the USA different to those of all the other NATO member states. Governments in Iceland have not shown any interest in participating in the foreign and security aspects of the EU (Kristinsson 1994). Security and defence matters do not put pressure on Iceland to open discussions with the EU concerning membership. This makes the situation in Iceland different from that in other states such as Finland (Bjarnason 2002: 306).[4] Archer and Sogner argue that leading politicians in Norway saw the EU as a source of security. EU membership was seen as an attractive option in security terms. For instance, the Labour government gave participation in the Common Foreign and Security Policy (CFSP) as a reason for joining the EU. This was also advocated by the Conservative Party (Archer *et al.* 1998: 27).

The special relationship between Iceland and the USA has also been based on economic grounds. Iceland received the highest assistance per capita under the Marshall Plan despite the fact that it benefited enormously, in economic terms, from the Second World War (Ingimundarson 1996: 141). For over a decade, the US government guaranteed Iceland a greater number of exemptions from the OEEC conditions than other nations were able to secure (Ingimundarson 2002: 327). The USA directly

12 *Domestic background and conceptual framework*

intervened to help Iceland out of a recession in the late 1960s and many Icelandic firms had favourable trading terms with the USA (Ingimundarson 2002). The US base in Iceland contributes considerably to the Icelandic economy. For instance, from 1970 to 1995, revenues from the base were over 2 per cent of GDP, and accounted for up to 20 per cent of foreign currency earnings in the 1950s (Snævarr 1993: 364). Furthermore, the US market has been important for Icelandic exports and is at present the third largest market after Britain and Germany. The third hypothesis examined in this book can be stated as follows: *The close relationship between Iceland and the United States of America in terms of security and economic and trade relations has had a profound influence on Iceland's response to European integration.*

Gstöhl offers a comprehensive theoretical approach in order to study why small, rich and open economies have been reluctant to participate in European integration (Gstöhl 2002). She offers an explanation 'by combining an analysis of economic interests in market integration with ideational interest in protecting national identity' (Gstöhl 2002: iv). Gstöhl partly agrees with Ingebritsen but claims that we have to look beyond the sectoral approach in order to fully understand the reluctance of states to participate in the European project. Gstöhl argues that integration preferences have to be explained by a combination of variables. This is because political constraints coexist with, and often dominate, economic interests. A better access for leading economic sectors to foreign markets 'may lose its temptation when domestic institutions, societal cleavages, foreign policy traditions, and experiences of foreign rule that touch on feelings of national identity come into play' (Gstöhl 2002: 211). Hence, Gstöhl emphasizes constructivist approaches, which claim that constructions of nation and statehood shape interests and policies, in order to understand the reluctance of states to take an active part in European integration. Gstöhl argues that both economic interests and national identity must be considered to explain integration policies. She argues that Norway, Sweden and Austria had for a long time good economic reasons to join the EU but did not 'because they suffered high political impediments to do so' (Gstöhl 2002: 214).

Neumann also criticizes Ingebritsen for not including national identity as an independent variable in explaining the Nordic states' different approaches to European integration (Neumann March 2001). Neumann argues that one of the key reasons why Norway rejected EU membership in 1972 and 1994 'was that the peasant and the farmer were able to present themselves as the embodiment of the nation' (Neumann March 2001: 92). Neumann continues 'We are talking here about the power of identity' (Neumann March 2001: 92). Neumann argues that the structure of the Norwegian discourse and the shape of political debates have 'a preserving influence on policy outcomes' in Norway (Neumann March 2001: 92). He calls for explanations of how Norway's agricultural and fisheries sectors were able to determine EU referendum outcomes and says 'Perhaps one should think of national identity as an independent variable' (Neumann March 2001: 92).

The fourth hypothesis to be examined in the book derives from Neumann's and Gstöhl's claims that national identity and political discourse can determine states' approaches to European integration: *Icelandic political discourse tends to polarize around nationalist themes, making it difficult for politicians to promote anything that seems to compromise Icelandic sovereignty and independence. For this reason, politicians are reluctant to advocate formal participation in the process of European integration.*

There is a call for an explanation of states' different approaches to European integration that is couched more in domestic terms (Bulmer 1983; Wallace 1999; Neumann March 2001; Archer *et al.* 1998; Gstöhl 2002). States' responses to the European project cannot be explained solely at the level of the international system; nor can they be explained by 'a single domestic variable' such as leading economic sectors, security matters or national identity. Thus, there is a search for 'new' variables and a new combined approach which may explain states' reactions to European integration.

It may be the case that the view of most of the Icelandic political elite towards the question of EU membership can be explained by Ingebritsen's sectoral approach, Neumann's national identity variable or a combination of these two approaches. However, it is tempting to look at the elite itself in order to find an explanation. This is particularly the case since the Icelandic political elite's position on EU membership distinguishes itself so sharply from the position of its counterparts in the other Nordic countries. The question arises whether the political elite in Iceland is in some way intrinsically different from the political elites in the other Nordic countries. Is there something in the elite's characteristics, conception of foreign policy, contacts or domestic power basis which may help us to understand its approach to European integration? Hence, the fifth hypothesis focuses on the Icelandic political elite: *The scepticism of the political elite in Iceland towards participation in European integration can be related to its 'realist' concept of foreign policy, its peripheral placement in Europe and its domestic power base in the regions outside Reykjavík.*

In the search for a wider and more precise explanation for states' responses to European integration, it may be useful to consider previous findings which indicate that the advantages and disadvantages of small administrations have to be taken into consideration when explaining the behaviour of small states in the EU context (Thorhallsson 2000). Administrative working procedures of small states concerning EU matters are characterized by informality, flexible decision making, greater manoeuvrability of officials and by guidelines, rather than instructions, being given to negotiators when they are dealing with issues that are not regarded as important. The size and characteristics of national administrations are a key variable in explaining the behaviour of states within the decision-making processes of the EU. Thus, Katzenstein (1985) misses an important variable in explaining the behaviour of small states in the international system by focussing only on their corporatist decision-making structure, a distinctive party system and an external variable: dependency on the world market (Thorhallsson 2000: 240).

The Icelandic national administration is very small compared to that of the other Nordic states, and its capacity to participate effectively in the EU has been put in doubt. For instance, the foreign service in Iceland employed only 150 people in April 2001, excluding locally employed personnel abroad, while the number of people working in the foreign services of the other Nordic countries ranged from 1,150 in Norway to 1,663 in Denmark (Ministries for Foreign Affairs in the Nordic Countries April 2001).

National administrations are confronted with several difficulties in managing negotiations within the EU (Wright 1996) and some of the smaller national administrations were not prepared to deal with EU business at the time of entry (Thorhallsson November 2001: 36–8). On the other hand, what consequences a small administration has for states' policy outcomes concerning possible EU membership remains an unanswered question. Are small administrations not able to provide ministers with sufficient information concerning pros and cons of EU membership in order for them to take a clear stand on the question of membership? Are politicians in small states forced to rely on interest groups to a greater extent in their policy approach to European integration than politicians in larger states due to the more limited capacity of their national administrations? Do politicians in small states hesitate to advocate EU membership if doubt has been cast on the capacity of their national administrations to deal efficiently with EU matters? The sixth hypothesis derives from the findings cited above concerning the size and characteristics of small national administrations and questions raised concerning the influence their smallness may have on the policy-making outcome concerning possible EU membership. The hypothesis states: *The smallness of the Icelandic administration and its limited capability have restricted Iceland's ability to participate in European integration. These factors have also made ministers more reliant on interest groups in their policy on Europe.*

The structure of the book

This book is divided into two sections and eleven chapters.

The first section, covering Chapters 2 to 4, analyses responses of successive Icelandic governments to European integration from the early days of European co-operation to Iceland's membership of the EEA and Schengen.

Chapter 2 provides a historical overview of the cautious position of Icelandic governments on European co-operation from the late 1940s up to the country's membership of EFTA and the signing of a free trade agreement with the EC in 1972. All attempts to open up the domestic market to foreign goods have met with strong resistance. Political parties have been very reluctant to open up the economy because major interest groups have campaigned against such a move, chief among them being the fisheries and agricultural pressure groups, and Icelandic governments have only opened the domestic economy to imports in return for, or in the expectation of, access to markets for Icelandic fish.

Chapter 3 focuses on the hotly-debated issue of membership of the EEA. It examines what factors encouraged the Icelandic government to participate in the EEA negotiation process and the government's policy objectives in the negotiations. It also analyses why the EEA Agreement met with such strong resistance both within the national parliament and from some pressure groups. The agreement upset the consensus on foreign economic policy that had existed since the debate on the membership of EFTA. In fact, it gave rise to a debate such as had not been seen in the Althingi for decades.

The aim of Chapter 4 is to show how closely integrated Iceland is, in fact, in the European project through its membership of Schengen. The chapter indicates why Iceland decided to participate in the scheme despite its traditional resistance to political integration in Europe.

The second section of the book, consisting of Chapters 5 to 11, provides a detailed analysis of the hypotheses stated above.

Chapter 5 examines to what extent Katzenstein's approach applies to Iceland. It focuses on how governments have responded to European and international constraints and to what extent they have sought to reduce Iceland's dependence by closer participation in European integration.

Chapter 6 analyses the importance of the fisheries sector in Iceland and its relationship with political parties and the government. It examines to what extent Ingebritsen's sectoral approach applies to Iceland, and compares the influence of the fisheries sector to that of the agricultural and industrial sectors on government policy on European affairs.

The influence Iceland's special relationship with the USA has had on its approach to European integration is examined in Chapter 7. The aim is to show how a small state is affected by its relationship with a powerful neighbour. Iceland has looked to the USA for protection and as a consequence a close relationship has been built up, both in terms of security and trade. The chapter will show how the defence agreement of 1951 has influenced the policy of the political elite towards Europe. It will also indicate how Icelandic trade relations and economic ties with the EU influenced the political elite's approach to Europe in the early days of the integration process.

Chapter 8 examines the elite's political discourse concerning independence and sovereignty. It indicates how national identity has influenced the approach of politicians towards the questions of Iceland's position in an integrated Europe.

Chapter 9 examines the background of the political elite in order to examine why it has not adopted the relatively pro-European attitude of other elites in Europe and the general public in Iceland. The chapter focuses on what distinguishes the Icelandic political elite from other elites in order to explain its scepticism towards European integration.

Chapter 10 examines what influence the small size of the national administration and its characteristics have had on the approach of governments to European integration. It analyses to what extent limited resources and special characteristics, such as lack of autonomy of officials and limited involvement in policy making, explain the approach of the Icelandic political leadership to European integration since the first round of the European debate took place in Iceland.

The final chapter provides a new theoretical approach on how a small state's reaction to European integration should be examined. It focuses on 'new' variables needed to explain the response of Iceland towards the European integration process. It argues that we need to look beyond the traditional variables that are used to explain the behaviour of small states in relation to European integration. Variables such as economic characteristics, military weakness, territorial size and the size of the population itself are useful tools in examining the activeness of states internationally. They can help to explain small states' promotion of free trade, neutrality or willingness to join a military alliance. Also, they may provide an account of states' behaviour in a military organization like NATO. However, they cannot provide a complete account of the approaches of small states to an institution such as the European Union. They lack the capacity to explain Iceland's approach to European integration.

'New' variables have to be examined in order to explain Iceland's approach to European integration. Variables such as the size and characteristics of the national administration, national identity, political discourse, perception of international relations and particular features of the domestic arena of the political elite, such as the electoral system and its peripheral placement in Europe, have to be taken into account in order to explain Iceland's approach towards European integration.

Notes

1 Archer and Sogner claim that security is a key variable in explaining the political elite's approach to European integration in Norway (Archer *et al.* 1998).
2 The vice-chairman of the party resigned from it and established a new party, the People's Movement (Þjóðvaki).
3 Katzenstein's analysis of the characteristics of small states is presented in his book: *Small States in World Markets: Industrial Policy in Europe* (Katzenstein

1985). He analyses the industrial adjustment strategy of seven small corporatist states: Sweden, Norway, Denmark, the Netherlands, Belgium, Switzerland and Austria. He compares the behaviour of these small states with five large states: Germany, France, the United Kingdom, the United States and Japan. Katzenstein has also written on Austria and Switzerland in his book: *Corporatism and Change: Austria, Switzerland and the Politics of Industry* (Katzenstein 1984).

4 Bjarnason is a leading figure in the Independence Party and its main specialist in foreign affairs. He is a former minister of education and culture (1995–2002) and became minister of justice in May 2003.

Bibliography

Archer, C. and Nugent, N. (2002) 'Introduction: Small States and the European Union', *Current Politics and Economics of Europe*, 11/1: 1–10.

Archer, C. and Sogner, I. (1998) *Norway, European Integration and Atlantic Security*, London: SAGE Publication.

Bjarnason, B. (2002) *Í hita kalda stríðsins*, Reykjavík: Nýja bókafélagið.

Bulmer, S. (1983) 'Domestic Politics and European Community Policy-Making', *Journal of Common Market Studies*, XXI/4.

EOS Gallup Europe (1996) *The European Union 'A View from the Top'*. Available online: http://europa.eu.int/comm/public_opinion/archives/top/top.pdf (accessed 9 April 2003).

Geser, H. and Höpflinger, F. (1975) 'Problems of Structural Differentiation in Small Societies: A Sociological Contribution to the Theory of Small States and Federalism', *Bulletin of the Sociological Institute of the University of Zurich*, 3: 59–64.

Griffiths, R.T. and Pharo, H. (1995) 'Small States and European Integration: Literature Survey and Evaluation', *ARENA*, working paper 19.

Gstöhl, S. (2002) *Reluctant Europeans: Norway, Sweden and Switzerland in the Process of Integration*, London: Lynne Rienner Publishers.

Ingebritsen, C. (1998) *The Nordic States and the European Unity*, Ithaca and London: Cornell University Press.

Ingimundarson, V. (1996) *Í eldlínu kalda stríðsins*, Reykjavík: Vaka–Helgafell.

—— (2002) 'Viðhorf Bandaríkjanna til íslenskrar hagstjórnar á 5. og 6. áratugnum', in J. Haralz (ed.) *Frá kreppu til viðreisnar: Pættir um hagstjórn á Íslandi á árunum 1930–1960*, Reykjavík: Hið Íslenska bókmenntafélag: 327–44.

Katzenstein, P. (1984) *Corporatism and Change: Austria, Switzerland and the Politics of Industry*, Ithaca and London: Cornell University Press.

—— (1985) *Small States in World Markets: Industrial Policy in Europe*, Ithaca and London: Cornell University Press.

—— (1997a) 'United Germany in an Integrating Europe', in P. Katzenstein (ed.) *Tamed Power: Germany in Europe*, Ithaca and London: Cornell University Press: 1–48.

—— (1997b) 'The Smaller European States, Germany and Europe', in P. Katzenstein (ed.) *Tamed Power: Germany in Europe*, Ithaca and London: Cornell University Press: 251–304.

Kautto, M., Fritell, J., Hvinden, B., Kvist, J., Uusitalo, H. and Fritzell, J. (2001) *Nordic Welfare States in the European Context*, London: Routledge.

18 Domestic background and conceptual framework

Kristinsson, G.H. (1994) 'Iceland and Norway: Peripheries in Doubt', in J. Redmond (ed.) *Prospective Europeans: New Members for the European Union*, New York and London: Harvester Wheatsheaf: 86–109.

—— (1996) 'Iceland and the European Union: Non-decision on Membership', in L. Miles (ed.) *The European Union and the Nordic States*, London: Routledge: 150–68.

Liberal Party (July 2001) 'No title'. Available online: http:www.xf.is/evropumal.htm (accessed July 2001).

—— (March 2003) *Málefnaskrá landsþings 7.–8. mars '03*. Available online: http:www.xf.is/index.php?xf=1=14&parent=1 (accessed 2 May 2003).

Ministries for Foreign Affairs in the Nordic Countries (April 2001) Data concerning the number of people working in foreign services in the Nordic states was provided by the Foreign Ministry in Denmark, Norway, Sweden, Finland and Iceland in April 2001.

Morgunblaðið (24 June 2001) 'Telur samningsmarkmiðin raunhæf', *Morgunblaðið*.

National Economic Institute (14 December 2001) *Historical Statistics 1901–2000*. Available online: http://www.ths.is/rit/sogulegt/english.htm (accessed 25 July 2002).

Neumann, I. (March 2001) 'The Nordic States and European Unity', *Cooperation and Conflict*, 36/1: 87–94.

Papadakis, M. and Starr, H. (1987) 'Opportunity, Willingness and Small States: The Relationship between Environment and Foreign Policy', in C. Herman, C. Kegley and J. Rosenau (eds) *New Directions in the Study of Foreign Policy*, London: Allen & Unwin: 409–32.

Progressive Party (19 April 2003) *Stefnuskrá*. Available online: http://www.xb.is/stefnuskra.lasso (accessed 19 April 2003).

Snævarr, S. (1993) Haglýsing Íslands, Reykjavík: Heimskringla.

Svasand, L. and Lindström, U. (1996) 'Scandinavian Political Parties and the European Union', in J. Gaffney (ed.) *Political Parties and the European Union*, London and New York: Routledge: 205–19.

Thorhallsson, B. (2000) *The Role of Small States in the European Union*, London: Ashgate.

—— (November 2001) 'Stjórnsýslumál', in E.B. Einarsson (ed.) *Ísland í Evrópu*, Reykjavík: Social Democratic Alliance: 29–54.

—— (2002) 'The Sceptical Political Elite Versus the Pro-European Public: The Case of Iceland', *Scandinavian Studies*, 74/3: 349–78.

Tillaga til þingsályktunar um stefnu Íslands í alþjóðasamskiptum (5 October 2000) 'A Parliamentary Resolution'. Available online: http://www.althingi.is/altext/126/s/0004.html (accessed 1 May 2003).

Wallace, W. (1999) 'Small European States and European Policy-Making: Strategies, Roles, Possibilities', in Between Autonomy and Influence: Small States and the European Union, *Proceedings from ARENA Annual Conference 1998*, Norway, ARENA, Report No. 1.

Wright, V. (1996) 'The National Co-ordination of European Policy-making: Negotiating the Quagmire', in J. Richardsson (ed.) *European Union, Power and Policy-Making*, London and New York: Routledge.

Part I

2 The first steps
Iceland's policy on European integration from the foundation of the republic to 1972

Baldur Thorhallsson and Hjalti Thor Vignisson

Introduction

After a brief account of conditions in Iceland in the decade after the end of the Second World War, the main part of this chapter examines the first three rounds of the debate on Iceland's participation in European economic and political integration. The first of these took place in the period 1957–59 when the government considered the implications for Iceland of joining the proposed free trade area to consist of the members of the Organization for European Economic Co-operation (OEEC); this proposal was made in response to the establishment of the European Economic Community (Alþingistíðindi B 1959: 561–2).

The second round of the 'European debate' followed in 1961–63 and concerned the question of whether or not to apply, together with Britain, Denmark, Norway and Ireland, to join the EEC. Icelandic officials considered closely the pros and cons for Iceland of forging closer bonds with European alliances, and controversy over the issue caused deep divisions in Icelandic society (Haralz 1992: 154).

The third round of the debate, in the years 1967–72, included the discussion of Iceland's membership of EFTA before 1970 and the moves towards the making of a free trade agreement with the EC. Discussions of whether or not to join EFTA were very similar to those that had taken place in the early 1960s, and once again, opinion was sharply divided.

In the following survey of these rounds, special effort will be made to identify the reasons why the Icelandic government turned its attention to the question of integration at the time, taking both economic and political factors into account. In the same way, an attempt will be made to explain what it was that politicians saw as the main obstacles to closer bonds with the rest of Europe in the form of participation in economic alliances.

The positions on European integration adopted by political parties and interest groups will be examined, and also the connections between them: during this period, and for a long time afterwards, there were close links between individual political parties and certain interest groups.

The situation in the first years of the republic

Iceland became wealthy during the Second World War, when the price of fish on the British market rose very steeply and the presence of the British, and particularly the American, armies in the country stimulated the domestic economy. In fact the war transformed Iceland's economy, but despite the resulting prosperity, economic management was unsophisticated and the economy was shackled by restrictive controls. As Europe was in ruins after the war, the USA gave it economic assistance in the form of Marshall Plan assistance. In the event, Iceland received more aid *per capita* under the Marshall Plan than any other country because Icelandic politicians exploited Iceland's strategic importance to the full when negotiating implementation of the aid programme (Snævarr 1998: 247).

The OEEC was established in 1948 to supervise aid under the Marshall Plan. As a recipient of this aid, Iceland was one of the founder members. The aim of the OEEC was to promote free trade between countries and to build up Europe's export industries. On the one hand, the Marshall Plan produced quick results (Benediktsson, E. *et al.* 1994: 12); on the other hand, the general opinion is that Iceland's participation in the plan retarded economic reform in the country (Ásgeirsson, J.F. 1998: 245; Benediktsson, E. 2000: 29; Snævarr 1998: 249) because capital was spent on direct investment instead of being used to achieve economic stability and free the economy from restrictive controls.

Iceland was not an active participant in the international institutions established after the war to manage global economic and trade issues such as the International Monetary Fund and the World Bank; nor did it join the General Agreement on Tariffs and Trade (GATT) (Benediktsson, E. 2003: 40). The economic upswing produced by the war itself and the Marshall Plan in Iceland had run its course by the early 1950s, and the government's restrictive policy was dominant in every sphere. While declaring its willingness to liberalize trade, the government justified its restrictive trappings with reference to the country's special position, its smallness and the sensitivity of its economy. The OEEC accepted these arguments, largely due to the position of the USA, which used its influence to ensure that Iceland's demands were met (Gunnarsson 1996: 89). For example, by 1957 some states had abolished all restrictions on trade in areas covered by the OEEC; abolition of 90 per cent of these restrictions was the guideline figure. Iceland distinguished itself by how slow it was to act: its 'liberalization percentage' had only reached 36 per cent in 1957 (Benediktsson, E. 2003: 46).

Iceland did not take part in the wave of adaptations to free trade that swept across Europe in the 1950s. There was little discussion in Iceland of the European Coal and Steel Community (ECSC), as its establishment could have few implications for Iceland's exports, which consisted almost entirely of marine products. Marine exports accounted for 92.3 per cent of all goods in 1952 (National Economic Institute 14 December 2001b). The extension of the nation's fisheries limit was a matter of far more interest to the Icelandic government; this was extended to 4 miles in 1952. To begin with, the government also showed little interest in the foundation of the European Economic Community.

First discussion of involvement in European integration

It was in 1957 when, under British leadership, the non-EEC countries of Europe began negotiations within the OEEC on the establishment of a free trade area in Western Europe that the Icelandic government first began a serious examination of the prospect of European integration. Iceland played an active part in the discussions within the OEEC at this time, but it was not clear then how much effect the proposed free trade area would have in Iceland. Gylfi P. Gíslason, a Social Democrat minister, was in charge of free trade issues in the left-wing government of 1956–58, and in fact remained in charge of them until 1971. He commissioned a report on the matter, which he presented to the Althingi in February 1958 (Gíslason November 1958). This stated that the effect of the establishment of the EEC on Iceland would be significant, though nowhere near as great as the effect on Britain and Denmark. In particular, further complications were foreseen for exports of unprocessed saltfish to Italy, chilled fish to Germany and frozen fish to France (Alþýðublaðið 22 February 1958).

However, these initial difficulties were seen as minor in comparison with the effect on Iceland's long-term interests: the country's rivals on these markets would be put in a much stronger competitive position. In addition, it was predicted that the EEC market would become steadily stronger, and so easy access to it would be a matter of vital importance. It was seen as a priority for Iceland to have the freest possible trade arrangements for its fish and other marine products throughout the proposed free trade area; on the other hand, various factors made it difficult for Iceland to be a full participant in the scheme unless it received certain special exemptions. The main obstacles were in the spheres of agriculture, manufacturing industry, trade with Eastern Europe, customs revenues for the Treasury and the development of power-intensive industry (Alþýðublaðið 23 February 1958). Within the OEEC, there was a lot of discussion of measures to meet the requirements of the less developed national economies, specifically those of Ireland, Iceland, Turkey and Greece (Alþýðublaðið 22 November 1957; Alþýðublaðið 30 November 1957).

According to the report, the only areas in which Iceland's agricultural sector would stand free competition would be the sale of fresh milk and lamb; domestic processed dairy products, beef, pork, chicken and vegetables would not be competitive against imports from abroad (Alþýðublaðið 23 February 1958). As regards manufacturing industry, Gíslason considered that certain occupations, which had developed under protective import tariffs, would require adaptation periods of at least 12–15 years. On the other hand, his view was that manufacturing industry enjoyed a smaller degree of protection than was generally believed (Alþýðublaðið 30 October 1957).

For a Western European country, Iceland had an unusually high volume of trade with Eastern Europe at this time: 33 per cent of its exports went to Eastern Bloc countries, including about 21 per cent to the USSR (National Economic Institute 14 December 2001a). The future of this trade would have been put in question if the country had taken part in the foundation of a free trade area.

The Progressive, Social Democratic and Independence parties seem to have taken the same position on the issue, while the People's Alliance stood apart. The first three parties were in favour of remaining vigilant and waiting to see how things developed. MPs of the Independence Party who discussed the report in the Althingi called for a discussion of the changes that would need to be made to the economy to make it possible to take part in the proposed free trade area (Morgunblaðið 28 November 1958). Ólafur Thors, the party chairman, saw joining the free trade area as the only way of tackling the problems that would result from its establishment (Alþingistíðindi B 1957: 1842–3). Einar Olgeirsson, an MP for the People's Alliance and one of Iceland's most prominent socialist leaders, adopted a resolute stance against Iceland's participation in the planned alliances in Europe. He predicted that 'German cartels' would dominate the proposed alliance and that the consequences of the alliance would be felt in the form of a lower standard of living, the collapse of certain occupations and serious jeopardy to the life of the Icelandic nation (Alþingistíðindi B 1957: 1813–19).

Nothing came of the proposed free trade area due to serious disagreements between the priorities of Britain and France. The outcome was that Britain, Sweden, Norway, Denmark, Austria, Switzerland and Portugal formed the European Free Trade Association (EFTA) in February 1959. Because of its fishery disputes with Britain, Iceland was not invited to join in the foundation of EFTA. Iceland was 'virtually at war with the U.K. over the 12 miles' (Benediktsson, E. 2003: 62); it had extended its fishing limit to 12 miles in 1958. 'It is conventional wisdom that while the U.K. and Iceland were engaged in these hostilities known as "cod wars", they could hardly have been partners in the same new trading organization' (Benediktsson, E. 2003: 40).

Membership of the EEC considered

The following years proved to be only a short lull before the question of Iceland's position in Europe came to the fore again. The political climate had changed: the Social Democratic Party and the Independence Party formed a coalition in 1959 that became referred to as the 'Government of

Reconstruction' (Viðreisnarstjórn) which stayed in office for three parliamentary terms, i.e. until 1971. It made radical changes to the country's economy, shifting it in the direction in which other countries in Western Europe had developed during the previous decades. One of the purposes of these changes was to enable Iceland to undertake the obligations involved in membership of free trade associations or economic alliances in Europe (Gíslason 1993: 59). When both EFTA and the EEC were established, free trade in fisheries products was for the most part excluded from their scope. The situation had been changing gradually, and there were plans among both the EFTA states and those of the EEC to abolish customs between the two entities (Jónsson 1976: 128). In addition, proposals on possible union or co-operation between EFTA and the EEC acted as a further stimulus on the Icelandic government to turn its attention to the issue of European integration. It was becoming necessary to examine the alternatives in order to secure Iceland's best interests for the future.

The government appointed a committee of officials headed by the minister of commerce, Gylfi Þ. Gíslason, in 1961 to examine the issue of free trade. The main aim of the committee was to discuss the possibility of Iceland joining EFTA in order to secure a better bargaining position with the EEC on free trade with fish. Three main points dominate the report submitted by the committee in April that year (Nefndin um fríverzlunarmál 12 April 1961).

First, the committee examined the changes affecting trade in marine products in Europe, and stated that if Iceland were to take part in free trade in the region, it was vital that the framework for trade in marine products should be as free as possible. The committee said the operations of EFTA embraced restricted free trade in marine products, and principally those that could be classified as industrial products. On the other hand, there was very limited access for Iceland's most important export product, frozen fish, on the British market. The committee referred to the EFTA resolution of February 1961 on increased trade in fish and other marine products. The committee foresaw radical changes in the trade structure in Europe in the years ahead, but due to the uncertainty as to the exact form they would take, said it was impossible to predict what consequences they would have for Iceland's exports.

Second, the committee discussed Iceland's position with regard to the market alliances in Europe. It did not foresee that EFTA was likely to last for long, as it had been formed primarily in order to secure a stronger position for its member states in possible negotiations with the EEC. The committee foresaw a merger of the two organizations in the immediate future as a possibility. Nevertheless, the committee's advice to the government was to abandon its 'wait and see' policy and apply to join EFTA. It based this, on the one hand, on the view that the merger of the EEC and EFTA might be delayed, in which case Iceland's competitive position would deteriorate seriously, and, on the other, on the view that membership of EFTA would guarantee Iceland a place in the company of some of the other major fishing nations of Europe (e.g. Denmark and Norway) and enable it to enjoy collaboration with these countries and with Sweden in other areas within EFTA.

Third, the committee examined Iceland's special position regarding free trade. Here, the same points emerged as had been seen as obstacles to the country's participating in a free trade area in the late 1950s: its important trade with Eastern Europe and the fact that its manufacturing industry was underdeveloped and poorly prepared to face foreign competition and that various matters concerning the agricultural sector, in particular the prohibition on export subsidies, would need special examination. The committee therefore emphasized that Iceland would need a long adaptation period – twice as long as was normally allowed – in order to dismantle its protective tariffs, and in addition it would be necessary to seek exemption so as to be able to continue its trade with Eastern Europe (Nefndin um fríverzlunarmál 12 April 1961: 1–10).

A great deal of activity followed after this report, including consultation with domestic interest groups (Nefndin um fríverzlunarmál 24 April 1961), extensive liaison with officials and politicians throughout the Nordic countries, interviews with the staff of international institutions and canvassing of the British position. Gíslason also explained the situation specifically to all the governments of the EEC countries (Benediktsson, E. 2000: 63).

Consultation and discussions abroad revealed that there were various obstacles to Iceland's membership of EFTA. For example the Secretary-General of EFTA considered it would be difficult to grant the exemptions that Iceland intended to seek (Andersen 30 August 1961). Furthermore, Britain's attitude to Iceland at this time was still not positive as a result of the dispute over fisheries limits that had taken place a few years previously (Ólafsson 22 July 1961). Moreover, the EEC announced that the EFTA states would be invited to negotiate membership on an individual basis, and not collectively (Kristinsson 1987: 57). Thus, one of the main motives that Iceland had for joining EFTA, being included in joint negotiations with the EEC, was no longer valid.

Britain and Denmark applied to join the EEC in August 1961; Norway and Ireland followed suit shortly afterwards and the neutral EFTA states applied for associate membership (Archer *et al.* 1998: 26). As the EEC member states had reached agreement on an external tariff on marine products, it had become even more urgent for Iceland to make an agreement with the community: the EEC's tariffs on saltfish and stockfish were due to rise by 13 per cent, its tariff on frozen fish was to become 10 per cent and canned fish products were to be subjected to tariffs of the order of 20–25 per cent (Jónsson 1976: 144–6). The tariffs that the EEC planned to impose meant that Iceland would have to double the average payments it made, in addition to which its competitive position, in comparison with that of fishing nations within the community, would deteriorate.

All the principal interest groups that the government consulted urged it in August 1961 to apply for membership of the EEC. These were the Agricultural Production Council, the Federation of Icelandic Co-operative Societies (SÍS), Icelandic Freezing Plants Corporation, the Union of Stockfish Producers, the Union of Icelandic Fish Producers (SÍF), the Federation of Icelandic Fishing Vessel Owners (LÍU), the Federation of Crafts and Industries, the Iceland Chamber of Commerce, the Retailers' Association, the Association of Icelandic Importers, Exporters and Wholesalers, the Confederation of Icelandic Employers and the Farmers' Association of Iceland (Morgunblaðið 18 August 1961). Earlier, Icelandic Freezing Plants Corporation had pressed the government to apply to join the EEC, but the Icelandic Federation of Labour had opposed such a move. One reason why the interest groups wanted to press ahead with an application with all speed was that they thought it would be easier for Iceland to achieve the terms it was aiming at before other states concluded their membership negotiations and the EEC was fully consolidated (Morgunblaðið 18 August 1961). Nevertheless, these groups did not call for membership at any price; they recognized that various points needed to be resolved before membership could be clinched, and in this attitude they were to a large extent in full agreement with the government. The Farmers' Association soon changed its position and opposed EEC membership; substantial doubts had arisen among farmers as to the merits of the community (Þjóðviljinn 10 September 1961; Tíminn 15 February 1963).

The ruling parties, the Conservatives and Social Democrats, were unanimous on the issue (Vísir 15 November 1962; Kristinsson 1987: 61–2). Gíslason led the debate, with the support of the Conservatives' leaders Ólafur Thors, party chairman and prime minister, and Bjarni Benediktsson, deputy party chairman, who held the portfolios of industry, justice and health. After extensive consultation with entities both in Iceland and abroad, the government soon decided that it was appropriate to apply for associate membership of the EEC, as it regarded various provisions of the Treaty of Rome as impractical for small states like Iceland (Benediktsson, B. 1961; Frjáls menning 1962: 47–8).

First, it was thought impossible for Iceland to accept the EEC's principle of equal rights to employment and right of establishment because of the smallness of the nation (Benediktsson, B. 1961; Independence Party 1961; Alþýðublaðið 6 February 1962). Second, various provisions regarding manufacturing industry, agriculture and trade with Eastern Europe were seen as an obstacle to full membership, and third, the government took the view that Iceland would need a long adaptation period in which to abolish its protective tariffs (Alþýðublaðið 14 July 1961). Fourth – and this was possibly the most important point – Iceland was not prepared to grant other countries the same rights as its own nationals had to catch fish in Icelandic waters (Alþýðublaðið 14 July 1961). Whether or not the EEC would have been prepared to accept Iceland's demands was never put to the test: the informal discussions between Icelandic officials and their foreign colleagues came to nothing after President de Gaulle declared his opposition to enlarging the EEC. Investigations by Icelandic officials of attitudes within the EEC Commission at the time indicated that it would have been difficult for Iceland to achieve its aims (Andersen 30 August 1961).

The Progressive Party and the People's Alliance were opposed to any form of membership of the national alliances in Europe, and were in favour of bilateral agreements with the EEC and EFTA, though the Progressives were less rigid in their position. Disputes arose between the Progressive Party and the government parties as to whether the Progressives had set themselves against the government's policy simply because it was in opposition; government leaders pointed to the policy of the Progressive Party when it had been in government at the time when the debate on the foundation of a free trade association in Europe had been at its height (Morgunblaðið 15 January 1963; Alþingistíðindi B 1962: 1563). In discussion of the issue of European membership, the People's Alliance appealed heavily to nationalistic sympathies (Þjóðviljinn 20 August 1961); the Progressives also used nationalistic arguments to some extent (Tíminn 8 January 1963).

When nothing came of the proposed enlargement of the EEC, the debate on Europe in Iceland died down. This was also the time of the 'herring boom', when huge catches and exports of herring brought more widespread economic prosperity than ever before. These developments reduced the government's interest in joining market alliances in Europe. Initially, instead, it channelled its efforts into finding a solution to Iceland's marketing problems through the negotiations on the 'Kennedy' round of GATT, which was then in progress. By early 1966 it seemed clear to the government that these negotiations would not meet its expectations, so it turned its attention to EFTA once again (Ásgeirsson, Þ. 22 January 1966). Icelandic officials monitored free-trade developments in Europe closely, gathering much of their information through collaboration with the other Nordic countries (Benediktsson, E. 2000: 65).

Iceland joins EFTA

Early in 1965 Britain examined means of strengthening EFTA, one of the ideas it proposed being to bring Iceland and Ireland into the association (GATT nefndin 20 April 1965). As a result of this, the Icelandic government committee appointed to monitor GATT negotiations turned its attention to the prospect of membership of EFTA, and submitted a report to the government in summer 1965 (GATT nefndin 1 July 1965). The main attraction of membership of EFTA, according to the report, was that it would facilitate Iceland's exports of fish and other marine products and improve their competitive position on the markets of Europe. The committee also expressed its concern at Iceland's position within the framework of Nordic co-operation, which had to some extent come under EFTA in the preceding years.

The main disadvantages of joining EFTA that the report named were the same as those that had been identified previously (GATT nefndin 1 July 1965: 2–3): means would have to be found to ensure a future for Iceland's manufacturing industries following the lowering of protective tariffs required for EFTA membership and it would be necessary to keep up trade with Eastern Europe, though this was no longer at the same high level as it had been. On the other hand, the committee no longer saw the provisions on equality as regards the right of establishment within the EFTA area as an obstacle to membership, since this right did not apply in the spheres of fisheries, agriculture, transport and the activities of banks and insurance companies (GATT nefndin 1 July 1965: 3). Despite the exemptions already applying to these sectors, the principle of equality in this area was a very sensitive issue in Icelandic politics, and the government investigated the possibility of securing a general exemption from it for Iceland (Ministry for Foreign Affairs 28–29 April 1966: 5).

Following on this report, the Icelandic government began examining the prospect of EFTA membership; this was favourably received by officials in the other Nordic countries (Ásgeirsson, P. et al. 7 May 1965). There had been some discussion of the issue in Iceland, particularly among leaders in manufacturing industry (Íslenskur iðnaður October–November 1964: 9; Íslenskur iðnaður August–September 1965: 7) and representatives of Icelandic Freezing Plants Corporation (IFPC) (Ministry of Commerce 20 May 1966; Hjaltason et al. 1997b: 22–6). For example, four representatives of the IFPC attended a meeting in the ministry of commerce in May 1966 to put questions about the EFTA scheme. Notes made at the meeting show that understanding of the workings of EFTA was not widespread, even among fish exporting companies (Ministry of Commerce 20 May 1966). According to a memo made by Iceland's minister–counsellor in Paris in 1964, the IFPC had great difficulty deciding its policy on the free trade issue. 'This is all the worse considering the fact that, as is common knowledge, these are the fastest-growing markets for our products' (Benediktsson, E. 8 January 1964). All the same, the IFPC saw Europe in a positive light and believed that extensive and constantly expanding markets were to be found there for frozen seafood (Hjaltason et al. 1997b: 22–6). However, EFTA did not emerge as a political issue until after the general election of April 1967.

The main motivation for opening negotiations with EFTA was the deteriorating position of Iceland's seafood exports on the European market, so securing favourable terms for these products was the precondition for

Iceland joining EFTA (Alþýðublaðið 2 April 1969). Here the aims of the fisheries interest groups and the government coincided: the aim was to secure tariff-free access to the markets for Icelandic fish exports without having to grant fishing rights in Icelandic waters to foreign trawling companies. The possibility of securing a free trade agreement with the EEC after joining EFTA was therefore one of the main reasons why the government pressed for membership of EFTA (Kristinsson 1987: 73).

The pros and cons of EFTA membership for Iceland were listed in a memo prepared in the ministry of commerce in October 1967 (Ministry of Commerce 30 October 1967). By this time the issue of EFTA had gained momentum. For example, the Association of Icelandic Canning Factories had sent the ministry of commerce a letter urging it to give careful consideration to the question of EFTA membership (Ministry of Commerce 28 July 1967). Icelandic officials also began broaching the issue with EFTA staff. They asked the Secretary-General whether it was realistic to expect that Iceland would gain completely free access to EFTA's markets for its fisheries exports; his view was that it was not (Ásgeirsson, Þ. 29 January 1968).

The 'Reconstruction Government' coalition was still in power at this time, and was unanimous in its policy and presentation of the issue. As before, the Social Democrat minister Gíslason was the main spokesman for membership, but was solidly supported by the Independence Party leaders, prime minister Bjarni Benediktsson and minister of industry, Jóhann Hafstein. For a long time the Progressive Party was undecided on the issue; even only eight days before the Althingi passed a resolution to apply to join EFTA, it had not decided on its position (EFTA-nefndin 4 November 1968). Its MPs had criticized the handling of the issue from the outset, however, and claimed that insufficient studies had been made of the consequences of membership for Iceland, and specifically for the country's manufacturing industries (Þjóðviljinn 9 November 1969).

Divisions of opinion cut deep into Icelandic society: on the day the Althingi voted to apply for membership, hundreds of people gathered outside the parliament building in protest, throwing stones at the building and eggs at government ministers (Þjóðviljinn 13 November 1968). In the vote on the resolution to apply for membership, 35 MPs voted in favour, 14 against and 11 abstained (Morgunblaðið 13 November 1969). It was supported by the government MPs and four members of the People's Alliance, and opposed by the Progressives and four People's Alliance members (Morgunblaðið 13 November 1969). The Progressive Party took the view that the time was not ripe to apply for membership, and proposed instead to take measures at home to strengthen the position of manufacturing industry and the economy as a whole. EFTA membership was not the answer to economic problems, it argued; the government must take measures of its own.

In the negotiations on Iceland's accession to EFTA, which began in

January 1969, the government aimed at securing four main targets (EFTA-nefndin 8 January 1969). First, the country was to enjoy all the concessions that EFTA had already implemented immediately on entry. Second, it would receive a certain number of years as a transition period in which to dismantle its tariffs and restrictions. Third, it would be permitted to continue trading with Eastern Europe and the USSR, and fourth, various bilateral issues would have to be resolved. One of these was that Iceland would need a special tariff-free export quota for its frozen fish sold to Britain if no agreement were reached on completely free trade in fisheries products. Iceland also sought support from the other Nordic countries to increase sales of lamb and strengthen the position of its manufacturing industries.

Almost all of these aims were secured (Benediktsson, E. 2000: 83–94). From the time of its entry, Iceland enjoyed in full the abolition of tariffs that had been implemented between the EFTA countries (Jónsson 1976: 156). It was also allowed to dismantle its import tariffs over a ten-year period. The EFTA states permitted Iceland to maintain its trade with the USSR, which consisted mostly of exports of fish in return for imports of fuel (Jónsson 1976: 156).

One of the most important demands that Iceland presented in its negotiations with EFTA was to secure broader access for its exports to Britain. The British negotiators, for their part, saw little to gain from Iceland's membership of EFTA, so talks with them did not go smoothly (Foreign Affairs Committee of the Althingi 13 December 1969: 5). The line adopted by Iceland was that if Britain did not take steps to open the way for Icelandic frozen fish, then trade would be far from balanced (Ásgeirsson, Þ. 31 March 1969: 5), since British manufacturers had open access to the Icelandic market but this was not the case for Icelandic seafood exports to Britain. Britain's proposal that the Nordic countries should receive a joint quota for frozen fish exports to Britain, which they could then divide between themselves, was completely unacceptable to Iceland. Eventually, Britain agreed to abolish the 10 per cent tariff on frozen fillets and also to establish a special minimum price system, which was regarded by officials and exporters in Iceland at the time as a highly satisfactory conclusion (Benediktsson, E. 2000: 91).

The other Nordic countries also met Iceland's demands. In February 1969, Bjarni Benediktsson proposed that the Nordic countries should set up an industrial development fund for Iceland, which was done in 1970. They also took measures to make it easier for Iceland to export lamb to their markets (Benediktsson, E. 2000: 92). The arguments Iceland used in pressing for these measures from the Nordic countries were the same as those that had applied to Britain: if Iceland were to open its market for imports of industrial goods from them with no adjustments made in return, the trading arrangements would not in fact be mutual (Ásgeirsson, Þ. 31 March 1969: 5–6).

When it came to a vote in the Althingi on the agreement negotiated with EFTA, the Progressive Party MPs abstained. The party was divided in its position on EFTA, and although many members were in favour, the party chairman, Eysteinn Jónsson, said one reason he was not supporting membership was that he did not wish to be responsible for the policy of the government (Eggertsson 1999: 69–70). Progressive Party members of the Althingi's committee on foreign affairs criticized Gíslason for not having secured from EFTA an exemption from its provisions on the right of establishment (Foreign Affairs Committee of the Althingi 13 December 1969). The reason that the Icelandic government had abandoned its demand for exemption was that this would have put it in a weaker bargaining position with Britain (Foreign Affairs Committee of the Althingi 13 December 1969: 4).

The People's Alliance adopted a firm stance against membership of EFTA, though three of its MPs broke away from the party and supported it. Two of them were leaders of the Icelandic Federation of Labour, and thus went against the policy of the federation, which followed the People's Alliance's policy. Opposition by the People's Alliance was based on fear that membership would lead to higher taxes and jeopardize the future of manufacturing industry, where any contraction would mean unemployment, and also that EFTA's provisions on the right of establishment would prove detrimental for Iceland and that membership would rule out a socialistically planned economy (Kristinsson 1987: 77).

Even though good terms had been secured on increased exports of lamb to the Nordic countries, interest groups in agriculture opposed EFTA membership. To begin with, agricultural leaders favoured membership, as they could see only benefits for the sector (EFTA-nefndin 22 August 1968). In 1969, however, farmers took a firm stance against the agreement, arguing that it would be to the detriment of Icelandic society and agriculture (Freyr 1969: 407). It can be assumed that the close connections between the agricultural sector and the Progressive Party influenced the position adopted by the agricultural interest groups on this issue.

Though membership of EFTA had serious implications for manufacturing industry in Iceland, interest groups in the sector were very much in favour of it, which made the government's path to EFTA membership much smoother (Benediktsson, E. 2000: 86). The government promised to take steps to solve the problems that the sector would face as a result of joining EFTA in areas such as taxation, finance, technical matters, customs and other aspects of business operations (Á döfinni 1993: 12).

In 1970 the EC began negotiations with Britain, Denmark, Norway and Ireland on their accession to the community (Gíslason 1980: 170–1; Jónsson 1976: 158–60; Ásgeirsson, P. 1972: 104). Thereafter, the EC agreed to open negotiations with other EFTA states on free trade agreements. Iceland was offered a free trade agreement covering industrial products. Obviously this held little attraction for Iceland: the government had always emphasized the fact that practically all the country's goods exports consisted of fish and other marine products (Ásgeirsson, Þ. 1972: 105). It was during these negotiations with the EC in 1972 that Iceland extended its fishing limits to 50 miles, which caused great difficulties: the problem was not only to have the EC agree to free trade in fish and marine products but also to keep the talks going at the same time as extending the fishing limits, which had direct and adverse effects on fishing enterprises in the EC countries (Ásgeirsson, Þ. 1972: 105). Nevertheless, Iceland managed to secure highly favourable terms in its free trade agreement, which received cross-party support when it was signed in 1972; the Progressive Party, the People's Alliance and the newly-formed Union of Liberals and Leftists had formed a government the previous year. The most important of all these was Protocol No. 6 to the agreement with the EC, which provided for free trade with most fish and marine products. This proved of great advantage to Icelandic fish exporters when it took effect; their competitiveness was no less important a factor here (Hjaltason *et al.* 1997a: 270; Jónsson 1976: 167). The protocol did not take effect until 1976 due to disputes between Iceland and the EC over fishing limits. Iceland extended these to 200 miles in 1975, this taking effect in 1976. Extension of the country's fishing limits (economic zone) was a dominating feature of Icelandic foreign policy from the end of the Second World War until the late 1970s (Benediktsson, E. 2003: 20).

Summary

Iceland was slow to turn its attention to the issue of free trade, and did not follow the policy of the other Nordic countries in this area. As the free trade arrangements introduced in Europe did not cover fish and other marine products, there was little economic incentive for Iceland to join in European integration, and there were also certain other economic and political factors that dissuaded the country from becoming more closely associated with the rest of Europe. Its economy was shackled in restrictions, and the struggle to extend its fishing limits was at its height. The country's restrictive economic policy played a large part in preventing it from taking part in the free trade area proposed by the OEEC states, and as a result of the extension of its fisheries limits to 50 miles in 1958 and the subsequent dispute with Britain, Iceland was not invited to join EFTA. Both domestic and external factors prevented it from participating in the movement towards European integration in the early 1960s when the government examined the pros and cons of joining EFTA or the EC. It was only near the end of the 1960s that the Icelandic government decided to participate in European integration; by this time Iceland had set aside many of its restrictive policies, higher tariffs were about to be imposed against its fish exports to Europe and the prosperity of the herring boom was a thing of the past.

The rhetoric in which the discussion of European integration was couched remained largely unchanged throughout this entire period, and the positions of political parties on the issue changed little. The People's Alliance was completely opposed to membership of the European alliances from the outset. For a long time the Progressive Party wavered in its position on free trade; it is likely that its spell in opposition from 1958 to 1971 influenced its position. The Social Democratic Party and the Independence Party were virtually indistinguishable in their position on the issue, and their leaders expressed their views in identical terms. Various interest groups took part in the debate. The agricultural unions and the Icelandic Federation of Labour fought against involvement in European integration. Even though they took little initiative, interest groups in the fisheries sector, on the other hand, were eager to maintain, and if possible improve, their position on the European market. Groupings in manufacturing industry were also in favour of more involvement in free trade, even though the sector enjoyed protective tariffs; this support was of great value to those who bore the brunt of the negotiating effort at the time.

The government took the initiative in assessing where the country stood in relation to the changes taking place in Europe at any given time, and the policy it adopted was that prime consideration should be given to the interests of the fisheries sector. Market access for fisheries exports was the factor that motivated the government to examine the options available regarding free trade. On the other hand, there were various obstacles in the way, and these had to be overcome before Iceland could join EFTA and make a free trade agreement with the EC.

In the opinion of interest groups and the political parties, Iceland's free trade agreement of 1972 with the EC secured a good competitive position for Icelandic fisheries products on the European market, and for more than a decade, no changes were made in the EC's internal market that could threaten this situation. For this reason, the issue of European integration was not on the Icelandic government's agenda during this time. It was only with the passing of the Single European Act and the finalization of the European Union's internal market that Iceland and the other EFTA states had to review their position.

Bibliography

Á döfinni [A journal published by the Federation of Icelandic Industries] (1993) 'Iðnaðurinn og upphaf EFTA aðildar', *Á döfinni* 2.
Alþingistíðindi B [Parliamentary record] (1957).
Alþingistíðindi B [Parliamentary record] (1959).
Alþingistíðindi B [Parliamentary record] (1962).
Alþýðublaðið [An Icelandic newspaper] (30 October 1957) 'Íslenzkur iðnaður er samkeppnishæfari en almennt er talið', *Alþýðublaðið*.

—— (22 November 1957) 'Um fríverzlun Evrópu', *Alþýðublaðið*.
—— (30 November 1957) 'Fríverzlunarnefnd OEEC heldur fundi í jan. um landbúnaðarvörur og lítt iðnvædd lönd', *Alþýðublaðið*.
—— (22 February 1958) 'Úr skýrzlu Gylfa Þ. Gíslasonar á alþingi – II', *Alþýðublaðið*.
—— (23 February 1958) 'Úr skýrzlu Gylfa Þ. Gíslasonar á alþingi – III', *Alþýðublaðið*.
—— (14 July 1961) 'Íslendingar og markaðsbandalög Evrópu – síðari hluti', *Alþýðublaðið*.
—— (6 February 1962) 'Aukaaðild hentar Íslandi bezt', *Alþýðublaðið*.
—— (2 April 1969) 'Freðfiskurinn gæti ráðið úrslitum um EFTA aðild', *Alþýðublaðið*.
Andersen, H.G. (30 August 1961) 'Memo', unpublished memo from the Icelandic ambassador in Brussels, Ministry of Commerce.
Archer, C. and Sogner, I. (1998) *Norway, European Integration and Atlantic Security*, London: SAGE.
Ásgeirsson, J.F. (1998) *Pétur Ben.*, Reykjavík: Mál og menning.
Ásgeirsson, Þ. and Benediktsson, E. (7 May 1965) 'Frásögn af viðtölum í Geneve 3–7 maí 1965 um hugsanlega aðild Íslands að EFTA', unpublished memo, Ministry of Commerce.
Ásgeirsson, Þ. (22 January 1966) 'Nokkrir punktar', unpublished memo, Ministry of Commerce.
—— (29 January 1968) 'Heimsókn á EFTA skrifstofuna', unpublished memo, Ministry of Commerce.
—— (31 March 1969) 'Viðtal dr. Gylfa Þ. Gíslasonar, viðskiptamálaráðherra við Anthony Crossland, viðskiptamálaráðherra Breta, í London 27. marz s.l.', unpublished memo, Ministry of Commerce.
—— (1972) 'Samningur Íslands við Efnahagsbandalag Evrópu', *Fjármálatíðindi*, 2: 104–8.
Benediktsson, B. (1961) 'Úr ræðu Bjarna Benediktssonar á landsfundi Sjálfstæðisflokksins 1961', unpublished speech, Independence Party.
Benediktsson, E. (8 January 1964) 'Tollalækkanir innan EFTA og tollabreytingar EBE', unpublished memo, Ministry of Commerce.
—— (2000) *Ísland og Evrópuþróunin 1950–2000*, Reykjavík: Fjölsýn forlag.
—— (2003) *Iceland and European Development*, Reykjavík: Almenna bókafélagið.
Benediktsson, E., Sigurjónsson, K. and Pálsson, S. (1994) *Upphaf Evrópusamvinnu Íslands*, Reykjavík: Institute of International Affairs in Iceland.
EFTA-nefndin [EFTA committee] (22 August 1968) 'Fundargerð', unpublished record of a meeting, Ministry of Commerce.
—— (4 November 1968) 'Fundargerð', unpublished record of a meeting, Ministry of Commerce.
—— (8 January 1969) 'Fundargerð', unpublished record of a meeting, Ministry of Commerce.
Eggertsson, D.B. (1999) *Steingrímur Hermansson, Ævisaga II*, Reykjavík: Vaka Helgafell.
Foreign Affairs Committee of the Althingi (13 December 1969) '393. fundur', unpublished record of a meeting, the prime minister's office.
Freyr [A journal published by the farmers association of Iceland] (1969) 'Aðalfundur Stéttarsambands bænda', *Freyr*, LVIII.

Frjáls menning (1962) *Sjálfstæði Íslands og þátttaka í Efnahagsbandalögum: Umræður á ráðstefnu Frjálsar menningar 27 janúar 1962*, Reykjavík, Frjáls menning.

GATT nefndin [The GATT committee] (20 April 1965) 'Aðild Íslands að EFTA', unpublished memo, Ministry of Commerce.

—— (1 July 1965) 'Rökin með og móti aðild að EFTA', unpublished memo, Ministry of Commerce.

Gíslason, G. (November 1958) *Skýrsla um fríverzlunarmálið: flutt á Alþingi 26 nóvember 1958 af iðnaðarráðherra, Gylfa Þ. Gíslasyni*, unpublished report, Althingi.

—— (1980) 'Hagsæld, tími og hamingja', *Fjármálatíðindi*, 1: 49–58.

—— (1993) *Viðreisnarárin*, Reykjavík: Almenna bókafélagið.

Gunnarsson, G.Á. (1996) 'Ísland og Marshallaðstoðin: Atvinnustefna og stjórnmálahagsmunir', *Saga, tímarit Sögufélagsins*, XXXIV: 85–130.

Haralz, J. (1992) 'Ísland úr fjarska', *Fjármálatíðindi*, 2: 151–8.

Hjaltason, J. and Hannibalsson, Ó. (1997a) *Með spriklið í sporðinum: Saga SH 1942–1996*, Reykjavík: Hið íslenska bókmenntafélag.

Hjaltason, J., Einarsson, H. and Hannibalsson, Ó. (1997b) *Yfir lönd yfir höf: Saga SH og dótturfyrirtækja SH erlendis 1942–1996*, Reykjavík: Hið íslenska bókmenntafélag.

Independence Party (1961) *Stjórnmálaályktun landsfundar Sjálfstæðisflokksins 1961*, Reykjavík: The Independence Party.

Íslenskur iðnaður [A journal published by the Federation of Icelandic Industries] (October–November 1964) 'Finnland og EFTA', *Íslenskur iðnaður*.

—— (August–September 1965) 'Norskur EFTA-sérfræðingur í heimsókn', *Íslenskur iðnaður*.

Jónsson, Ó.H. (1976) 'Ísland og efnahagsbandalögin', *Fjármálatíðindi*, 2: 124–74.

Kristinsson, G.H. (1987) *Ísland og Evrópubandalagið*, Reykjavík: Icelandic commission on security and international affairs.

Ministry of Commerce (20 May 1966) 'Til minnis', unpublished memo, Ministry of Commerce.

—— (28 July 1967) 'Memo', unpublished memo, Ministry of Commerce.

—— (30 October 1967) 'Aðild Íslands að EFTA,' unpublished memo, Ministry of Commerce.

Ministry for Foreign Affairs (28–29 April 1966) 'Frásögn af norrænum "handelschefs" – fundi í Reykjavík dagana 28. og 29. apríl 1966', unpublished record of a meeting, Ministry for Foreign Affairs.

Morgunblaðið [An Icelandic newspaper] (28 November 1958) 'Breytingar á hagkerfi undirstaða þátttöku í fríverzlun', *Morgunblaðið*.

—— (18 August 1961) 'Samtök meginatvinnuveganna styðja: Inntökubeiðni í Efnahagsbandalagið', *Morgunblaðið*.

—— (15 January 1963) 'Vinstri stjórnin vildi aðild að fríverzlunarsamningi við EBE', *Morgunblaðið*.

—— (13 November 1969) 'Samþykkt með 35 gegn 14', *Morgunblaðið*.

National Economic Institute (14 December 2001a) *Merchandise exports by countries 1901–2000, percentage breakdown*. Available online: http://www.ths.is/rit/sogulegt/a0709.xls (accessed 12 March 2003).

—— (14 December 2001b) *Percentage breakdown of export of goods (fob) by industries 1901–2000*. Available online: http://www.ths.is/rit/sogulegt/a0704.xls (accessed 13 March 2003).

Nefndin um fríverzlunarmál [The committee on free trade] (12 April 1961) 'Álitsgerð', unpublished report, Ministry of Commerce.

—— (24 April 1961) 'Samstarf við hin ýmsu hagsmunasamtök um undirbúning að aðild Íslands að fríverzluninni', unpublished memo, Ministry of Commerce.

Ólafsson, D. (22 July 1961) 'Afstaða Íslands gagnvart markaðsbandalögunum', unpublished memo, Ministry of Commerce.

Snævarr, S. (1998) 'Ísland og alþjóðaefnahagsstofnanir 1945–1960', in G.J. Guðmundsson and E.K. Björnsson (eds) *Íslenska söguþingið 28.–31. maí 1997*, Reykjavík: Sagnfræðistofnun Háskóla Íslands og Sagnfræðifélag Íslands.

Tíminn [An Icelandic newspaper] (8 January 1963) 'Örlagamálið', *Tíminn*.

—— (15 February 1963) 'Hér er á ferðinni eitt mesta sjálfstæðismál Íslendinga', *Tíminn*.

Vísir [An Icelandic newspaper] (15 November 1962) 'Einhugur um EBE', *Vísir*.

Þjóðviljinn [An Icelandic newspaper] (20 August 1961) 'Níðingsverk í undirbúningi', *Þjóðviljinn*.

—— (10 September 1961) 'Ekki má veita útlendingum jafnrétti til atvinnurekstrar eða atvinnu', *Þjóðviljinn*.

—— (13 November 1968) 'Mótmæli við Alþingi í gær', *Þjóðviljinn*.

—— (9 November 1969) 'Alþýðubandalagið og Framsókn telja umsókn um aðild að EFTA ótímabæra', *Þjóðviljinn*.

3 A controversial step
Membership of the EEA

Baldur Thorhallsson and Hjalti Thor Vignisson

Introduction

As an associate member of the European Union under the European Economic Area Agreement, Iceland is deeply involved in European integration. It is part of the EU's internal market, which is in a state of constant development, in addition to which it benefits from collaboration with the EU in other areas, e.g. education and science. The EEA Agreement was hotly disputed before Iceland's accession: many considered that it involved an assignment of sovereignty and was therefore at variance with the Icelandic constitution. Advocates of the agreement, on the other hand, emphasized that it would secure better access to the European market for Icelandic fisheries exports; this argument won support for their cause. However, the EEA Agreement concerns more than merely access to markets. Under it, Iceland is obliged to adopt EU legislation, so ensuring implementation of the 'four freedoms' and incorporates about 80 per cent of EU legislation.[1]

Below follows an account of the background to Iceland's formulation of a policy on the EEA and its accession to the EEA Agreement. This begins with the Luxembourg Declaration of 1984 and ends with the ratification of the agreement by the Althingi early in 1993. The first part of the chapter examines the lead-up to negotiations and the motives that led Iceland and the other EFTA states to take part in them. An account is also given of the progress of the negotiations and the aims that Iceland sought to achieve. The second part of the chapter traces the stance taken by the political parties and interest groups on membership of the EEA. Finally, a brief survey is given of what the government sees as the results of EEA membership for Iceland.

Background and negotiations

Changes occurred in Europe's free trade structures in the mid-1980s that made it imperative for Iceland to make a response. These began with the Luxembourg Declaration of April 1984 (Gstöhl 1996: 48–54; Gstöhl 2002: 147–9). At first, the increased collaboration between the EC and EFTA allowed for under the declaration was not seen as being of significance for Iceland, as no mention was made of liberalizing trade in fish and other marine products; consequently there was little economic motivation for Iceland to participate in the process. The declaration only mentioned industrial products and the harmonization of standards, the elimination of certain technical barriers and unfair trading practices, etc.

Many EFTA states, particularly Sweden, thought the aims stated in the Luxembourg Declaration nowhere near satisfactory; Sweden's large industrial enterprises were highly dependent on developments in the rest of Europe (Gstöhl 2002: 152). Following the publication of the EC's white paper of 1985 on the completion of the internal market, and the passing of the Single European Act in 1986, the EFTA states pressed harder for closer co-operation with the EC. There was good reason for this: according to the 'Checchini Report,' the establishment of the internal market would result in a gain of 5.3 per cent of GDP for the EC states (Gstöhl 2002: 148). Various economists estimated that the EFTA states' terms of trade would worsen by 5 per cent if they remained outside the internal market (Stephensen 1996: 29). The negotiations that took place between EFTA and the EC following the Luxembourg Declaration nevertheless received little attention in Iceland; this was also the case elsewhere in Europe (Gstöhl 1996: 51; Gstöhl 2002: 148–9).

In Iceland's case, the reason for giving close attention to developments in Europe was rather different: the enlargement of the EC in 1986 with the entry of Portugal and Spain, the two countries that were by far the largest buyers of Icelandic saltfish. This is illustrated by the fact that about 23 per cent of the country's saltfish sales were to EC countries in 1985, while in 1986 the figure was over 95 per cent (Valdimarsson *et al.* 1997: 51–2). Tariffs and quotas on trade in saltfish were not adopted until Spain and Portugal entered the community, and probably in response to demands by fishing enterprises in those countries. Nevertheless it was not until 1988 that interest groups in Iceland took up this issue: the previous two years had been good ones for Icelandic exporters because of poor fish catches elsewhere in Europe. Norway and Canada had dealt with the situation by making agreements with Portugal on the exchange of fishing rights and free market access for fish products. Canada had also made a similar agreement with Spain (Stephensen 1996: 52–6). An agreement of this type was out of the question for the Icelandic government, which had never been prepared to trade fishing rights in return for market access. Under agreements with the EC and EFTA in the early 1970s, about half of Iceland's fisheries exports were tariff-free. These consisted mainly of frozen fillets. In 1991, tariffs on saltfish and fresh fish were far more important considerations in Iceland's negotiations for improved access to the European markets. That year, 46.2 per cent of the tariffs paid by Iceland to the EC related to saltfish and 41.6 per cent to fresh fish (DV 2 August 1991).[2]

It was after the initiative by Jacques Delors, president of the European Commission, on increased co-operation between EFTA and the EC in the European Parliament in 1989 that the debate on European integration really got into its stride in Iceland. The prime ministers of the EFTA states met shortly afterwards in Oslo, where they welcomed Delors' initiative and declared their will to examine ways of achieving closer co-operation between the two organizations. Iceland almost failed to take part in this declaration: it only managed to have the other EFTA states agree to free trade in fisheries products at an extraordinary meeting just before the press conference at which the outcome of the meeting was made known (Stephensen 1996: 39). The prime minister (1983–87 and 1988–91) and chairman of the Progressive Party, Steingrímur Hermannsson, stressed both at the meeting and after he returned to Iceland that Iceland had stated a proviso regarding the free movement of capital, services and workers. On the other hand, the minister for foreign affairs (1988–95) and the chairman of the Social Democratic Party, Jón Baldvin Hannibalsson, said at the end of the meeting that Iceland intended to play a full part in the forthcoming negotiations with the EC, and stated no provisos regarding the 'four freedoms' (Stephensen 1996: 36–40).

From the outset of the negotiations, Iceland held out stubbornly to secure free trade in fisheries products, and difficult situations arose. The EC found it difficult to agree to treat fish and marine products in the same way as manufactured goods (Stephensen 1996: 55–7). It saw free trade in fish in the context of the other aspects of its common fisheries policy. For its part, the Icelandic government ruled out the possibility of allowing fishing in Icelandic waters in exchange for better access to markets, and completely refused to have trade related to the common fisheries policy (Benediktsson 2003: 23). An illustration of the tense atmosphere of the negotiations can be seen in the fact that the Icelandic delegation walked out of a session in April 1991 in protest at the EC delegates' assertion that they had only been authorized to agree to waive tariffs on fisheries products in return for fishing rights in the waters of the EFTA states. After this incident the Icelandic team decided not to attend a joint meeting with EC representatives. However, the Icelandic negotiators returned to the negotiating table a few days later, and the government issued a statement reiterating its demand for market access for fisheries products without concessions on fishing rights in return. The final outcome, in which tariff-free status was achieved for 90 per cent of Iceland's fisheries products, was generally regarded as extremely good from Iceland's point of view (Stephensen 1996: 56; Morgunblaðið 23 October 1991).

In all essential points, Iceland also secured its other aims in these negotiations. Under the agreement, agricultural imports are limited and Iceland managed to state provisos on investment by foreign parties in the fisheries and power sectors, in addition to which non-nationals are not permitted to purchase coastal properties with perquisite rights (Stephensen

1996: 55–7). Regarding the right to employment and residence, Iceland is authorized to take special security measures, i.e. to limit the influx of people under certain circumstances; this involved recognition of the country's special position in terms of its small population. Nevertheless, the Icelandic government declared its intention to participate in the agreement on this point (Stephensen 1996: 63).

Attitudes of the political parties and sectoral interest groups

Hannibalsson, the minister for foreign affairs, piloted Iceland's accession to the EEA Agreement from the beginning and made it a priority to have it ratified. At the beginning of the negotiations between EFTA and the EC that led to the EEA Agreement, Iceland's government was a three-party coalition of the Progressive and Social Democratic parties and the People's Alliance that ruled from 1988 to 1991.[3] The priorities of each of these parties at the time merit special attention.

The SDP supported the agreement, but elements in the Progressive Party and the People's Alliance felt dubious about it. This did not prevent the government from playing a full part in talks on the establishment of the EEA, and the parties did not publicly criticize the progress of negotiations (Stephensen 1996: 87). The attitude of the Icelandic government was similar to that of the other EFTA governments, i.e. it was prepared to support the 'four freedoms', providing that they were not linked to access to Icelandic fishing grounds (Benediktsson 2003: 197).

It is believed that the scepticism of the Progressive Party and the People's Alliance towards the agreement influenced Hannibalsson when he decided to break free of the coalition after the general elections of 1991 and form a government with the conservative Independence Party. Individual MPs of the People's Alliance were believed to be opposed to the agreement, and as the three coalition parties had a parliamentary majority of only one vote, the government would have had serious difficulty ensuring that it was accepted. While the Conservatives were in opposition they had stressed that Iceland should take part in the EEA Agreement, while at the same time making a special agreement with the EC on free trade in fish and marine products.

The positions of the various parties on European integration were to become more sharply defined later on, and in this context it is interesting to take account of whether they were in government or in opposition at the time. The People's Alliance and over half of the Progressive MPs opposed the EEA Agreement after these parties were in opposition; after the Conservatives came into the government, they abandoned their position that Iceland should make a bilateral agreement with the EC, parallel with the EEA Agreement. There are other examples of the effects on a party's policy of whether or not it was in government. When participation in a European free trade area in 1957–59 was first seriously discussed, the

Progressive Party was in government and took part in formulating the 'wait and see' policy; in 1959, when the party found itself in opposition, it declared itself firmly opposed to Iceland's membership of alliances in Europe. The People's Alliance fought hard against membership of EFTA in 1970, and the Progressives did not support membership; in 1971, when these parties formed a government, their ministers raised no objection to membership and worked on a free trade agreement with the EC.

Although the Social Democrats and the Conservatives stood together in the latter stages of the negotiation of the EEA Agreement, certain differences can be seen in their policies. The SDP saw the EEA Agreement as a defence of Icelandic businesses against foreign competitors. The party was in favour of Iceland's undertaking the obligations involved in the 'four freedoms,' with the exception that it could not accept foreign investment in the country's fisheries sector; this objection it shared with other political parties in Iceland. In the debate that took place in Iceland on the EEA Agreement, disputes centred on its institutional provisions; both legal experts and laymen were divided as to whether accession to the agreement involved a violation of the constitution. The Social Democrats did not see the institutional provisions as such a serious obstacle as many critics made them out to be. It did not see signature of the agreement as an assignment of sovereignty, and if this were to be the case, then it saw no objection to sharing sovereignty with other nations (Stephensen 1996: 103–16).

From the outset, the Independence Party emphasized that the purpose of agreements with the EC was to obtain the freest possible access to markets in Europe for Icelandic fisheries products, while foreign investment in the fisheries sector would not be permitted and Iceland was to retain control of its fishing grounds. The party was also in favour of maintaining certain restrictions on agricultural imports, but otherwise it was in favour of the 'four freedoms'. For a time, the agricultural provisions of the agreement shook the foundations of the coalition. The Conservatives aimed at protecting domestic agricultural produce against imports, and managed to do so (Stephensen 1996: 55). There had always been considerable connections between the Independence Party and the country's farmers; the SDP, on the other hand, had never had any connections with the agricultural sector. Just over 15 per cent of the Conservative MPs during the 1991–95 parliamentary term had worked in agriculture; by contrast, none of the Social Democratic MPs had worked in the sector (see further the examination of party-sector connections in Chapter 6).

When the EEA Agreement had been drafted, by which time the Progressive Party was in opposition, deep dissent developed within the party as to whether it should support or reject the agreement. Seven of its MPs, led by Hermannsson, the chairman of the Progressives and former prime minister, voted against the agreement as they thought it incompatible with the constitution. Six Progressive MPs, led by the party's deputy chairman, Halldór Ásgrímsson, abstained when the vote was taken; they regarded the agreement as being too important for the country's export enterprises to warrant opposing it. These six Progressive MPs were unwilling to bear political responsibility for its acceptance in the Althingi, as there was a possibility that it might be shown to be unconstitutional, so they abstained from the vote. The Progressive Party as a whole, which had always been very closely associated with the agricultural sector, called some aspects of the 'four freedoms' into question. It wanted to limit the influx of foreign agricultural products into Iceland and, like the other parties, it was not prepared to permit foreign investment in the fishery sector. Regarding the right of employment and residence, the Progressives wanted to have special provisions under which it would be possible, in times of serious unemployment, to take measures to reduce the influx of foreign workers.

The People's Alliance (together with the Women's Alliance, which will be examined further below) was one of the strongest opponents of the EEA Agreement. It had serious doubts about the 'four freedoms,' specifically regarding agricultural imports, foreign investment in the fishing industry and the free movement of capital and persons. As with the other parties, however, there were shades of opinion within the People's Alliance. For example, Svavar Gestsson, one of its leaders, said he would not cancel the agreement if the party came to power unless a bilateral agreement with the EC were in existence (Alþýðublaðið 22 October 1992). Nevertheless, all the MPs of the People's Alliance voted against the EEA Agreement in the Althingi.

The Women's Alliance was opposed to the agreement from the outset, and it did not change its stance. One of its MPs, Ingibjörg Sólrún Gísladóttir, nevertheless abstained from voting on it and declared that she was basically in favour of accession (Stephensen 1996: 145). Other members were not at all prepared to contribute towards the assignment of power to international institutions. In their opinion, membership of the EEA would transform fundamental aspects of society, since Iceland would become part of an institution in which democracy was not active; it would be completely powerless to influence the collective operations and women's interests would not be served: nowhere in the Treaty of Rome were their interests guaranteed (Ástgeirsdóttir August 1991; Einarsdóttir August 1992).

The debate in the Althingi over EEA membership was the most intensive since the discussion about EFTA membership in the late 1960s. Moreover, over 34,000 voters (about 19 per cent of the electorate at the time) signed a petition against the EEA Agreement. Vociferous demands were made for a referendum on the EEA Agreement. The feeling was such that the president, Vigdís Finnbogadóttir, even considered refusing to sign the act ratifying the Agreement. Finally she made an announcement explaining that she was signing it in accordance with the traditional non-political role of the presidential office. It is a very unusual step for the president in Iceland to explain publicly why he or she signs a particular bill or agreement.

Sectoral interest groups took a keen interest in the matter. Those in the fisheries and manufacturing sectors were very much in favour of securing advantageous terms with the EC, though their policies rested on different premises. Fish exporters had for some time been pressurizing the government in order to try to secure better market access in the EC countries (Benediktsson 2003: 192) and engaged the manager of the Union of Icelandic Fish Producers in full-time employment for a year in order to defend the interests of the fishing industry in negotiations with the EC (Tíminn 5 December 1991). As has been described above, higher tariffs on saltfish imports to the EC were becoming a more and more important issue for Icelandic exporters, and in this connection leaders of the fishing industry spoke about the need for a fifth freedom: free trade in fish products (Gunnarsson 8 May 1991). Besides these demands, interest groups in the fisheries sector also stressed that they were not prepared to trade fishing rights in exchange for market access.

In October 1991, when the draft of the EEA Agreement was ready, interest groups in the fisheries sector declared their support of it. Under the draft agreement, Iceland was to yield fishing rights to 3,000 tons of redfish equivalents to the EC in exchange for 30,000 tons of capelin. Fisheries leaders saw this as acceptable, both because an exchange was involved and also because it was explained that 70 per cent of this 3,000-ton quota would consist of grenadier, a fish species that was not utilized to any appreciable extent by Iceland at the time (Morgunblaðið 29 November 1991). Later, the EC requested to use this 3,000-ton quota solely for redfish (Morgunblaðið 29 November 1991). When this was revealed, the fisheries groups declared that they no longer supported the draft text of the agreement (Tíminn 28 November 1991). Iceland's fisheries minister, a Conservative MP, said there was no alternative but to take account of the views of the interest groups and try to have changes made to the agreement (Morgunblaðið 28 November 1991). In the event, however, the EC secured its demands and the interest groups accepted the situation and supported membership of the EEA.

Interest groups in the manufacturing sector saw the agreement as guaranteeing better operational conditions. They looked forward to enjoying tax, currency and exchange-rate structures of the same type as those in their competitors' countries. Industrial leaders believed that with greater liberalization in the fields of banking, insurance, transport and types of service with a bearing on industrial enterprises, their material supplies would become cheaper, which would strengthen the sector in Iceland (Davíðsson 12 July 1991). The Federation of Icelandic Industries regarded Icelandic control of the country's fishing grounds as the precondition for entering into the agreement, so echoing the claims of almost all other entities that stated their position. By contrast, the federation was in favour of allowing foreign investment in the fishing industry.

Both the Confederation of Icelandic Employers and the Iceland

Chamber of Commerce were in favour of EEA membership, and saw the outcome of the negotiations as better than anyone had dared to hope (Egilsson 23 October 1991; Morgunblaðið 23 October 1991). Spokesmen for these organizations agreed with the industrial interest groups that Iceland's exporting industries would be placed in a far better position and new opportunities would open up. The Icelandic Federation of Labour was concerned mainly with the implications of the EEA Agreement's provisions on employment, residence and the right of establishment. Its leadership stressed that certain provisos would have to be made regarding the EEA's rules on the employment market so as to enable Iceland to restrict the influx of foreign workers if it proved to be too large (Skúlason 31 November 1991).

The agricultural interest groups were opposed to the EEA Agreement. Liberalization of imports of vegetables, flowers and processed dairy products was not to their liking, and they were against the changes in the ownership of land that the EEA Agreement would entail (Morgunblaðið 3 October 1991). Iceland's agricultural sector receives substantial support of many types from the state, and the government has been very reluctant to open the way for foreign agricultural imports. There is also a system of large direct grants for production, exports and other aspects of agriculture. In terms of producer subsidy equivalents (PSE), Iceland's farmers receive considerably more support than their counterparts in the EU, the OECD and the USA (Snævarr 2002).[4]

The effects of the EEA Agreement

Examples of the benefits enjoyed by Iceland under the EEA Agreement are listed in a report published by the ministry for foreign affairs in 2002 on Iceland's position in European co-operation in 2002. Market access has improved; Iceland is taking a greater part in European co-operative projects (particularly in research and development); there has been a greater influx of capital into the economy; there has been greater harmonization of economic and commercial legislation, increased liberalization and a stimulus in the direction of more modern administrative practices.

According to the report, the EEA Agreement has given Iceland access to those elements that are to its greatest advantage, while at the same time permitting it to stand aloof from aspects of European co-operation that are not so attractive to it (Ministry for Foreign Affairs April 2000: 7–12). First among these aspects is of course the common fisheries policy; furthermore, the EEA Agreement does not require acceptance of the EU's common agricultural policy, with the result that Iceland is able to control its agricultural sector in a way that is largely independent of the other states, e.g. as regards subsidies and protective tariffs. The report also states that non-participation in the EU's trade puts Iceland in an advantageous position, since it has not been involved in the trade disputes that have arisen between the EU and third countries; the USA and Japan are named specifically in this context.

Various aspects of the agreement's institutional provisions have caused the Icelandic government concern due to its lack of influence on policy and decision making. Nevertheless, it sees it as a distinct advantage for Iceland not to be involved in the EU's supranational institutions: the consequence of this is that the country's right of self-determination is stronger in the EEA than it would be in the EU.

On the other hand, the report points out that there have been cases where new legislation is proposed in the EU that is not based directly on the existing framework of the EEA Agreement, but the right of the EFTA states to be involved in its preparation has simply been forgotten. Thus, says the report, it is essential for the EFTA states to be on the alert at all times (Ministry for Foreign Affairs April 2000: 9)

The EU is in a state of constant development; when the EEA Agreement was made, it was based on the institutional structures and decision-making processes that were then in force in the EU. Both the EU's intergovernmental conferences in Maastricht and Amsterdam have advanced co-operation within the EU; as a result, the premises on which the EEA Agreement was built have changed (Ministry for Foreign Affairs April 2000: 18–21). Changes in co-operation between the EU member states that are not reflected in the EEA Agreement are numerous; three of the most important will be mentioned below.

First, the EU member states have increased their co-operation in the field of internal affairs and justice. Iceland and Norway both participate in Schengen, but various other developments are afoot in this field that could be of significance for Iceland, for example the establishment of an information centre about drug offences in Lisbon, EUROPOL and aviation security. Second, it is likely that the adoption of the euro will have a profound influence on Iceland as time passes, and particularly if it is adopted by Denmark, Sweden and Britain. Nevertheless, various arguments have been presented against its adoption in Iceland. Among other things, it has been pointed out that economic cycles in Iceland follow a completely different pattern from those in the EU countries. Third, the EFTA states are not involved in the EU's co-operation in the fields of security and defence. This has caused the Icelandic government concern at the prospect that with a stronger defence base in the EU, the transatlantic partnership, which is important to Iceland, will be weakened.

Besides these points, which are related directly to Iceland's position in European co-operation, there are various other factors that are also of importance. The main one of these is the future of Nordic co-operation. Denmark, Finland and Sweden are all members of the EU. This imposes a heavy burden on the administrative organs of their states; as a result, they are not able to give as much attention as before to co-operation with the other Nordic countries. Furthermore, the solidarity that the Nordic countries often demonstrated within the World Trade Organization and the United Nations has been weakened (Ministry for Foreign Affairs April 2000: 29).

Summary

The EEA Agreement was a highly controversial issue in Iceland, and a heated debate raged over it both in the Althingi and in the press. From the outset, the Social Democratic Party piloted the progress of the agreement, changing its partner in government half way through the process. With the exception of the Women's Alliance, which was in opposition the whole time, the other political parties changed their position on the agreement slightly according to whether they were in government or in opposition. It is interesting to note that all the parties (with the exception of the SDP in its position on foreign investment in the fishing industry) stated provisos regarding some aspects of the 'four freedoms'.

Iceland achieved nearly all the objectives that it set out to achieve in its negotiations on the agreement. The main emphasis was on ensuring access to the EU markets without having to grant the EU countries fishing rights in Icelandic waters and allowing foreign investment in the fishing industry. The Icelandic government was also very keen to limit imports of agricultural products. However, Icelandic fish exports do not enjoy absolutely tariff-free access to the EU markets, and another cause for concern is that the EU is undergoing constant development, which means that some of the premises of the EEA Agreement have changed since it was made.

While negotiations on the EEA Agreement were in progress between EFTA and the EC, the landscape in Europe changed with the fall of the iron curtain. By the time the agreement took effect, the majority of the EFTA states had applied for EU membership. The Icelandic government, however, never considered joining the other Nordic countries that applied for membership of the EU at this period. Applying for EU membership was never on the government's agenda.

Notes

1 Information from the ministry for foreign affairs. However, it is difficult to state precisely how much of EU legislation the EFTA/EEA states have implemented.
2 Customs tariffs on fresh fish were divided as follows: 15.1 per cent due to fresh sole, 13.5 per cent due to fresh whole cod and 13 per cent due to fresh and chilled fillets.
3 In 1989 they were joined by the Citizens' Party, a splinter group originating in the Independence Party. The Citizens' Party first put forward candidates in the general elections of 1987 and gained seven seats. In the 1991 elections, however, it fared extremely badly and did not receive a single seat.
4 When the PSE (producer subsidy equivalent) was calculated in 1998, farmers in Iceland, Switzerland, Norway and Japan were found to receive considerably higher levels of state support than farmers in the EU, the OECD and the USA

that year (Snævarr 2002). The PSE was developed by the OECD to facilitate comparison between countries. It takes into account the quantities produced, the price paid to producers on the domestic market, world market prices, direct payments from the state, production levies, all other payments from the state and feed price adjustments. The PSE shows the sum that would have to be paid to the producer if all state subsidies were abolished (Agricultural Statistical Service 2002).

Bibliography

Agricultural Statistical Service (2002) 'Opinber stuðningur við landbúnað'. Available online: http://www.hag.is/kaflik.pdf (accessed 24 April 2002).
Alþýðublaðið [An Icelandic newspaper] (22 October 1992) 'Mun ekki segja EES upp', Alþýðublaðið.
Ástgeirsdóttir, K. (August 1991) 'Af hverju ekki EB og EES?', Vera [A feminist magazine].
Benediktsson, E. (2003) Iceland and the European Development, Reykjavík: Almenna bókafélagið.
Davíðsson, Ó. (12 July 1991) 'Íslenskt atvinnulíf og evrópskt efnahagssvæði', Morgunblaðið [An Icelandic newspaper].
DV [An Icelandic newspaper] (2 August 1991) 'Um helmingur alls tolls til EB er vegna saltfisks', DV.
Egilsson, V. (23 October 1991) 'Stóraukin samkeppni og bylting í fiskvinnslu', Morgunblaðið [An Icelandic Newspaper].
Einarsdóttir, K. (August 1992) 'EES-samningurinn er ekki vegabréf fyrir konur', Vera [A feminist magazine].
Gstöhl, S. (1996) 'The Nordic countries and the European Economic Area (EEA)', in L. Miles (ed.) The European Union and the Nordic Countries, London and New York: Routledge.
—— (2002) Reluctant Europeans. Norway, Sweden and Switzerland in the Process of Integration, London: Lynne Rienner Publishers.
Gunnarsson, M. (8 May 1991) 'Leggja þarf áherzlu á þörf okkar fyrir "fimmta frelsið"', Morgunblaðið [An Icelandic newspaper].
Ministry for Foreign Affairs (April 2000) Staða Íslands í Evrópusamstarfi: Skýrsla Halldórs Ásgrímssonar utanríkisráðherra til Alþingis, Reykjavík: Ministry for Foreign Affairs.
Morgunblaðið [An Icelandic newspaper] (3 October 1991) 'EES samningum í núverandi mynd hafnað með öllu', Morgunblaðið.
—— (23 October 1991) 'Merkilegra skref en EFTA samningurinn', Morgunblaðið.
—— (28 November 1991) 'Útilokað annað en að taka tillit til atvinnurekenda', Morgunblaðið. Available online: http://safn.mbl.is/ (accessed 7 March 2002).
—— (29 November 1991) 'Jón Baldvin vissi að langhali yrði ekki samþykktur', Morgunblaðið. Available online: http://safn.mbl.is/ (accessed 7 March 2002).
Skúlason, A. (31 November 1991) 'Nauðsynlegar tryggingar', DV [An Icelandic newspaper].
Snævarr, S. (2002) 'Landbúnaður'. Availble online: http://www.hag.hi.is/deild/namsvefur/namskvor01vi/haglysing/landbunadur.ppt (accessed 24 April 2002).
Stephensen, Ó.P. (1996) Áfangi á Evrópuför, Reykjavík: The University of Iceland Press.

Tíminn [An Icelandic newspaper] (28 November 1991) 'Jákvæð stemmning á fölsku forsendum', *Tíminn*.
—— (5 December 1991) 'Magnús sérstakur „utanríkisráðherra" sjávarútvegsins', *Tíminn*.
Valdimarsson, V.U. and Bjarnarson, H. (1997) *Saltfiskur í sögu þjóðar – síðara bindi*, Reykjavík: Hið íslenska bókmenntafélag.

4 Deeply involved in the European project
Membership of Schengen

Stefán Eiríksson

Introduction

Iceland began full participation in the Schengen scheme on 25 March 2001, following several years' preparations and the appropriate negotiation process. Formal preparations can be said to have begun in 1995, when the prime ministers of the Nordic countries declared, after a meeting in Reykjavík on 27 February that year, that it would be in the best interests of the Nordic Passport Union for the Nordic countries to adopt a common, positive attitude on participation in co-operation under the Schengen Convention. The present chapter examines the main reasons why Iceland decided to become involved in the scheme, what this entails and how Iceland's participation is both different from, and at the same time closer than, its ordinary collaboration with the EU, e.g. under the EEA Agreement.

The Schengen scheme

Co-operation under the Schengen scheme began with the signing of the Schengen Agreement on 14 June 1985, followed by the Convention implementing the Schengen Agreement of 1985, which is dated 19 June 1990; the latter is referred to as 'the Schengen Convention'. Five states, Belgium, France, the Netherlands, Luxembourg and Germany, signed the Schengen Agreement in 1985 and subsequently the Schengen Convention in 1990. Implementation of the Convention began formally on 26 March 1995, by which time Portugal and Spain had joined the Convention.[1]

The main purpose of the scheme is to guarantee the free movement of persons across the borders of the member states without identification checks at the borders. Under the scheme, the member states collaborate closely on implementation of border control on the outer borders of the area and on the issue of visas and various support measures such as collaboration between police authorities on specific matters, e.g. in dealing with drug smuggling, the extradition of criminals, legal assistance in criminal proceedings, the handling of applications for asylum, etc. Initially, collaboration under the Schengen Convention took place entirely outside the institutions of the EU, even though it was directed mainly at removing obstacles to the free movement of individuals, which is one of the main aims of the Treaty of Rome. Thus, it began as traditional international collaboration in which all decisions were based on unanimous agreement by the participating states in each individual case (Kristjánsson 1999: 180–2).

The Treaty of Amsterdam, which was signed in October 1997, included a protocol, which subordinated the Schengen scheme to the legal and institutional framework of the EU, at the same time permitting the 13 member states of the EU that had already joined the Convention to continue their co-operation within the framework of the EU. Discussions aimed at incorporating the Schengen scheme, and also other aspects of judicial and internal affairs,[2] in the functions of the EU had already been in progress for some years, particularly in connection with the Maastricht Treaty in 1991, but the idea did not meet with broad support to begin with (de Zwaan 1998: 15).

No further examination will be made here of the reasons for the change in attitude by the EU states in the period between the Maastricht Treaty and the Amsterdam Treaty regarding co-operation in the field of justice and home affairs. However, this development resulted in a fundamental change: co-operation between the EU states in this field was brought within the framework of the EU, and was therefore no longer classified as traditional international co-operation outside the institutional framework of the EU; Schengen had been a good example of such co-operation. This was certainly a fundamental change regarding the EU states, but it also had an effect on other states, and in particular on Iceland and Norway's participation in the Schengen scheme.

The background to Iceland's entry into Schengen

Together with the other Nordic countries, Iceland had already become a member of Schengen when the EU states decided to make co-operation in this area into part of the workings of the EU. It was after the declaration by the Nordic prime ministers in 1995 that the Nordic countries began negotiations on participation in the Schengen scheme, which at that time took the form of traditional international co-operation, as has been described above. Denmark had already applied for the status of an observer member of Schengen; this can be said to have led to the five Nordic countries' having to make up their minds as to whether, and if so, how, they were to continue with the Nordic Passport Union.[3] If Denmark alone were to join the Schengen scheme without the other Nordic countries, it would have meant that the outer borders of the Schengen area would have been drawn through the Nordic countries, thus entailing the end of the Nordic Passport Union. In the light of this, Denmark stated a proviso in its application for membership of the Schengen scheme making it subject to the condition that the Nordic Passport Union would continue to exist.

At that time, the Nordic Passport Union was one of the key elements in Nordic co-operation, and all the Nordic governments took the view that their citizens would not accept the end of freedom of movement between the Nordic countries without passports, which they had enjoyed for 40 years. Furthermore, it was also feared that this would jeopardise other forms of co-operation that had developed in connection with the passport union, particularly in the fields of policing, legal assistance in criminal matters, etc. (Tillaga til þingsályktunar 18 November 1999: 2–3). Taking these considerations into account, the Nordic prime ministers stated a policy that envisaged the development of the Nordic Passport Union within the framework of Schengen.

It can be said that there were three possible lines of development at this point. First, the Nordic countries could have continued with the Nordic Passport Union and remained outside the Schengen area. Second, the Nordic Passport Union could have been abolished and Sweden, Denmark and Finland (as EU members) could have joined the Schengen scheme, with border inspection adopted between the Nordic countries e.g. along the long border between Norway and Sweden. The third possibility, and the one that was in fact adopted, involved all the Nordic countries gaining access to the Schengen Convention (Anderson et al. 2001: 122–3).

Negotiations on access to the Convention by the Nordic countries proceeded smoothly and a co-operation agreement between Iceland and Norway and the Schengen member states was signed in Luxembourg on 19 December 1996, together with the membership agreements of Denmark, Finland and Sweden.

As a result of the changes made to the Schengen scheme when it was incorporated in the legal and institutional framework of the EU, Iceland and Norway had to renegotiate their membership of the scheme. It can be said that the two states were in a strong position in the light of the fact that they had already signed a co-operative agreement with the Schengen states and were therefore *de facto* members of the Schengen area when the EU decided to take it over. The Schengen Protocol to the Amsterdam Treaty therefore contained a special reference to the position of Iceland and Norway and called on the EU Council of Ministers to make special agreements with Iceland and Norway on participation of those states in the implementation, application and development of the Schengen Acquis (de Zwaan 1998: 21–2).

Iceland and Norway therefore began negotiations with the Council on participation in the Schengen scheme in 1998. One of the two main aims that Iceland had was to ensure that when it came to formulating new rules for the Schengen area, Iceland would retain the same level of influence that it had had under the co-operation agreement of 1996, which expressly stated that Iceland and Norway were to play a full part in the implementation and formulation of Schengen rules in all fields, with the exception that they would not participate in voting. Iceland's other main aim was that no monitoring function over Iceland's implementation of the Convention would be exercised by international institutions unless Iceland itself were involved in such institutions in a manner at least comparable to its involvement in the institutions of the EEA. These negotiation aims were based partly on an opinion given by three professors of Law at the University of Iceland in December 1997 on the question of whether the proposed agreement on Iceland's participation in the Schengen scheme, after it was brought under the EU following the Amsterdam Treaty, was compatible with the provisions of the Icelandic constitution. Iceland's main aims were secured in the agreement on participation by Norway and Iceland in the implementation, application and development of the Schengen Acquis, which was concluded late in 1998 and signed in Brussels on 18 May 1999 (Tillaga til þingsályktunar 18 November 1999: 3).

Iceland's participation in the implementation, application and development of the Schengen Acquis

In order to make it possible to accede to the demands by Iceland and Norway for the same sort of influence on the formation of the Acquis as they had had under the co-operation agreement of 1996, it was necessary to locate the workings of the scheme outside the traditional decision-making framework of the EU. A special committee, the mixed committee, was established; its function under the participation agreement of 18 May 1999 is to discuss all matters arising that fall under the scope of the Convention. The mixed committee is intended to reflect the composition of EU committees in this area and it therefore meets to discuss many aspects of the matters covered by the Convention, from expert to ministerial level. However, Iceland and Norway do not participate in voting, when this takes place; the two states therefore take independent decisions in each individual instance concerning the approval of additions to the Acquis. If they do not accept new rules, this entails the termination of the agreement, following the conciliation process provided for in the agreement itself. No independent supervisory or judicial system was established for Iceland and Norway (Kristjánsson 1999: 191).

Iceland's involvement in the development and formulation of the Schengen Aquis differs in various ways from its involvement in comparable processes in the framework of the EEA Agreement, and in some ways the country is in a better position. In the functions of the EEA Agreement, Iceland's involvement is restricted to the specialist committees of the European Commission and it is not able to take part in discussions on the Commission's proposals when these are submitted for treatment by the EU Council of Ministers. Involvement at this level is fully guaranteed, on the other hand, under the co-operation agreement on participation in the formulation of the Schengen Acquis.

The decision-making process in Schengen is complex, particularly for the EU states, due to its having been removed, to a large extent, from the EU's traditional framework. In principle, a solution of this type ought to have been unthinkable in terms of the legal and institutional structure of the EU. However, the strong position of Iceland and Norway, which was due not least to the fact that they were members of Schengen when it was taken over by the EU, and that the inclusion of Iceland and Norway was a precondition for participation by the other Nordic countries, secured the adoption of this outcome (Kuijper 2000: 350–1). It is also worth mentioning that it is almost impossible to monitor the long border between Sweden and Norway. This may have helped Norway and Iceland to secure their terms.

The arguments advanced for Iceland's participation

As is traced above, Iceland's positive attitude towards involvement in the Schengen scheme was first and foremost a reflection of the fact that the other Nordic countries (initially Denmark) had a strong interest in joining the scheme. Denmark applied for membership in May 1994, Sweden and Finland in June 1995. They stated the proviso that it would be possible to maintain the Nordic Passport Union. It was clear that Iceland and Norway could never become full members of the Schengen Convention, since paragraph 1 of Article 140 of the Convention states that membership is open only to EU member states. The Nordic countries took the view that a solution would have to be found concerning Iceland and Norway to avoid the collapse of the Nordic Passport Union, with unforeseeable consequences for Nordic co-operation in general (Kristjánsson 1999: 189).

However, the future of Nordic co-operation was not the only argument cited for participation by Iceland in the Schengen scheme, even though it was the most important one from Iceland's point of view. It was also argued that participation would involve Iceland in broad co-operation with all the Schengen states in the fields of policing and policy on foreign nationals, and that this would strengthen the country's position in the fight against international organized crime. Thus, the bolstering of international co-operation in these fields was one of the arguments advanced for Iceland's involvement in Schengen. Naturally, the main aim of the Schengen Convention, i.e. to facilitate the movement of persons between the member states, was also named as a reason why Iceland should become involved, but it cannot be regarded as the main motivation behind the Icelandic government's attitude towards participation.

In public discussion of the issue, little emphasis was placed on the political significance of the Schengen scheme for Iceland as regards the country's possible membership of the EU, though when reasons for participation were listed it was mentioned that the general policy of the government at any given time to strengthen co-operation with the EU could not be ignored (Kristjánsson 1999: 190). Shortly before Iceland began full participation in Schengen, the minister for foreign affairs was quoted in a newspaper interview as saying that no conclusion could be drawn regarding a change in position towards the EU on the part of the Icelandic government from the fact that it was taking part in the Schengen scheme. He said that this participation was based on specific political aims: to preserve the Nordic Passport Union and at the same time to strengthen co-operation with EU member states in the sphere of policing. The minister also said it was clear in his mind that the Schengen Convention gave Iceland a unique opportunity to exert an influence on EU policy in the areas involved. In fact, he said, the opportunities involved were unique in relations between the EU and a non-EU state. In the Schengen scheme, contrary to the situation under the EEA Agreement, Iceland had an influence on the substance of decisions at all levels of the process, both within the Commission and the Council of Ministers. Quite apart from whatever views people might have on whether or not Iceland should participate in Schengen, he said, they should welcome the fact that it had gained influence in this forum (Morgunblaðið 22 March 2001).

Naturally, Iceland's position on the EU was also touched upon in debates in the Althingi late in 1999 in connection with the ratification of the agreement on Iceland's participation in the implementation, application and development of the Schengen Acquis. In these debates the minister of justice said there was no avoiding the fact that by entering into co-operation with the EU in the fields covered by the Schengen Convention, Iceland was entering into new territory in co-operation with the EU. Undeniably it was not an easy matter to establish channels for such co-operation that could satisfy the demands of Iceland's constitutional structure and at the same time take into account the structure of the EU. The minister said these matters had been addressed successfully in the co-operation agreement, since Iceland's participation in the decision-making process had been guaranteed without the institutions of the EU being given authority over Iceland. The minister also mentioned that it had been guaranteed in the Schengen scheme that ministers from the member countries could engage in formal political consultation regarding their co-operation, and experience had already shown that this had created an active forum for political consultation between Iceland and the EU member states in this field (Pétursdóttir 1999).

Iceland's participation in Schengen was not a major issue among the public or the politicians in Iceland. There was a broad consensus in the Althingi in favour of participation, opposed only by the Left Green Movement and a small minority of the Independence Party. From their point of view there were many drawbacks to participation, for example the huge cost involved, and in the view of the Left Greens, participation in

Schengen was simply another step towards EU membership. They argued that Iceland should have opted for another solution since no application for EU membership was on the agenda in the foreseeable future. In their view, a bilateral agreement with the EU on involvement in Schengen would have been more appropriate in the circumstances (Nefndarálit 20 March 2000a; Nefndarálit 20 March 2000b). Despite this criticism, Iceland's participation in Schengen was approved by the Althingi with a large majority.

Summary

It is clear that Iceland's involvement in the Schengen scheme is one chapter of many in the history of relations between Iceland and the EU. It can be said that Iceland neither took the initiative nor had any particular interest in joining the Schengen scheme, but external circumstances, and in particular concern over the future of the Nordic Passport Union, led to a decision to apply to join it. The fact that Iceland and Norway had already been admitted to Schengen in 1997, when it was brought under the EU, and that the three Nordic EU member states made it a condition for their participation in Schengen that Iceland and Norway be included, put the two states in a unique bargaining position vis-à-vis the EU Council of Ministers when it came to negotiations on their continued participation. As a result, Iceland secured the aims it set out with when the negotiations began, and the outcome was a co-operation mechanism that is without parallel in relations between the EU and a state outside the Union.

One must concur with the aforementioned caution by Iceland's minister for foreign affairs not to interpret Iceland's participation in Schengen as an indication of a change in government policy on EU membership. On the other hand, there is no ignoring the fact that in this specific field of the EU's functions, Iceland is as close as it is possible to come to working as a full member state. It has been pointed out, for example, that the position of Iceland and Norway in Schengen is very similar to that of Denmark, which enjoys a special position in this area following its rejection of the Maastricht Treaty in a national referendum. Furthermore, Iceland and Norway are in a stronger position in this area than are Britain and Ireland, which participate only partially in the Schengen scheme (Kuijper 2000: 351–2). On the other hand, Iceland is not involved in the functions of the EU in other areas of justice and home affairs, i.e. those not covered by the Schengen Convention, since the EEA Agreement does not cover co-operation in the fields of justice and home affairs.

The situation of Iceland and Norway in the Schengen scheme is in many ways unique, as is mentioned above. Under the participation agreement of 18 May 1999, Iceland and Norway head the Mixed Committee at the level of ministers and ambassadors during the second half of every year, i.e. the chair rotates between them. Therefore the relevant ministers from Iceland

and Norway frequently control the debate among EU ministers on EU matters, i.e. Schengen issues. This illustrates the strong position Iceland and Norway occupy under their agreements.

Whatever policy the Icelandic government adopts in the coming years on EU membership, it is clear that Iceland is already a full participant in the EU in the field covered by Schengen. In this field, it is almost on an equal footing with most of the EU member states, and on an even better footing than some of them in terms of influence on the implementation, application and development of the Aquis in this specific and restricted area of co-operation within the EU.

Notes

1 Subsequently, all member states of the EU have begun full participation in the Convention, with the exception of Britain and Ireland, which have, however, applied to participate in specific parts of the scheme. Two states that are not EU members, Iceland and Norway, also participate in the scheme.
2 Collaboration under the Convention is classified as being in the field of justice and home affairs, or, as it is now generally termed, 'co-operation on freedom, security and justice'. This field covers, primarily, co-operation on policing, policy on foreign nationals, judicial affairs and co-operation in the field of law in areas relating to criminal justice and private law, e.g. the enforcement of judgements and in the field of family law.
3 The Nordic Passport Union was founded by an agreement between four of the Nordic countries that was signed on 12 July 1957. Iceland became a party to the agreement on 24 September 1965.

Bibliography

Anderson, A. and Bort, E. (2001) *The Frontiers of the European Union*, New York: Palgrave.
Kristjánsson, H.S. (1999) 'Hvert fara landamæraverðirnir? Ísland, Schengen og Amsterdamsáttmálinn', *Úlfljótur* 2: 177–213.
Kuijper, P.J. (2000) 'Some legal problems associated with the communitarization of policy on visas, asylum and immigration under the Amsterdam Treaty and incorporation of the Schengen Acquis', *Common Market Law Review* 2: 345–66.
Morgunblaðið (22 March 2001) 'Opnar dyr á mikilvægum sviðum', *Morgunblaðið*. Available online: http://safn.mbl.is/ (accessed 3 May 2003).
Nefndarálit um tillögu til þingsályktunar um fullgildingu samnings sem ráð Evrópusambandsins og lýðveldið Ísland og konungsríkið Noregur gera með sér um þátttöku hinna síðarnefndu í framkvæmd, beitingu og þróun Schengen-gerðanna (20 March 2000a) 'nefndarálit frá 1. minni hluta utanríkismálanefndar' [the first minority opinion on the Schengen bill]. Available online: http://www.althingi.is/altext/125/s/0791.html (accessed 3 May 2003).
—— (20 March 2000b) 'nefndarálit frá 2. minni hluta utanríkismálanefndar' [the second minority opinion on the Schengen bill]. Available online: http://www.althingi.is/altext/125/s/0792.html (accessed 3 May 2003).
Pétursdóttir, S. (7 December 1999) 'Speech at the Althingi'. Available online: http://www.althingi.is/altext/125/12/r07222821.sgml (accessed 3 May 2003).

Tillaga til þingsályktunar um fullgildingu samnings sem ráð Evrópusambandsins og lýðveldið Ísland og konungsríkið Noregur gera með sér um þátttöku hinna síðarnefndu í framkvæmd, beitingu og þróun Schengen-gerðanna (18 November 1999) 'a parliamentary resolution'. Available online: http://www.althingi.is/altext/125/s/0240.html (accessed 3 May 2003).

de Zwaan, J.W. (1998) 'Schengen and its incorporation into the new treaty: the negotiating process', in M. den Boer (ed.) *Schengen's Final Days? The Incorporation of Schengen into the New TEU, External Borders and Information System*, Maastricht: European Institute of Public Administration.

Part II

5 Partial engagement
A practical solution

Baldur Thorhallsson

Introduction

Katzenstein's analysis of how European and German influences manifest themselves in different institutions and policy sectors in ten small European states offers an ideal framework for understanding how small states respond to European integration (Katzenstein 1997a, 1997b). Katzenstein regards small states as having various economic and political characteristics in common (Katzenstein 1984, 1985) which influence their policy on Germany and European integration. The concept of economic and political vulnerability is never far away in his approach, e.g. he sees small states as seeking closer economic and political integration to 'tie down the Germans' in order to diffuse their growing bilateral dependence on Germany in a variety of multilateral arrangements (Katzenstein 1997b: 254). Katzenstein's argument coincides with Wallace's claim that multilateral institutions provide small states with a framework to promote their interests and exercise greater leverage over large states (Wallace 1999: 11–13). Wallace argues that small states can be expected to support stronger multilateral institutions and 'play an active and constructive role within them' (Wallace 1999: 13). He argues that Denmark, Sweden and Norway have 'hesitated to accept this logic' (Wallace 1999: 13) but in the end they have all accepted participation in European integration as a solution.

Katzenstein argues that Germany has had a direct effect on the process of European integration through its unification, economic power, and collective memories of German domination and atrocities. Small states experience these effects variously as German or European influences, or as a mixture of both (Katzenstein 1997b: 259–60). Katzenstein argues that small states which are deeply involved in European integration, such as the Benelux states, experience the influence of Germany and European integration as soft constraints. On the other hand, small states which take only a limited part in European integration, such as the central European states, experience these effects as hard constraints (Katzenstein 1997b: 260–1). Thus, the more deeply involved a small state becomes in the European integration process, the more it comes to experience European and international constraints as soft constraints. This is because 'Europe and Germany provide a soft institutional environment for the small European states that leaves considerable leeway for distinct national choices within a broadly converging European pattern' (Katzenstein 1997b: 271). Iceland has taken decisive steps which have deepened its involvement in the European integration process, as previous chapters have indicated. Thus, the first hypothesis to be tested in the present study can be stated as follows: *Participation in European integration eases European and international constraints on Iceland.*

Constraints on Iceland

The early days of European integration were not designed to minimize European and international constraints on Iceland. The European Coal and Steel Community did not serve Icelandic interests and the creation of the EEC was not seen as doing so either. Iceland did not show any interest whatsoever in taking part in these organizations, and nor did the member states which created them show any interest in bringing Iceland on board. On the other hand, governments in Iceland were wary of possible constraints that closer European co-operation might place on fish exports to Europe. However, the government came to the conclusion that participation in the free trade area discussed by the OEEC members would be too costly. Free trade with fish was not on the agenda of the OEEC members and the benefits were not seen as outweighing the costs. The Icelandic economy was characterized by restrictions and the government was not willing to open it up for imports of agricultural and industrial products. Plans for major industries and considerable trade with states in Eastern Europe were seen as standing in the way of participation, and the government was not willing to sacrifice its revenues from tariffs.

The situation changed swiftly in the early 1960s. Applications from Britain, Norway, Denmark and Ireland to join the EEC in 1961 were seen by many as having considerable negative consequences for the Icelandic economy. The government saw the potential membership of Iceland's most important trading partners as entailing unbearable constraints on its fish exports. Thus, it started to look into the question of membership of the EEC: the interests of the Icelandic fishing industry had to be guaranteed. The fact that the government was willing to consider membership of the EEC seriously somewhat supports Katzenstein's thesis that small states seek to diffuse and reduce their dependence through closer European integration. However, this explanation fails to account for the full picture, since a considerable number of obstacles were in the way which had to be solved before Iceland could join the EEC, as is discussed above. These obstacles led the government to come to the conclusion that associate membership of the EEC would serve Icelandic interests better than full membership. Contrary to Katzenstein's claims, full participation in the

EEC was seen as placing unbearable constraints on Iceland's small economy and society.

De Gaulle's veto, which prevented Britain from joining the EEC, led to a policy change in Iceland and put associate membership on hold. The country's economy was flourishing thanks to the 'herring boom' and the government sought to limit the impact of higher tariffs to the EEC market by taking part in GATT. Participation in European integration was not regarded as the only option open to the government. This supports Katzenstein's claim that a small state does have a choice as to what extent it wants to take part in the European project. The government decided to live with tariffs in the EEC market, helped by the external effect of increased fish catches and a potential better market access for fish stemming from the GATT agreements. This also supports Katzenstein's argument that states' decisions on whether or not to participate in European integration should be related to external factors as well as past and present domestic choices.

The government decided to join EFTA in the hope of a free trade agreement with the EC. EFTA membership was seen by some politicians and interest groups as hardening European constraints on Iceland, but the government emphasized that it would lead to better market access for fish exports to Europe. The government's hopes for a free trade agreement with the EC were realized, and Iceland was gradually drawn into closer European co-operation without having to take a full part in the European project. The free trade agreement was seen as softening international and European constraints because it gave Icelandic fish better access to the European market. However, full participation in the EC was not seen as likely to further ease international and European constraints on Iceland. In the early 1970s, when two of the Nordic countries, Denmark and Norway, sought membership, the Icelandic government did not even consider the possibility of following them. Membership of the EC was seen as entailing unbearable constraints for Iceland. Partial involvement in European integration was regarded as softening these constraints to a greater extent than full participation.

From the mid-1980s onward, the Icelandic government became increasingly worried that the completion of the EU's internal market would jeopardise Icelandic interests. It joined the negotiations leading to the signing of the EEA Agreement in the hope of securing better market access for Iceland's fish exports and in order to guarantee the benefits gained by the existing free trade agreement with the EU. However, all political parties in Iceland, except for the small Social Democratic Party, were deeply worried that some aspects of the EU's 'four freedoms' would have devastating effects on Iceland's economy and society. The EEA was far from being seen as a safeguard of Icelandic interests. On the other hand, the foreign minister from 1988 to 1995 and leader of the SDP argued that Iceland had got all for nothing through the EEA Agreement. He emphasized that it would give Iceland better access to the European market for its fish exports and got the Independence Party to support his approach. The majority of the Althingi came to the conclusion that the EEA Agreement alleviated European and international constraints on Iceland. Full membership of the EU was not seen as likely to ease these constraints further; on the contrary, it was seen as likely to lead to unbearable constraints for fishing and farming interests in Iceland. When Norway, Finland and Sweden sought EU membership in the early 1990s, the government of Iceland did not consider an EU application as an option. Membership of the EU was unthinkable and would mean considerable sacrifices for Iceland.

As is discussed in Chapter 3, membership of the EEA is thought to have served Icelandic interests. It gives Iceland access to the EU market for its fish with limited tariffs, at the same time giving Icelandic politicians and interest groups considerable leeway over their own decisions within the fishing and farming sectors. The aim of Icelandic policy makers is to gain the maximum possible economic benefit from European integration without sacrificing their direct control in the economically important fishing sector and the politically important farming sector. Politicians are also wary about a possible backlash if they advocate a transfer of power from Reykjavík to Brussels (see Chapter 9 for a detailed discussion of this point). Therefore they accepted the EEA Agreement but rejected EU membership on the grounds that it would increase European and international constraints on Iceland. Icelandic policy makers have been willing to sacrifice the seat that EU membership would grant them at the negotiation table in Brussels, since they regard the domestic cost as too high.

Iceland's membership of Schengen further demonstrates this. When the Nordic Passport Union was threatened by further co-operation in the area of justice and domestic affairs within the EU, Iceland had to react in order to guarantee the long-established free movement of Icelanders in the Nordic region. Once again, European integration was seen as jeopardizing Icelandic interests and leading to considerable constraints on its citizens. The government opted for closer integration to ease these constraints, but without a full commitment to the project.

Summary

The case of Iceland supports Katzenstein's thesis in the sense that Iceland has sought to diffuse and reduce its dependence through a cautious step-by-step approach to closer European integration. It also supports his claim that small states do have a choice as to whether or not they participate in European integration. Policy makers in Iceland decided not to join the proposed free trade area that was the subject of negotiations in 1957–59 nor EFTA in the early and mid-1960s, and on all occasions that the question has arisen, Icelandic governments have decided not to apply for EU membership. The case of Iceland also supports Katzenstein's claim that if a small state decides to participate in European integration, it does have a choice as to what extent it participates in it. Iceland has decided to be only partially engaged in the European project through its membership of the EEA and Schengen, 'preferring autonomy to full commitment' (Wallace 1999: 14). Katzenstein's thesis is also supported by the way decisions in Iceland have been shaped by external influences following on from European integration, i.e. how Icelandic governments have reacted to developments on the Continent. The outcome has been a request for closer engagement in the European project. For instance, the Icelandic government decided to seek associate membership of the EEC in the early 1960s as a result of the decisions of its most important trading partners to apply for EEC membership, and when Britain's membership was rejected, Iceland dropped its policy of becoming an associate member of the EEC. Iceland was not invited to become a founder member of EFTA because of its fishing dispute with Britain, and its decisions to join EFTA, the EEA and Schengen resulted from the increased constraints that European integration put on its small economy and society.

However, Katzenstein's thesis does not fit the case of Iceland when it comes to the question of full engagement in European integration. Full participation by Iceland in European integration has been regarded by all governments and most politicians and interest groups as entailing unbearable constraints on the country. This is contrary to what Katzenstein claims, i.e. that the softness or hardness of European constraints 'depends on the depth and extent of a state's participation in the European integration process' (Katzenstein 1997b: 272). Also, the political elite in Iceland does not regard the deepening of European integration as a desirable extension of the European process (Katzenstein 1997b: 258). The deepening of European integration has been seen by most politicians and interest groups as leading to increased constraints on the country. Politicians have hesitated to respond positively to new steps taken in the integration process, as they are fearful of the constraints that closer involvement in the European project might impose on Iceland. They have taken decisive steps to bring Iceland closer to the European core but have never sought to take it all the way to Brussels. The further constraints involved in full participation in the European project are seen as prohibitive, while partial engagement is seen as a way of easing the constraints imposed by complete abstention.

Thus, Katzenstein's thesis fails to explain why the political elite in Iceland does not regard the European integration process in the same light as other elites in Europe. It fails to explain why partial engagement in the European process is regarded as easing European and international constraints on Iceland while full membership of the EU is seen as likely to increase these constraints. Consequently, the answer to this question must be sought in other theories that have been put forward in order to explain Iceland's approach to European integration.

Bibliography

Katzenstein, P. (1984) *Corporatism and Change: Austria, Switzerland and the Politics of Industry*, Ithaca and London: Cornell University Press.
—— (1985) *Small States in World Markets: Industrial Policy in Europe*, Ithaca and London: Cornell University Press.
—— (1997a) 'United Germany in an integrating Europe', in P. Katzenstein (ed.) *Tamed Power: Germany in Europe*, Ithaca and London: Cornell University Press: 1–48.
—— (1997b) 'The smaller European states, Germany and Europe' in P. Katzenstein (ed.) *Tamed Power: Germany in Europe*, Ithaca and London: Cornell University Press: 251–304.
Wallace, W. (1999) 'Small European states and European policy-making: strategies, roles possibilities', in *Between Autonomy and Influence: Small States and the European Union, Proceedings from ARENA Annual Conference 1998*, Norway, ARENA, Report No. 1.

6 Life is first and foremost saltfish[1]

Baldur Thorhallsson and Hjalti Thor Vignisson

Introduction

Prosperity in Iceland is not least owing to the results achieved in the catching, processing and marketing of fish and other marine products. At the beginning of the twentieth century, Iceland was one of the poorest countries in Europe, and was characterized by subsistence farming. Industrialization began with the foundation of the bank Íslandsbanki in 1904 and increased foreign investment in fishing. Fishing from motorized boats, and shortly afterwards from trawlers, brought Iceland out of poverty into wealth. The first three decades of the last century were, in fact, the first period of transformation of the Icelandic economy. At this time industry was underdeveloped, and agriculture and fisheries towered above other economic sectors in importance. Interest groups in these sectors were extremely powerful and had strong connections with the government, and to a large extent they structured the operational environment of their sectors themselves. Most members of parliament had experience of working in these sectors, and agriculture and fisheries have enjoyed a special position in Icelandic politics ever since (Kristinsson *et al.* 1992: 43–5). The second phase of transformation of Iceland's economy took place during the Second World War. At the end of the war, Iceland was one of the wealthiest countries in Europe.

The aim of this chapter is to describe the position of the fishing industry in Iceland's economy and the influence it has on government policy regarding Iceland's involvement in European integration, focussing particularly on the period following the conclusion of the EEA Agreement.

Ingebritsen's sectoral approach will be used to examine whether the leading economic sector in Iceland, the fishing sector, has determined Iceland's response to European integration. This chapter will test Ingebritsen's claim that the importance of the fishing sector and its significant role in government policy making explain Iceland's attitude to European integration. In order to apply the sectoral approach to the case of Iceland, the second hypothesis can be stated as follows: *Priorities of fisheries interest groups have been the controlling factor in the reluctance of Iceland to participate in European integration.*

Few attempts have been made to analyse the relationship between the fishing sector and the government in Iceland. This chapter will provide evidence on this complex relationship and how it compares with the relationship between the agrarian and industrial sectors on the one hand and the government on the other.

First, a survey of the development of the fishing industry is given, with some key statistics showing the importance of the industry in the economy, its share of GDP and the proportion of the workforce employed in fisheries. An account is also given of the pattern in exports of Icelandic fish products, the markets to which they have been sold and the obstacles that have made market access difficult. The focus here is mainly on the situation in Europe over the past decade.

Second, there is a discussion of the attitude of interest groups within the industry towards Icelandic participation in European integration, and particularly the question of Icelandic membership of the EU.

The third part of the chapter examines the influence of fisheries interest groups on Iceland's policy towards European integration. It describes the connection between the fisheries sector, individual political parties and non-governmental organizations and participation by fisheries interest groups in the formulation of government policy towards European involvement. To illustrate the depth and extent of this influence, connections between the fisheries sector and the government are compared with those of the agricultural and industrial sectors. This is done by examining connections between members of the Althingi and the three sectors during the period in which the European dimension has been a political issue in Iceland.

Fourth comes an examination of the positions of the various political parties towards EU membership, showing how they are related to the fisheries sector and reflect opposition to the EU's fisheries policy.

The fifth section examines the possible effects of Iceland's membership of the EU on the fisheries sector, with reference to studies of the implications of the EU's common fisheries policy for the sector. The question is raised whether, as has often been claimed, the EU's common fisheries policy excludes the possibility of Icelandic membership.

Development of the fisheries sector in Iceland

Some of the most productive fishing grounds in the world are located around Iceland. The position of the island, together with the pattern in the ocean currents in the vicinity, is the underlying reason for the flourishing marine life found in the waters around the country (Hugason 2002: 32). Though the country has been populated for more than a thousand years, Icelanders only began utilizing the marine resources on a significant scale in the early twentieth century. This was due both to a shortage of capital and a lack of practical expertise. The ruling class was also extremely conservative, for a long time opposing attempts by people to leave the land and establish homes along the coast (Hálfdanarson 1993: 39–52).

The spirit of progress that spread across Europe following the Enlightenment eventually reached Iceland in full around the 1900s, following which the revolution in the fishing industry spread to other areas of life and influenced the basic structure of society in the country. Changes in population distribution took place rapidly: people flocked from the countryside to the towns and villages that sprang up quickly along the coast close to the fishing grounds. These developments also drew a finer distinction between workers and employers: economic classes began to form, accompanied by the establishment of unions to protect their interests.

The agricultural sector was strongly represented in the governmental structure, and the constituency-based electoral system was not revised to take full account of the considerable changes in population distribution that took place during the twentieth century. The result of this was that sparsely-populated regions were more heavily represented in elections, returning proportionally more members to the Althingi than Reykjavík and its surrounding areas. Gradually, moves have been made to equalize representation, but there is still a long way to go before votes will carry equal weight.

Another consequence of the electoral system is that interest groups in the fisheries and agricultural sectors have had a greater say in the formulation of legislation applying to these sectors than has been the case in other occupations, since agriculture and fisheries tend to be the major occupations in the sparsely-populated regions.

The Second World War put Iceland among the richest countries of the world, and a new phase in its history began. Nevertheless, fisheries still play a dominant role in the country's economy, even though the government has made every attempt to diversify both employment and exports in recent years. Figures on the relative size of the fishing industry over the period 1940–2000 show that it is still by far the most important occupation in the country, even though its importance has declined.

As can be seen from Table 6.1, the share of the fishing industry in total employment has declined considerably, and the same applies to the contribution made by the industry to GDP. On the other hand, the fishing industry has numerous connections with other occupations. For example, banks, insurance companies, public relations companies, accounting firms, consultancies and financial institutions have to some extent specialized themselves in meeting its needs. The extent of these connections has not been assessed methodically, but it has been estimated that the proportion of GDP generated by the fisheries sector and the occupations that support it could be as great as 35–40 per cent (Snævarr 1993: 156). A report prepared by a committee appointed by the ministries of industry and commerce on

70 *Life is first and foremost saltfish*

Table 6.1 Contribution of the fishing industry to the Icelandic economy, percentages of total

Year	Employment	GDP	Marine products in total	
			Exports of goods	Exports of goods and services
1940	20.2	28.2	95.1	95.1
1950	16.2	–	89.8	65.9
1960	16.3	–	91.0	61.8
1970	14.4	15.7	77.2	48.1
1980	14.4	16.5	74.9	59.2
1990	11.6	15.0	75.5	55.9
2000	9.0	9.9	63.7	41.3

Source: National Economic Institute 25 July 2002.

Note
Data on GDP by sector in Iceland is not available from 1945 to 1973. The figure for GDP by the fishery sector for 1970 is the figure for 1973. The figure for GDP by the fishery sector in the year 2000 is estimated.

the connections between manufacturing industry and the fisheries sector revealed that industries of many different types have very close connections with the fishing industry. Examples of such industries are catch-gear manufacturers, food canning and smoking enterprises, ship builders and ship repairers, companies producing cardboard and paper products, metalworkers and manufacturers and repairers of electrical appliances and meters for the fishing industry (Ministries of Industry and Commerce, October 1995). Changes in the fortunes of the fishing industry, nearly all of which originate in external factors such as reductions in catches and drops in prices on overseas markets (Magnússon 1997), can therefore have serious consequences for these occupations (Ministries of Industry and Commerce, October 1995).

With the emergence of a stock market in Iceland in the 1990s, the ownership and managerial connections in the economy became more visible. From a report by the Competition and Fair Trade Authority (2001), it is clear that a large number of companies have interests in the fishing industry. Banks, insurance companies, oil companies and transport companies, for example, have extensive interests, and they are likely to purchase commercial goodwill by buying shares in the fishing sector. The Competition and Fair Trade Authority revealed the existence of two groups of companies that have strong mutual ownership and managerial connections. An examination of the shareholdings of these groups in the fisheries sector reveals an interesting picture. The first of these groups consists of Burðarás, Eimskip, Icelandair, Sjóva-Almennar and Skeljungur. This group owns large shareholdings in the largest fisheries enterprises in Iceland.[2] The second group consists of companies that emerged from the

Life is first and foremost saltfish 71

collapse of the co-operative movement: Olíufélagið, Samskip, the Co-Operative Pension Fund and the insurance company Vátryggingafélag Íslands. Together, they own considerable shares in many fisheries companies, though these shareholdings are not as great as those of the first group.[3]

From the foregoing it is clear that to evaluate the importance of the fisheries sector and the numbers of people and enterprises that have a direct interest in its fortunes, it is necessary to define the sector as consisting of more than merely those companies that engage in the catching and processing of fisheries products. Interests and involvement in fisheries in Iceland run deep through society and affect the performance and welfare of a wide range of other enterprises and sectors.

As is stated above, the importance of the fishing industry appears clearly from its share in goods exports, as is shown in Table 6.1. Iceland's goods exports are very one-sided, with fisheries products accounting for nearly 64 per cent of the total in 2000. The proportion of services has been rising, however, and tourism now generates considerable amounts of foreign currency. Part of service earnings, however, are due to the export of fish and other marine products. When it is borne in mind how large a part fisheries products play in goods exports, it is not surprising that Iceland's position on European integration has been based first and foremost on securing its fisheries exports the best possible position on the European market: Western Europe is by far Iceland's most important market, as can be seen from Figure 6.1.

Combining the shares for EFTA and the EU during the 1990s illustrates well the implications of European integration for Iceland: about 70 per

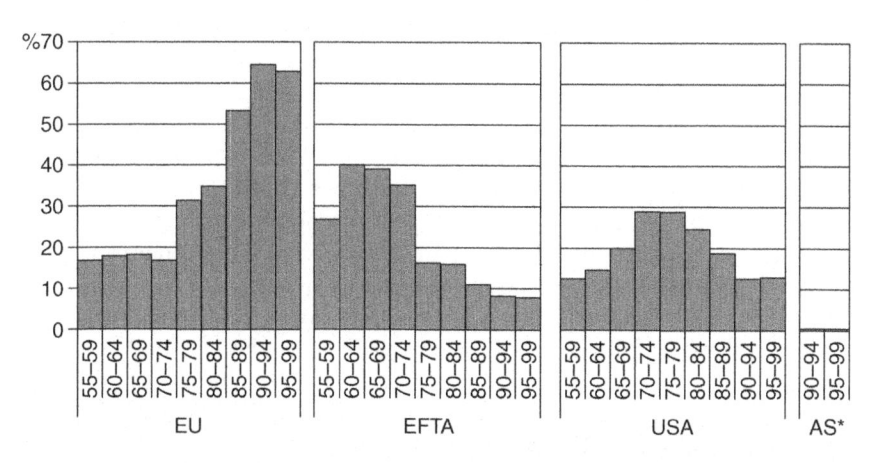

Figure 6.1 Shares of individual market areas in Iceland's goods exports, 1955–99.
Source: Statistics Iceland 2001.

Note
*Applicant states.

cent of the country's exports were made to the European Economic Area (EEA, embracing the EFTA and EU states). The enlargement of the EC/EU increased its importance for Iceland, major stages in this process being the admission of Britain, Denmark and Ireland in 1973 and of Spain and Portugal in 1986, as can be seen from Figure 6.1.

Britain has long been the most important market country for Icelandic goods: more than 18.2 per cent of Iceland's goods exports in 2001 went to Britain. Germany follows close behind in importance, taking 14.9 per cent of Iceland's goods exports that same year. The USA has long been an important market too, particularly during the 20 years from the mid-1960s to the mid-1980s; in 2001 it purchased 10.3 per cent of Iceland's goods exports.

As has been examined in detail in Chapters 2 and 3, changes in access to the European markets for Icelandic seafood and other marine products have always given a stimulus to discussion of the question of joining in European integration. The changes currently taking place in the market in Europe with the expansion of the EU and the adoption of the euro will not initially have any great effect on Iceland's position.

Iceland enjoys tariff-free access for most of its seafood exports to the EEA countries, and the share in its exports taken by those countries that are now joining the EU is very small: only about 1 per cent of Iceland's goods exports during the five-year period 1997–2001 went to the ten countries due to join the EU in 2004 (Statistics Iceland 2003). On the other hand, seafood exports to these countries are expanding rapidly, particularly those of herring, which account for half the seafood that Iceland sells to these markets: the volume increased more than 400-fold, from 53 tons to 21,337 tons, during the four years from 1999 to 2002 (Morgunblaðið 10 April 2003a). The Icelandic government conducted long and complex negotiations with the EU on the adaptation of the EEA Agreement to take account of the expansion of the Union. One of Iceland's main aims in these negotiations was to retain the tariff-free status that its exports had enjoyed in the countries applying to join the EU; it was foreseeable that high tariffs would be imposed on certain types of fish products that had enjoyed exemption under the free trade agreements between EFTA and the countries concerned. The EU eventually acceded to Iceland's request for exemption from tariffs rather than export quotas, with the result, for example, that Icelandic exporters no longer have to pay a tariff of 15 per cent on exports of herring to EU countries. For its part, Iceland agreed to increase its payments to the EU by a factor of five, to about €6 million per year, for the period 2004–09, after which the need for support for the poorer countries of the EU is to be reviewed.

Norway, on the other hand, pays the largest share of the contribution made by the EFTA/EEA states (about €227 million), and Liechtenstein only about €600,000 (Morgunblaðið 10 April 2003b). *Morgunblaðið* stated: 'A satisfactory conclusion regarding monetary matters resulted in the EU showing greater willingness to reach an agreement regarding tariffs' (Morgunblaðið 10 April 2003b). For example, the EU abandoned its demand that Iceland permit nationals of the EU countries to invest in fisheries enterprises in Iceland; the EU negotiators had presented this as an absolute condition for reaching any agreement on broader access to its markets (Morgunblaðið 10 April 2003b). On the other hand, the EFTA/EEA states made no headway on being more definitely involved in decisions regarding the EU legislation that are adopted throughout the EEA.

Currency developments in Europe, on the other hand, can have serious implications for Iceland, particularly if the euro grows stronger while the Icelandic krona weakens and/or fluctuates greatly in strength. Forty-three per cent of Iceland's exports in 2000 were made to the euro area, and if Britain, Denmark and Sweden had been part of it then 68 per cent of Iceland's earnings would have been in euros. Leaders of the Confederation of Icelandic Employers and the Federation of Icelandic Industries have declared that if these countries adopt the euro, it would increase the pressure on the Icelandic government to re-examine the pros and cons of joining the EU (Geirsson 15 May 2001; Hannesson July 2001). Ásgrímsson, Iceland's foreign minister, has also stated that if these countries adopt the euro, this would have an important effect on the EU debate in Iceland. It would provoke many questions about the possibility of keeping the Icelandic krona reasonably strong in the future (Fréttablaðið 27 June 2001). Davíð Oddsson, the prime minister, on the other hand, maintains that Iceland's economy does not keep time with that of the rest of Europe, and that Europe's economic management would never respond to cycles in Iceland's economy; consequently, he says, membership of the euro area is not an option for Iceland. As Iceland's economy is very special, it is vital for the country to be under flexible economic management (Oddsson 26 March 2002). To a certain extent, Ásgrímsson concurs with these views, particularly as regards the different nature of economic cycles in Iceland and the EU. On the other hand, he says that Iceland must examine its position on the euro. For example, he says, failure to adopt the euro could result in foreign companies being less inclined to set up branches in Iceland and interest levels in the country being higher in the long term (Ásgrímsson 15 March 2002).

Attitude of the fishing industry towards EU membership

The Confederation of Fisheries Employers (SAS) was founded at the turn of the year 1988–89, and one of its concerns was policy formulation for the fisheries sector on European integration.[4] It defined three preconditions on which Iceland could play an active role in the internal market of the EU. First, only Icelanders were to have the right to exploit the resources in the sea around the country; second, Iceland was to receive free and unhindered access to the markets of the EU, and third, state subsidies to the fisheries in the EU would have to be discontinued so as not to distort the competitive position of companies within the market. The confederation then came to the conclusion that EU membership was not an attractive proposition for two main reasons: first, the uncertainty surrounding the EU's fisheries policy in the future (which was to be reviewed before 2002) and second because of how inefficient the EU's fisheries management had proved.

Employers in the fishing industry have not changed their position in recent years. The question of EU membership has come up at annual general meetings of the Federation of Icelandic Fishing Vessel Owners (LÍÚ), and its leaders have repeated their position on Europe many times, orally and in the press. For example, an economist at the LÍÚ has said it is out of the question for Iceland's vessel owners to enter the EU, because the country would lose control of its fishing grounds, and in any case the EEA Agreement is perfectly adequate as far as trade is concerned (Hjartarson 6 October 2000). Kristján Ragnarsson, chairman of the LÍÚ, endorsed this view, saying he found it particularly objectionable that the power of decision on total permissible catches in Iceland waters would be transferred to Brussels, in addition to which foreign parties would be permitted to invest in the country's fishing industry. Also, he said, it was not an attractive prospect to submit to the EU's common fisheries policy, since its implementation had, in his opinion, been a complete disaster (Ragnarsson 9 November 2000). At the annual general meeting of the LÍÚ in 2002, Ragnarsson listed further reasons why Iceland could not join the EU. It would be completely without influence in the Union; it already had almost free access to the markets of the EU; there would be a great danger of quota jumping; Iceland would no longer negotiate its own agreements with third countries on the utilization of shared stocks and it had no business adopting the euro because its economy was completely different from that of other parts of Europe (Ragnarsson 11 November 2002). Shortly before this, Ragnarsson had declared that he could not see that the EU's common fisheries policy would be amended in such a way as to become acceptable to Iceland. In this connection, he said he 'could not face the ultimate implications of the idea that decisions on the right to make catches in our economic zone, and what we catch and how we utilize it, would be transferred to Brussels' (Aldarhvörf 6 November 2000).

Sectoral influences on government policy on Europe

Ingebritsen maintains that the establishment of the EU's internal market and the collapse of the Soviet Union opened up various possibilities for the Nordic countries, particularly Sweden and Finland, as regards changes in policy on international affairs. She states that the sectoral approach illustrates how and why the Nordic states have responded in a different way to European integration, showing how their leading sectors put pressure on their governments to adopt a positive or negative attitude towards Europe. She argues that leading sectors influence governments' political process in three ways (Ingebritsen 1998: 157–63).

First, they can exert an influence through their connections with government committees that are engaged on European issues. In Sweden, manufacturing industry was in a strong position in this respect, as five industrial managers were members of the 19-man committee that discussed European issues in the preparations for Sweden's entry into the EU. Icelandic governments have also appointed committees to examine European dimensions when it has been necessary to take decisions on moves towards closer union but representatives of leading interest groups have never been invited to participate in them.

Second, occupational sectors can influence government policy through their connections with the political parties. There are numerous examples of parties and interest groups developing side by side; for example, agrarian parties were closely associated with agricultural unions in the early twentieth century, and the same applies to social democratic parties and the trade union movement. Connections between members of Iceland's parliament, the Althingi, and the occupational sectors are extremely close, as will be examined below. On the other hand, connections between the agricultural sector and MPs have been as close, until recently, as connections between the fisheries sector and MPs.

Third, occupational sectors can influence government policy on European integration by participating in social movements that are founded in connection with the debate on the issue. In Iceland there are organizations campaigning both for and against EU membership. Also when the EEA Agreement still lay in the future, an organization was founded to oppose acceptance of its terms. However, no evidence has been found to support the assertion that the main sectors participated directly in these movements.

An attempt will be made below to evaluate the influence that interests in the fishing industry have had in these three ways on Icelandic government policy towards European integration, and to compare it with the influence exerted by representatives of agricultural and industrial interests.

Government committees and the occupational sectors

Since the debate on European integration first arose in Iceland at the end of the 1950s, four government committees have examined aspects of the question: the committee on free trade in 1961, the GATT Committee, which functioned in the mid-1960s; the EFTA Committee, which was appointed after the general election of 1967 and the European Policy Committee, which started work in May 1988.

The government appointed a committee on free trade in 1961 to discuss the possibility of joining EFTA. The aim was to gain access to the EEC, i.e. to gain tariff-free access for Icelandic fish to its market, by membership of EFTA. The committee consisted of officials and the minister of commerce, Gylfi Þ. Gíslason. The committee consulted a wide range of interested parties, as is described in Chapter 2. In summer 1961, when the government was still deciding what policy to adopt, the minister of commerce summoned representatives of the interest groups to a meeting in order to find out their positions. By August all interest groups had submitted their opinions. All, except for two, urged the government to apply for membership of the EEC subject to certain conditions; for further details, see the discussion in Chapter 2 (Morgunblaðið 18 August 1961).

When considering membership of EFTA, the government established a committee to examine the question in 1967; the committee of officials dealing with Iceland's membership of GATT also discussed the possibility of its entry into EFTA in 1965. There is nothing in the records to indicate that the GATT Committee sought to consult interest groups in the occupational sectors. Its work on the possibility of joining EFTA seems to have consisted solely of internal discussion between the committee members of the pros and cons for Iceland and the preparation of a report on the prospect of membership of EFTA (GATT Committee 26 April 1965; GATT Committee 15 June 1965; GATT Committee 1 July 1965; GATT Committee 7 July 1965). On the other hand, the GATT Committee stated in the course of its discussions that it would be desirable to establish a special EFTA Committee consisting of the same persons as were in the GATT Committee, together with representatives of interest groups; in this connection it mentioned the Iceland Chamber of Commerce, the Federation of Icelandic Co-Operative Societies (SÍS), the Federation of Icelandic Industries, the Icelandic Federation of Labour, the Agricultural Production Council, the Union of Fishery Workers and the Federation of Icelandic Fishing Vessel Owners (LÍÚ) (GATT Committee 24 June 1965).

When the EFTA Committee was appointed after the general elections of 1967, the GATT Committee's recommendation on including representatives of sectoral interest groups was ignored and it consisted solely of representatives of the political parties. Nonetheless, the EFTA Committee acquainted itself with the views of a large number of occupational organizations and enterprises. There is nothing to indicate that any one occupation or sector was accorded more weight than another in the committee's work (EFTA Committee 13 August 1968; EFTA Committee 15 August 1968; EFTA Committee 20 August 1968; EFTA Committee 22 August 1968; EFTA Committee 14 October 1968; EFTA Committee 16 October 1968), though it is true to say that the committee made special efforts to explore the position of the leaders of a wide range of industrial trades (EFTA Committee 21 February 1969; EFTA Committee 3 March 1969; EFTA Committee 4 March 1969; EFTA Committee 6 March 1969;

EFTA Committee 7 March 1969).[5] Membership of EFTA had considerable consequences for manufacturing industry and trades, so it is not surprising that the committee wanted to know the attitude of employers in industry towards joining EFTA. The committee also held meetings with representatives of the Confederation of Icelandic Employers, the Icelandic Federation of Labour and organizations representing agriculture, commerce and the fishing industry (EFTA Committee 13 August 1968; EFTA Committee 20 August 1968; EFTA Committee 22 August 1968; EFTA Committee 14 October 1968; EFTA Committee 16 October 1968).

When attention turned to the EEA Agreement, the same method was applied as when the question of EFTA membership arose: a committee representing the political parties was established. Named the European Policy Committee, it canvassed opinion in many areas of society: government officials, academics, ministers and interest groups. Seventeen representatives of sectoral interests attended meetings with the European Policy Committee, including eight from the fisheries sector, four from trade unions, three representatives of manufacturing industries and two from employers' associations (European Policy Committee 1990: 278–82).

On three of the seven occasions when participation in European integration has been a prominent issue in Icelandic politics, the government has appointed committees to examine it. On two of these occasions, Iceland has taken its most important steps as regards closer participation in the integrative process, through its membership first of EFTA and then of the EEA. It is interesting to note that interest groups have not been represented in any of the committees that have been appointed. Thus, the fisheries does not determine the policy-making outcome of these committees. Ingebritsen's sectoral approach does not fit the case of Iceland in this respect. These committees have either consisted exclusively of government officials or else of representatives of the political parties. They have, on the other hand, sought the co-operation of the interest groups, i.e. summoned their representatives to meetings and/or asked them for a formal expression of opinion on the issue under discussion at any given time. There is nothing in the work of these committees to suggest other than that the interest groups are not treated in more or less the same way as regards this consultation process and the scope they have to influence the committees. There is nothing to suggest that interest groups in manufacturing industry and agriculture have not been in just as good a position as the fisheries sector as regards influencing the policy of the committees, since considerable liaison has also taken place with these sectors. Thus, the fishing industry does not stand out as a special case as regards the opportunity to influence the work of the committees.

In his annual end-of-year article in December 2002, the prime minister, Davíð Oddsson, proposed the establishment of an all-party Committee on Europe, the role of which would be 'to approach the question from a number of different angles, at the same time being able to break free of the worst nonsense that currently sets its stamp on the discussion' (Oddsson 31 December 2002). The prime minister proposed that political parties should nominate representatives to sit on this committee. No suggestion was made of including representatives of the occupational sectors on the committee. Thus, the leading economic sector, the fishing industry, was not given any special treatment. In their initial response, the leaders of the various parties showed no absolute opposition to the idea, though not all were equally enthusiastic about it (Morgunblaðið 3 January 2003). This was particularly the case with the chairman of the Social Democratic Alliance (SDA), who accused the prime minister of trying to stifle discussion of the issue before the upcoming election debate. Following the article the prime minister sent letters to all party leaders inviting their nominations to the committee: each party was to nominate two representatives, except the Liberal Party, which was allocated one seat on the committee. The prime minister's letter stated that representatives could propose what matters the committee should examine, and that its work should lead to a report. No time limit was mentioned (Fréttastofa útvarpsins 26 March 2003). The Liberal Party and the Left Green Movement made their nominations, but the SDA ignored the letter and made no formal response to it. The Progressive Party made no nomination either; although this cannot be interpreted as opposition to the idea of the committee *per se*, it indicates a lack of enthusiasm about it. The chairman of the SDA stated, late in March, that there was no need for haste in convening the committee; it would be the role of the next government to discuss European affairs (Skarphéðinsson 26 March 2003). The prime minister has made no appointments to the committee so far, which seems to be a result of the opposition of the SDA and the limited enthusiasm shown by other party leaders.

The political parties and the occupational sectors

As is mentioned above, Ingebritsen believes that the occupational sectors are able to influence policy on Europe by participation in the work of the political parties. Various studies indicate strongly that the interplay between the political parties and the occupational sectors in Iceland has been very close (Grímsson 1978; Gunnarsson 1989; Kristinsson *et al.* 1992). Employment policy in Iceland has been formulated by consultation with the individual sectors rather than overall consultation between employers, workers and the state (Kristinsson *et al.* 1992; Gunnarsson 1989). The political parties have had a powerful hold on society, though this has weakened slightly as time passes. When this hold was at its strongest, the political parties were involved in such areas as pricing, money supply, the allocation of building lots and appointments to civil service positions, and also had considerable power in the media and book publishing houses (Kristinsson *et al.* 1992: 21).

Life is first and foremost saltfish 79

For a long time the Independence Party has had close connections with interest groups in commerce and the fishing industry, e.g. the Iceland Chamber of Commerce, the Confederation of Icelandic Employers and the Federation of Icelandic Fishing Vessel Owners. As Iceland's agrarian party, the Progressive Party has worked closely with interest groups in agriculture. The Social Democratic Party (SDP) and the People's Alliance were less closely involved in the economy. The SDP was closely connected with the trade union movement up until 1942, after which the People's Alliance was more closely associated with it. Policy on employment grew out of a complex interaction between the political parties and interest groups, exactly who was involved in policy decisions depending on who was in power at any given time. The composition of the group that took the decisions changed according to the changing political climate (Gunnarsson 1989: 50). Moreover, it has often been difficult to draw the line between the part played by the interest groups and that played by the state in policy formulation. Frequently, members of the Althingi have had strong connections with interest groups or individual sectors, and have therefore been in a position to serve two masters as opportunities have presented themselves (Kristjánsson 1994: 22; Grímsson 1978: 18).

Kristinsson considers that the legislature has a strong control over the executive in Iceland and plays a key role in employment policy. Iceland's executive sector developed rather later than its legislature, and was extremely small and weak. It resembles the British executive in that great store is set by obedience to political power (Kristinsson *et al.* 1992: 16).

In order to identify possible influence by three occupational sectors (fisheries, agriculture and industry) on government policy, an examination will be made of connections between members of the Althingi and these sectors. Connections between members of the three parliamentary standing committees that discuss these matters and the respective sectors will also be examined. The extent of all connections with each political party will be assessed.

Through an examination of the extent of these connections it should be possible to attempt to assess possible influence by the occupational sectors on the policy of the legislature and the government. The examination will focus on connections during the electoral periods when the issue of Europe has been most under discussion, i.e. the seven rounds of discussion listed in Chapter 1. The first of these took place near the end of the 1950s, when Britain proposed to the OEEC the establishment of a free trade association in Western Europe, and the seventh is currently in progress. The examination concentrates on the principal members of the Althingi, i.e. those actually elected, and does not include deputies who may have taken their place.

Members of the Althingi are regarded as having connections to the occupational sectors if it is stated in *Alþingismannatal* (a published collection of biographical sketches of members of the Althingi) or on the

80 *Life is first and foremost saltfish*

Althingi's website that they worked for more than one year in one of the relevant sectors or held qualifications in a relevant occupation (e.g. a certificate as a ship's mate or a qualification in agriculture or an industrial trade). Those who worked for the co-operatives and the co-operative movement are regarded as having connections with agriculture and fisheries, as these business operations spanned both sectors.

In some cases it happens that although connections exist between a member of the Althingi and a sector, they are not substantial. It must be borne in mind, however, that it is difficult to gather accurate statistics on connections. For example, those MPs who hold shares in companies in the fishing industry or other industries are not included, as it is impossible to identify all such connections. For this reason, the extent of connections is almost certainly not over-estimated.

Thus, MPs' listing of their own job experience is seen as the best way of reviewing their connections with the occupational sectors: in practically all cases, MPs can be presumed to regard such connections as being to their credit.

Table 6.2 shows the connections between MPs and individual occupational sectors in the parliamentary periods during which European membership or integration has been a prominent political issue. It is clear that in terms of these connections, agriculture and fisheries have historically been in a far stronger position than other industries. It is particularly interesting to note the strong 'representation' of the fishing industry among MPs during the first three rounds of the European issue in Iceland, and it should also be noted that it is still considerable. The connections between MPs and agriculture up until the middle of the 1990s were considerable, but this is not surprising. What is more interesting is that connections between MPs and agriculture have weakened in recent years, while those with the fishing industry strengthened after the middle of the 1990s, compared with the previous decade. Moreover, it is interesting that the level of

Table 6.2 Percentages of MPs with connections to individual occupational sectors in seven parliamentary terms

Term	Connections to		
	fisheries	*agriculture*	*industry*
1956–58	38.5	36.6	11.5
1959–63	33.3	25.0	9.6
1967–71	38.3	26.7	11.6
1987–91	23.7	28.6	12.7
1991–95	17.7	23.8	16.1
1995–99	28.5	15.8	14.3
1999–03	27.0	12.7	14.3

Source: Jónsdóttir *et al.* 1996; Althingi 2002.

connections between MPs and agriculture is similar to the level of connections between MPs and manufacturing industry since the mid-1990s, i.e. during the last three rounds of the European debate: the question of an EU application in 1994–95, participation in the Schengen scheme 1998–2000 and the current round.

Figures 6.2 to 6.4 show these connections broken down by political party. Some of the MPs in all parties, with the exception of the Left Green Movement, have connections with the fishing industry (see Fig. 6.2.). What is interesting is the relatively constant proportion of Conservative MPs (26–37 per cent) with connections with the fishing industry during the seven parliamentary terms. It is also interesting to note that half or more of the Progressive MPs had connections with the fishing industry during the first three terms, i.e. up until 1971. These connections weakened in the fourth term (1987) and only two of the 12 Progressive MPs in 1999 had connections with the fishing sector. There were substantial connections between MPs of the People's Alliance and the SDP and the fishing industry, especially in the earlier terms, but they waned as timed passed in the case of the People's Alliance and became unsteadier in the case of the SDP.

It must be remembered, on the other hand, that connections between the SDP and the fishing industry were of a different nature from those of the Independence and Progressive parties: SDP MPs came from the ranks of ordinary seamen, and were not owners or managers of fishing or

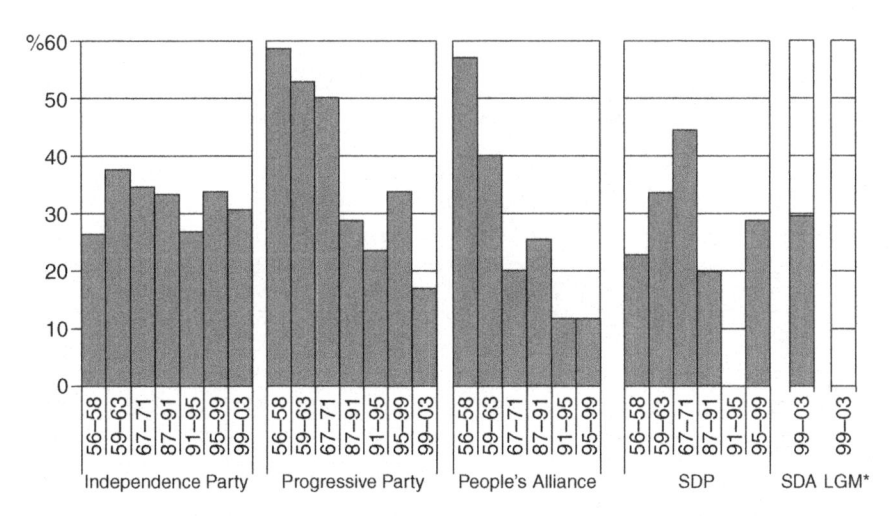

Figure 6.2 Percentages of MPs with connections to the fishery sector in seven parliamentary terms, by party.

Source: Jónsdóttir *et al.* 1996; Althingi 2002.

Note
*Left Green Movement.

fish-processing companies, as was often the case with the latter two parties. Most of the People's Alliance MPs who had connections with the fishing industry were from the ranks of ordinary seamen, though there were exceptions. A considerable proportion (30 per cent) of MPs of the recently-founded Social Democratic Alliance (SDA) have connections with the fishing sector, but these connections resemble those of the SDP more than those of other parties. None of the MPs of the Left Green Movement has connections with the fisheries sector.

It is not surprising, when examining connections between MPs and the agricultural sector, to find the high level of connections with the Progressives revealed by Figure 6.3. The party is in a unique position in this respect. Nonetheless, the connection has weakened and by 1999 only a third of the Progressive MPs had connections with the sector, though of course this is still a considerable proportion. Some Conservative MPs have also had connections with the agricultural sector, but their numbers declined over the period in question. No SDP or SDA MPs have had connections with the agricultural sector. In the case of the People's Alliance, connections were hardly significant, but two of the six current Left Green MPs have connections with agriculture.

Figure 6.4 shows the level of connections between MPs and manufacturing industry, by party. In all cases, the proportions fluctuate widely over the period, though members of all parties had some connections with the sector during the first two parliamentary terms of the 1990s and in the case

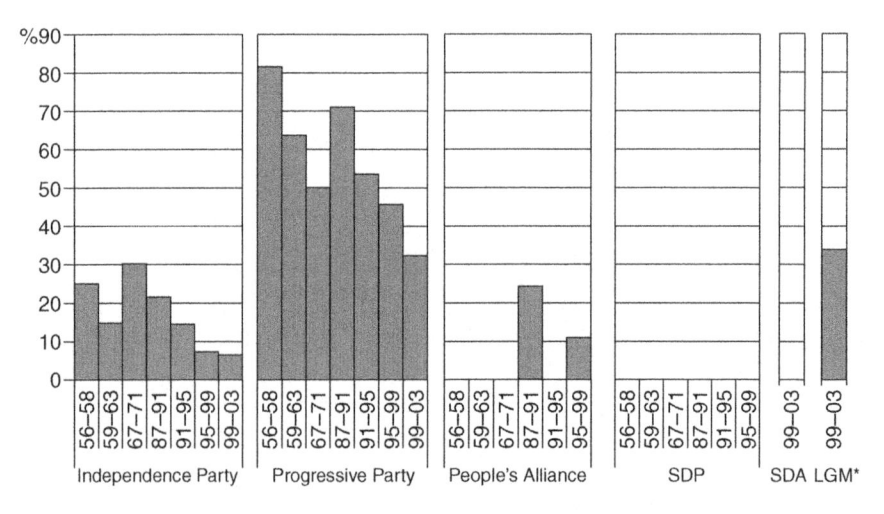

Figure 6.3 Percentages of MPs with connections to the agricultural sector in seven parliamentary terms, by party.

Source: Jónsdóttir *et al.* 1996; Althingi 2002.

Note
*Left Green Movement.

Life is first and foremost saltfish 83

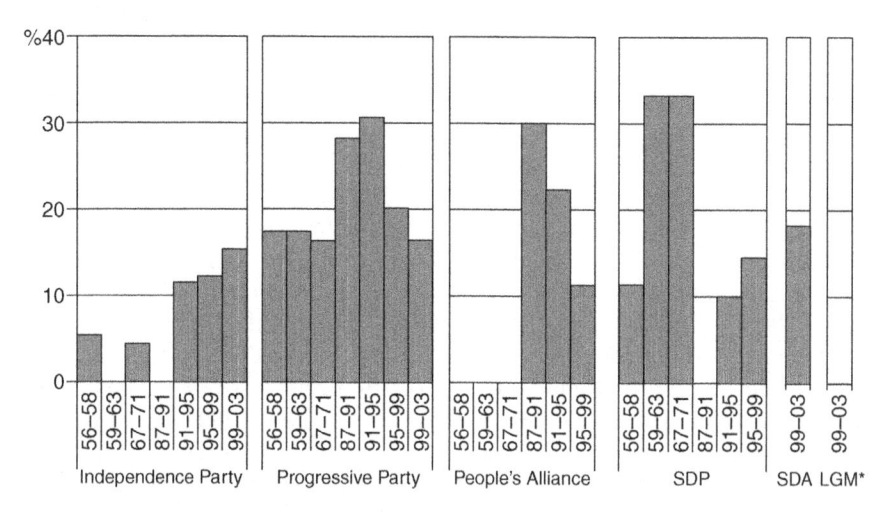

Figure 6.4 Percentages of MPs with connections to the industrial sector in seven parliamentary terms, by party.

Source: Jónsdóttir *et al.* 1996; Althingi 2002.

Note
*Left Green Movement.

of the Conservatives the level was reasonably constant during the entire decade. The Progressives' connections with industry have diminished to some extent over the years, but they have at all times had some MPs with connections to the sector. During the parliamentary term 1999–2003, the three largest parties had similar levels of connection with industry. The SDP's connections with industry around 1960 and 1970 were substantial, involving over 30 per cent of its MPs. That party's connection with industry through its MPs had dried up completely in 1987, when the first connections between MPs of the People's Alliance and industry are recorded. Of course it must be borne in mind that the SDP and the People's Alliance had rather smaller groups of MPs than the Independence and Progressive parties, thus magnifying the effect on these statistics of changes in the numbers of their MPs returned from one parliamentary term to another.

Overall, fishing emerges as the sector that has had connections with all the major political parties, and in this it distinguishes itself from the other sectors. Moreover, the level of connections between fisheries and the political parties has also been relatively stable, while that of agriculture has declined rapidly and that of manufacturing industry has fluctuated widely.

From the above breakdown by parties, it emerges that the Independence Party has had far stronger connections with the fishing industry than with the other sectors, and also that these connections have been more constant. Connections between Conservative MPs and agriculture have waned considerably, and their connections with industry can not be regarded as substantial. Through its MPs, the Progressive Party had considerable connections with the fishing industry during the periods in question, but its connections with agriculture were stronger. The Progressives also had some connections with industry, more, in fact, than those of the Conservatives. Connections between the SDP and the People's Alliance and the fishing industry through their MPs were greater than with the agricultural and industrial sectors, but both did have some connections with industry. As has been demonstrated above, the SDA's sectoral connections through its MPs included fisheries and industry, but not agriculture. Thus, a considerable number of MPs from all the parties named above have had connections with the fishing industry. The only exception is the Left Green Movement. It should therefore have been simple for interest groups within the fisheries sector to make their views known among MPs.

An examination of the composition of parliamentary standing committees with a view to whether their members have connections with specific occupational sectors produces interesting results. Table 6.3 presents a survey of the connections between the members of the committees on agriculture, fisheries and industry and the relevant sectors.

Connections between the members of the standing committees on agriculture and fisheries and the respective sectors have been extremely strong; in the case of the committee on industry the situation has been rather different. During four of the seven parliamentary terms under consideration, more than half of the MPs sitting on the committee on fisheries have had connections with the fisheries sector. About half or more of the members of the committee on agriculture had connections with that sector up until the elections of 1995. What is interesting to note is that while the number of MPs who served on the committee on fisheries and had connections with the fishing industry rose during the 1990s, there was

Table 6.3 Percentages of MPs with connections to individual occupational sectors in the Althingi's relevant standing committees

Term	Connections to		
	fisheries	*agriculture*	*industry*
1956–58	30.0	70.0	22.2
1959–63	60.0	60.0	30.0
1967–71	71.4	53.3	24.4
1987–91	57.1	50.0	23.1
1991–95	33.3	55.5	22.2
1995–99	44.4	44.4	33.3
1999–03	55.5	22.2	11.1

Source: Jónsdóttir *et al.* 1996; Althingi 2002.

a decline in the numbers of those with connections with agriculture on the agriculture committee.

It is of course not surprising that MPs who have connections with particular sectors will seek appointment to the relevant committees within the Althingi. On the other hand, the high proportion of members of the committees on fisheries and agriculture who have connections with the respective sectors is in striking contrast to the far lower proportion of members of the committee on industry who have any connection with that sector. The fact that MPs who have connections with particular sectors seek to work on matters connected with those sectors within the Althingi probably indicates that they would not neglect opportunities of securing the best outcome for the relevant sectors when it comes to negotiating agreements with groupings of states in Europe or elsewhere. Most of the individuals concerned have, or had, many years of experience of work in the relevant occupations and many still have direct personal interests in their prosperity. For these reasons, most of them should be in regular and direct contact with interested parties in the sectors. They should have considerable scope, in the case of fisheries and agriculture, to influence the policies adopted by the Althingi as a whole, and considerably more than can be said of MPs with connections with the industrial sector. Manufacturing industry has not acquired a stronger representation in the Althingi, while the leverage enjoyed by the fishing industry has anything but declined, especially in the light of the increase in the last few years in the number of members of the standing committee on fisheries who have connections with the sector. In the case of agriculture, the decline in the number of MPs with connections with the sector, both in the general assembly of the Althingi and in the standing committee on agriculture, would seem to indicate that agriculture has less leverage as regards policy making.

To illustrate further the influence of interest groups in the fishing industry on government fisheries policy, reference may be made to two other studies. Halldór Jónsson came to the conclusion that the present fisheries management system in Iceland was almost exclusively formulated by the Fisheries Congress, the meeting of interested parties in the sector (Jónsson 1990). Both discussion by the Althingi and the initiative taken by the executive were very limited, and Jónsson's view is therefore that the system was established by the interested parties in the fishing industry. Kristinn Hugason has recently made a more extensive examination of this same topic. He disagrees with Jónsson and argues that the policy-making process that led to the introduction of the present fisheries management system was characterized by consultation with the relevant sector and involved interaction between the state and the interested parties. He demonstrates that neither the interested parties nor the executive played a dominant role in establishing the fisheries management system, and that it was introduced as a result of collaboration between the two. While

Jónsson and Hugason disagree in their accounts of the present fisheries management system in Iceland, it is nevertheless striking that the interest groups in the fisheries sector play major roles in both. This leads to the question of whether it is natural that employers in the fisheries sector should wield so much influence and power. According to Hugason, politicians did not regard this as a problematic issue; he demonstrates that practically all the MPs who discussed the matter regarded it as necessary that interested parties should play a part in determining policy (Hugason 2002: 186).

It is clear from the foregoing that substantial connections exist between the legislature in Iceland and the fisheries sector. All the main political parties in existence during the relevant periods had, or still have, appreciable connections with the fishing industry. MPs appear to regard it as a priority that interested parties in the fishing industry should be involved in the formulation of government policy, and accordingly they play their part in presenting the industry's point of view, as is indicated by their involvement in the parliamentary committee on fisheries. Thus, Ingebritsen's theory regarding substantial connections between Iceland's political parties and the country's leading sector appears to be founded on fact. On the other hand, it must be borne in mind that connections between the Althingi and the agricultural sector were also considerable during the relevant periods, though they have weakened rapidly in the last few years. It would therefore appear that the agricultural sector was also in a position to exercise considerable influence in the Althingi during the first five parliamentary terms under examination. This potential influence of the agrarian sector is particularly interesting when considering the influence of the regions in Icelandic politics, as will be discussed in Chapter 9. It is an overstatement that the fisheries sector is the controlling variable in explaining Iceland's approach to European integration. The role of other sectors, particularly the agrarian sector, have to be taken into account as well as other indicators, as will be indicted in the next chapters.

Social movements and the occupational sectors

The third way in which the occupational sectors are able to influence government policy on European integration is, according to Ingebritsen, through social movements. Three social movements have arisen in Iceland to participate in the European debate. The first of these was *Samstaða um óháð Ísland* (Stance on an Independent Iceland) which was founded by those who were opposed to the country's joining of the EEA. In its policy manifesto, published in August 1991, it stated that its aim was to support free international trade on a broad basis, but that Iceland should not become dependent on trade alliances and should retain full sovereignty (Morgunblaðið 31 August 1991). Members also called for the EEA Agreement to be submitted to a referendum by the electorate. The movement was very active, and managed to establish branches in many parts of the country. It had strong connections with both the People's Alliance and the Women's Alliance; in fact, its first chairman was one of the MPs of the Women's Alliance. The connections with both political parties are clear from the composition of the movement's committee in 1991 and 1995. By contrast, there were no discernable connections between *Samstaða um óháð Ísland* and any occupational sectors.

This was very different from the situation in Norway in the early 1990s, when the agricultural and fisheries sectors made extensive use of the organization *Nej till EG* to influence the debate on the question of joining the European Union (Ingebritsen 1998: 160). The anti-EU movement in Norway had a great deal of influence on the debate in that country, and its activities spread across the whole country prior to the second referendum held in Norway on the question of EU membership (Ingebritsen 1998: 160).

Though supporters of EEA membership formed no organization to counteract *Samstaða um óháð Ísland*, various entities supported the government in securing its aims. For example, the Iceland Chamber of Commerce, the Confederation of Icelandic Employers and other employers' unions launched an advertising campaign to promote their point of view.

The European issue faded somewhat into the background after the 1995 elections, and gradually the activities of *Samstaða um óháð Ísland* died down and came to a halt. The probable explanation for this is that the EEA Agreement had been implemented in Iceland and there was therefore little likelihood that it would be cancelled by an Icelandic government.

The launch of the pro-EU organization *Evrópusamtökin* by supporters of Iceland's entry into the EU followed straight on the cessation of activity by *Samstaða um óháð Ísland* in May 1995. *Evrópusamtökin* has two main aims: to stimulate informed and unprejudiced discussion in Iceland of the collaboration between the countries of Europe and to work towards Iceland's application to join the EU (Morgunblaðið 27 May 1995). As with *Samstaða um óháð Ísland*, the founders of *Evrópusamtökin* spanned practically the entire political spectrum, and once again some leading politicians took part in its foundation and sat in its first committee and council of representatives. No clear connections can be discerned between the occupational sectors and *Evrópusamtökin*, however, though it is interesting to note that at least two prominent members of the Federation of Icelandic Industries sat on its first and only representative council, which was appointed at its foundation meeting. The association was reasonably active to begin with, but as the years passed it proved very difficult to get people to take part in its work and almost impossible to find people to sit in its committee, particularly from the Conservatives, and it almost ceased to function altogether. In 2001 a new committee was elected and a call was made to resuscitate the organization. Members of the SDA and the

Progressive Party youth wings were prominent in the new committee. However, the association has not opened an office or had a paid employee in its service, with the exception of one month, March 2003, when an attempt was made to inject more life into the movement in connection with its annual general meeting. Members of the SDA are conspicuous in the association's new committee, both as principals and alternates, including one ex-MP, but it also includes some members of the Progressive Party. The association has had difficulty raising funds and did not maintain an active website from 1997 to spring 2003.

In summer 2002, opponents of the proposal that Iceland should join the EU founded *Heimssýn* (a movement of Euro-sceptics). Its members come from many sections of society; conspicuous among them are members of the Conservatives and of the groupings that are furthest to the left in the political spectrum, and also the managers and directors of some fishing-vessel operating companies. *Heimssýn* has been active since its foundation. It has a manager in a more or less full-time position and office in central Reykjavík open half the day, and it runs an active website. The principals and alternates elected to its committee in March 2003 include some well-known figures from all the political parties. It is particularly noteworthy that the committee includes a Conservative MP and three former MPs, one a former chairman of the Progressive Party and ex-prime minister and one a former chairman of the People's Alliance and ex-minister of finance, who is currently chairman of the movement. It is interesting that the manager of *Heimssýn* was chairman of the foreign affairs committee of the national congress of the Independence Party in March 2003.

It is clear that there is some grassroots political activity afoot in Iceland in connection with the issue of European integration, and that both those who support and those who oppose the idea that the country should apply to join the EU are rallying and preparing to fight the issue out. Specific occupational sectors have not involved themselves directly in the activities of these movements either for or against Iceland's participation in European integration; those individuals who have connections with particular sectors appear to take part in the work of the social movements on their own initiative. Naturally, involvement by these individuals in the work of the movements strengthens the movements' standing and support base. On the other hand, sectoral interest groups appear to have chosen to campaign alone and without enlisting the assistance of these movements, at least up to the present time. Ingebritsen's theory regarding connections between the leading sectors and social movements for and against European integration therefore appears to be ill-founded.

Despite making some attempts to do so, the pro-EU organization *Evrópusamtökin* has not succeeded in linking its operations to those parties in the business world that have spoken out in favour of membership of the EU. Nor has it managed to raise funding to open an office and engage an employee, and enterprises and interest groups that favour membership of the EU have not been willing to have their names associated directly with it. This goes completely against Ingebritsen's theory, and is interesting, e.g. in the light of the fact that the Federation of Icelandic Industries has been very much in favour of Iceland's joining the EU, and extensively campaigned for membership, and the Iceland Chamber of Commerce has advocated membership. The anti-EU organization *Heimssýn* has been far more successful in raising funds for its activities, which has resulted in its gaining considerable prominence. None the less, no enterprises or sectoral interest groups have been willing to be associated directly with it either, even though it is clear that some parties regard it as being in their interests if an organization opposed to Iceland's membership of the EU is prominent in discussions of the issue of European integration.

The political parties, the fisheries sector and the prospect of EU membership

The implications for Iceland's fishing industry of the country's possible accession to the European Union's common fisheries policy constitute a key factor in the position of all political parties regarding membership of the Union. All political parties agree that it would be out of the question to permit foreign fishing vessels to make catches inside Iceland's 200-mile fisheries jurisdiction in connection with membership of the EU. This principle is endorsed with equal emphasis by the Independence Party, which is opposed to EU membership, and the Social Democratic Alliance, which is in favour of applying to join the EU.

The Conservatives' stance against EU membership is based mainly on their reluctance to give up Iceland's authority over its fishing grounds. Resolutions approved by the party in 1999 and 2001 state that EU membership would entail serious disadvantages, with the position of the fishing industry mentioned specifically in this context. The party has also pointed to the expenses that Iceland would incur in connection with the enlargement of the Union (Independence Party October 2001) and also higher company taxes and more complex regulations following from EU membership (Independence Party 1999). The Conservative minister of fisheries in 2000 stated that the main obstacle in the way of Iceland's joining the EU was the Union's common fisheries policy. If this were removed, he said, Iceland could conceivably apply to join (Útvegurinn December 2000). In an interview with Icelandic National Television, the minister said he could not face the idea of

> going cap in hand to Brussels to negotiate for something that Iceland already has full control of ... and it would mean that we would have to go through all the wars we fought for control of our fishing zone at least once a year in Brussels.

(Aldarhvörf 6 November 2000).

In the resolution on foreign affairs passed after its national congress in March 2003, the Independence Party declared its satisfaction with the EEA Agreement and reiterated its opposition to membership of the EU. The disadvantages of EU membership for Iceland are enumerated: 'First among these is the EU's common fisheries policy, which is completely unacceptable for Iceland' (Independence Party 30 March 2003). Direct payments made by Iceland to the EU would be considerable, and would increase on enlargement of the Union. The resolution warned against making use of the EU's subsidy system and pointed out that it was better to develop profitable industries. In addition, it said that 'Joining in the EU's common currency would prove to be of disadvantage to Iceland. Consequently, the Independence Party considers that membership of the EU would not be in the interests of the Icelandic people' (Independence Party 30 March 2003).

For the Progressive Party, the implications for the fishing industry also constitute a substantial obstacle in the way of Iceland's joining the EU. The party's chairman and minister of foreign affairs, Halldór Ásgrímsson, said it was first and foremost the EU's fisheries policy, and to some extent its agricultural policy, that prevented Iceland from joining the Union (Ásgrímsson 18 January 2002; Ásgrímsson 14 March 2002). On the other hand, he considered that the EU's fisheries policy was moving in the right direction, though in terms of Iceland's interests it was still a long way from where its implementation 'could be considered acceptable from Iceland's point of view' (Ásgrímsson 18 January 2002). Furthermore, he considered that the arrangement that Norway negotiated with the Union in 1994 would not be satisfactory for Iceland (Ásgrímsson 18 January 2002). He said there could be no objection to conferring with the other states within the EU on aims and principles in fisheries management, but that a thirty-man ministerial council including representatives of many landlocked countries should have the final say in determining total catches in Icelandic waters was unacceptable (Ásgrímsson 18 January 2002).

Ásgrímsson investigated possible ways of overcoming the hindrances posed to Iceland's membership of the EU by its common fisheries policy. In a speech he made in Berlin in March 2000, which aroused attention both in Iceland and Norway, he explained why Iceland could not join the common fisheries policy and why Iceland's fishing grounds should not be subject to common control if Iceland were to join the EU (Ásgrímsson 14 March 2002). He said it was natural for the EU countries to have a common fisheries policy where the fish stocks were truly joint resources, moving through the economic zones of several states, but that this was not the case as regards Iceland. The economic zones of Iceland and the EU do not overlap, and the bulk of the commercial fish species in Icelandic waters are non-shared stocks, not migrating significantly outside Iceland's economic zone. Ásgrímsson said that in view of the importance of fishing for Iceland, it could never accept the transfer of authority over its fishing grounds outside its borders. For this reason, he said Iceland could never participate in the common fisheries policy regarding non-shared fish stocks. In his view, on the other hand, the position was different concerning those stocks that Iceland shared with the EU. The key point in his speech is that the fishery resources in Icelandic waters are not common but belong exclusively to Iceland. To illustrate his argument, he asked whether Finland would be prepared to have its forests under common control by all the countries of Europe, or whether Britain would agree to common control of its oil reserves (Ásgrímsson 14 March 2002).

The Progressive Party's Committee on Europe was established in 2000 and submitted its report at the beginning of 2001. This focussed particularly on fisheries, agriculture and regional development, but also included briefer examinations of issues such as administration and defence (Evrópunefnd Framsóknarmanna 22 January 2001). The committee proposed nine main goals to be set regarding fisheries in any possible negotiations between Iceland and the EU (Evrópunefnd Framsóknarmanna 22 January 2001: 4). These were, first, that it should be guaranteed that only Icelanders would be able to utilize the fishery resources around the country; second, that Iceland's economic zone would be a special administrative area under Icelandic supervision; third, that the principle of subsidiarity would be observed when taking decisions on fisheries management; fourth, that Iceland would be in charge of supervising and monitoring its economic zone; fifth, that a collapse in fish catches elsewhere in the EU would not result in increased catches by foreign vessels being permitted in Iceland's fisheries jurisdiction; sixth, that determination of the total catches permitted in Icelandic waters would be in accordance with Icelandic marine biologists' recommendations; seventh, that the economic bonds between vessel-operating companies and Iceland would be ensured, e.g. as regards management, ownership and entitlements to dispose of assets and utilize catch quotas; eighth, that Icelandic exporters of marine products would not be put at a competitive disadvantage vis-à-vis foreign companies, e.g. as regards support measures, and finally, ninth, that Icelandic fishing companies would have the right to fish on the high seas, where they would be subject to the ordinary rules applying to such fishing. The committee stated its view that Iceland could be optimistic about its chances of securing, in the course of its negotiations on membership of the EU, solutions to the majority of the problems relating to the fisheries sector; in this context it referred to the agreement secured by Norway in 1994 (Evrópunefnd Framsóknarmanna 22 January 2001: 8).

The Progressive Party Congress held in February 2003 was cautious in its declarations, stating that it was still desirable to try to secure amendments to the EEA Agreement to keep pace with the eastward enlargement of the EU. The congress was in favour of continuing discussion of the issue of European integration by the party on the basis of the report by its committee on Europe, in addition to which it wanted to promote continuing discussion of the issue by the public (Progressive Party 12 March 2003). The party reiterated that the most important aspect of Iceland's foreign policy was 'to stand guard over the nation's sovereignty over the resources of the sea' (Progressive Party March 2003). It held open the option of applying for membership of the EU, stating that the party congress was to be reconvened specially to discuss the issue before any application was made.

Össur Skarphéðinsson, chairman of the Social Democratic Alliance, considers membership of the EU to entail more advantages than drawbacks. He believes that the adaptations required in the sphere of fisheries are not such an obstacle as some people have maintained, and that the EU's common fisheries policy could even be of advantage for Iceland in some ways (Skarphéðinsson 26 June 2002). His opinion is that it would be possible to ensure Icelandic control over its fisheries jurisdiction through negotiation with the EU, but if this did not prove possible then membership could never be viable (Skarphéðinsson 26 June 2002). The SDA held a special referendum on its policy on Europe in October 2002. The question put to party members was as follows: 'Should the SDA's policy be that Iceland should define what it seeks to secure in negotiations and request negotiations on EU membership, and that any possible agreement should then be submitted to the nation in a referendum, to be either approved or rejected?' Voting papers were posted to all party members, and the response rate was about 35 per cent. Of those who answered, 81.5 per cent said 'yes', 15.7 per cent said 'no' and 2.8 per cent returned spoiled papers.

The European issue was high on the agenda of the SDA's party congress in 2001, by which time the party's report on the question of European integration, *Ísland í Evrópu* (Iceland into Europe) was complete. It was clear before the congress that there was considerable disagreement within the party over the question of EU membership, and it was decided that all party members should vote in a referendum in autumn 2002 on what steps to take.

The section dealing with fisheries in the SDA's report is interesting because it defines the objectives to be secured in possible negotiations on membership of the EU. The authors of this section are of the opinion that the special circumstances applying to Iceland because of the importance of the fisheries for the nation's economy would be recognized by the EU and therefore that it would be possible to reach agreement on a wide range of points concerning the fishing industry. They regard it as unrealistic to assume that Iceland could manage to stand outside the EU's common fisheries policy, but say that this need not be an obstacle. According to the authors, there are nine broad aims regarding the fishing industry that the SDA should seek to secure in the course of negotiations with the EU. These are: first, that Iceland should not have to yield up catch quotas on joining the EU; second, that the position of manager of the Union's fisheries policy should be awarded to an Icelander; third, that the rules on catch performance history and relative stability be established on a permanent basis; fourth, that marine biologists' proposals be observed as guidelines in determining total permitted catches in Icelandic waters; fifth, that Iceland should be to a large extent exempt from the EU's centralized fishing management control and be able to determine fisheries management in its own jurisdiction in all main respects, e.g. regarding monitoring and rapid responses to protect stocks; sixth, that catches of under-exploited stocks should not be increased; seventh, that the principle of subsidiarity should be observed in the management of fisheries in Icelandic waters; eighth, that there should be economic bonds between fishing vessel operators and the Icelandic economy and, ninth, that approximately half the vessels fishing in Icelandic waters should be obliged to land their catches in Icelandic ports and the other half should only be permitted to land them in selected ports in the European markets (Ágústsson et al. 2001: 87–118). These negotiation objectives are not unlike those stated in the Progressive Party's report. Little discussion took place of the question of EU membership at the SDA congress before the general elections in spring 2003, but it was reiterated in the party's election manifesto that the alliance was in favour of going ahead with negotiations with the EU aimed at membership, and that if an agreement could be reached, it should be submitted to the electorate for approval or rejection (Social Democratic Alliance 8 April 2003).

The Left Green Movement is vigorously opposed to Iceland's joining the EU. It bases this stance on a number of considerations, e.g. employment rights, environmental protection, national sovereignty and control by Iceland of its natural resources (Left Green Movement 21 March 2003). It is in favour of developing relations between Iceland and the EU along the lines of bilateral contact. The party's chairman, Steingrímur J. Sigfússon, is not as optimistic as the SDA chairman regarding the possible outcome of negotiations with the EU (Sigfússon 7 April 2002). He believes that if Iceland were to join the EU, foreign fishing fleets would flock to its fishing grounds, Iceland would lose the right to negotiate regarding its own interests in the spheres of fisheries management, and economic control, which has long taken the performance of the fishing industry into account, would no longer be in Icelandic hands (Sigfússon 7 April 2002).

It will be clear from the above survey that four of Iceland's largest political parties give a great deal of weight to the interests of the fishing industry when they discuss the prospect of Iceland's joining the EU. All agree that Icelandic control of the resource would have to be clear and permanent; what distinguishes between them is how likely they think it is that these aims could be achieved in negotiations on membership of the EU.

The fisheries sector and the EU's common fisheries policy

The most extensive examination of the EU's common fisheries policy that has been made in Iceland to date with regard to potential Icelandic membership of the Union is that by Úlfar Hauksson (Hauksson 2002). He considers it is unrealistic to assume that Iceland could secure substantial exemptions from the policy; he bases this view partly on the experience gained in Norway (Hauksson 2002: 158). He then goes on to pose the question whether Iceland could accept the EU's policy and even whether it could benefit from doing so.

The key element in the EU's common fisheries policy is the principle by which, all other things being equal, member states are guaranteed relatively stable catches of each fish stock (Hauksson 2002: 64). In accordance with this principle, and the fact that Iceland has been the only nation to exploit marine resources in its waters since the 1970s,[6] no change would be made regarding Iceland's right to make catches from non-shared stocks within its 200-mile fisheries jurisdiction (Hauksson 2002: 158–9). Various species found in the waters around Iceland are either under-exploited or not utilized at all by Iceland; it is conceivable that fishermen from other countries could find it tempting to utilize them. If Iceland wished to deny foreign fishing fleets access to its fisheries jurisdiction to make catches from these stocks, it is likely that it could manage to do so. Thus, Iceland would still retain the control it has had up to now over access to the waters covered by its fisheries jurisdiction and shares in total catches made in Icelandic waters. When it comes to shared stocks, on the other hand, the situation would be more complicated (Hauksson 2002: 160). The fisheries jurisdictions of Iceland and the EU do not meet, but both parties utilize stocks that are either found in international waters or migrate in and out of national fisheries jurisdictions. Hauksson believes that there would be no problem regarding shared stocks which migrate into Iceland's jurisdiction and out again, and which are also utilized by other nations. If Iceland wanted to keep its fisheries jurisdiction for itself, it could do so. If the EU demanded to be allowed to catch part of its fishing quotas in Icelandic waters, then Iceland would be able to demand, in return, to be allowed to make part of its authorized catches from shared stocks in the EU's jurisdiction. Thus, there would be a balanced mutual exchange.

As has been described above, Icelandic politicians have expressed serious concern as to how fishing in Icelandic waters would be managed if Iceland were to join the EU. Hauksson believes this concern is baseless, and that the politicians are exaggerating the danger. He argues that the final decision would be taken in Brussels at a meeting which would be attended by Iceland's minister of fisheries, with his colleagues from the other EU countries, to negotiate total catch figures, and the minister would have with him the recommendations of Iceland's Marine Research Institute. Hauksson believes that the figures proposed by the Icelandic minister would be approved virtually without discussion because no other country would have any interests to defend in Iceland's fishing grounds (Hauksson 2002: 161). Nevertheless this point has caused Icelandic government officials a great deal of anxiety, as can be seen clearly from the comments by the country's fisheries and foreign ministers quoted earlier in this chapter: both say it would be completely unacceptable if an Icelandic minister of fisheries were to have to confer with other ministers in the EU to determine total fish catches in Icelandic waters.

Iceland managed to secure its aim of preventing foreign capital from entering its fisheries sector, both in the EEA Agreement and in the negotiations on the adaptation of that agreement to the enlargement of the EU. Not everyone is in full agreement that this is a good thing, however; for example the minister for foreign affairs has said he would be in favour of changing the law on foreign ownership shares in Icelandic fisheries enterprises, and some Icelandic vessel operators have also proposed doing so (Hauksson 2002: 164). The prime minister, on the other hand, has taken a different line and said it would be out of the question to permit foreign investment in Iceland's fishing industry (Fréttastofa útvarpsins November 2002). This view is echoed by the leadership of the Federation of Icelandic Fishing Vessel Owners and the chairman of the Althingi's standing committee on fisheries from 1999–2003, who is a member of the Independence Party (Arngrímsson 16 March 2003; Guðfinnsson 5 November 2002).

Hauksson believes that while it would be virtually impossible to prevent foreign investment in the fishing industry if Iceland were to join the EU, various things could be done to ensure that fishing enterprises would be economically bound to Iceland. To support this view he cites the measures taken by Britain to deal with the problem of 'quota jumping' (which occurs when foreign vessel operators buy a share in a vessel operating company in another country but land the catch in their own country). Hauksson believes that Iceland could prevent quota jumping, e.g. by obliging fishing ships based in Iceland to land their catches in Icelandic ports (Hauksson 2002: 166; Ministry for Foreign Affairs April 2000: 236).

Although Hauksson believes that it should be possible to negotiate an acceptable solution with the EU without it making a permanent exemption from its common fisheries policy, there remain various points which the Icelandic government regards as obstacles to Icelandic endorsement of the policy. Its reluctance to submit to the EU's rules on the setting of quotas in Brussels has already been mentioned, and it has been pointed out that various features of Iceland's fisheries management system would have to be changed if the country were to join the EU. Iceland would still be able to allocate fishing permits on the basis of the quota system, but it would be obliged to refer decisions on technical matters, e.g. net gauge sizes, catch-gear collisions, the closure of certain areas to fishing at short notice to protect stocks, monitoring mechanisms, etc., to the Council of Ministers in Brussels (Ministry for Foreign Affairs April 2000: 232). This would be more cumbersome and less efficient than the present system, and the resulting delays in implementation could be damaging because it is often necessary to respond quickly to changing conditions in the sea.

The argument that because Icelanders are the only parties with experience of catching fish inside their 200-mile limits, little or nothing would change even if the final decision on total catches made in Icelandic waters were to be transferred to Brussels, has not proved sufficiently strong to convince leaders of the fishing industry, or most MPs, of the advantages of joining the EU. Leaders of the Federation of Icelandic Fishing Vessel Owners and the prime minister have stated that it would be out of the question to submit to the EU's common fisheries policy, because even though the principle of relative stability would ensure Iceland's position at present, there is no guarantee that it will always apply (Morgunblaðið 8 May 2002; Ragnarsson 9 November 2000). The paramount consideration is that Iceland can not accept others' having the right to determine whether or not Icelanders will be the only ones permitted to utilize the natural resources in the waters around their country.

Summary

Fishing (together with fish processing, marketing and exporting) is by far the most important occupation in Iceland and its fortunes have implications throughout Icelandic society, particularly for the many companies that have business dealings with, or ownership shares in, fisheries enterprises. Fisheries products still account for a large share of Iceland's goods exports. Exports of services have been steadily increasing, however, and the share of the fisheries sector in exports of goods and services has now dropped to about 40%. The fisheries sector share in GDP has also fallen from 15 per cent in 1990 to around 10 per cent in 2000.

Interest groups in the fisheries sector have been opposed to the idea of Iceland joining the European Union. These groups exert influence in a number of subtle ways, and studies indicate that decisions influencing the operational environment of the fishing industry are more often than not taken in the course of a complex process of interaction between MPs and the interest groups. In many cases, furthermore, MPs have connections with the fisheries sector and use their influence in areas that concern its operations. Many MPs with connections with the fishing industry have sat for several consecutive terms in the Althingi and sought to serve on its standing committee on fisheries. There are also close connections between the fishing industry and MPs in all the main parties represented in the Althingi.

In the light of the above, it must be concluded that the fisheries sector has considerable scope for influencing government policy towards participation in European integration. This impression is reinforced if the leverage of the fisheries sector is compared with that of manufacturing industry, at least as far as is indicated in terms of MPs' connections with the respective sectors and the composition of the respective standing committees of the Althingi. On the other hand, there is nothing to indicate that the fisheries sector has been able to exert much more influence than the agricultural sector, except perhaps during the past few years, during which the number of MPs connected with agriculture has fallen, whereas the number of MPs connected with the fisheries sector has risen recently after a temporary decline.

MPs of two of the largest parties, the Independence Party and Progressive Party, have had substantial connections with both agriculture and the fishing industry. MPs of the Progressive Party have been slightly more closely connected with agriculture than with the fishing industry during the past 30 years, while the opposite has applied to the Independence Party: its connections with agriculture have weakened steadily while those with fisheries have remained reasonably steady. One or both of these parties has been in power ever since the creation of the Republic, with the exception of two short periods of minority governments under SDP leadership.

It is clear from the above that the part of Ingebritsen's theory concerning the scope that leading sectors have to influence party policies through close contacts with them applies in the case of Iceland's fisheries. The sector has considerable connections with the political parties, and in the opinion of the political parties, the EU's common fisheries policy is the chief political obstacle to Iceland's joining the Union. Leaders of all the political parties agree in saying that membership of the EU is out of the question if it involves submitting to the common fisheries policy. They differ as to whether they believe it would be possible to secure exemptions from certain parts of the policy or negotiate different terms to some extent. On the other hand, opposition to membership of the common fisheries policy seems to be stated occasionally in order to prevent further discussion on the question of EU membership. In other words, rejection of the policy is used as an excuse not to take the issue any further. What undermines Ingebritsen's theory is that the influence of the fisheries sector on the government's policy on Europe is not found to fit two of the three parts of the theory. The fisheries sector has not been in a better position than other sectors to influence the policy making of committees formed by government to discuss Iceland's approach to Europe, and it has not exerted a direct influence on the work of social movements. Regarding the third part, i.e. the connections between the fisheries sector and the political parties, these are appreciable, and, as stated above, the sector appears to be in a good position to exert an influence. On the other hand it must be borne in mind in this connection that agriculture has been in just as good a position, to judge by MPs' connections with that sector.

Thus, evidence is not found to support the hypothesis based on Ingebritsen's sectoral approach and stated at the beginning of this chapter, that *priorities of fisheries interest groups have been the controlling factor in*

98   *Life is first and foremost saltfish*

the reluctance of Iceland to participate in European integration. More factors need to be studied in order to gain a comprehensive understanding of the Icelandic government's reluctance to take part in European integration. For instance, it is important (as Ingebritsen mentions, in fact) to take account of factors such as the relationship of the government to the USA under the defence agreement. It is also necessary to compare and examine national identity, the rhetoric of the political elite and the elite's perception of international relations. Moreover, it is necessary to examine the characteristics of the political elite, its domestic power base and the smallness of the national administration in Iceland in order to appreciate how far the fishing industry moulds government policy on Europe and the parts played by the above factors in this policy. The fisheries sector is far from being the only controlling variable, overshadowing all others, in explaining Iceland's response to European integration. The sectoral approach fails to take into account key variables in explaining a small state's approach to European integration. The limited attention which the sectoral approach gives to other indicators makes it overestimate the importance of the fisheries sector on governments' policy towards the question whether or not to join the EU. Ingebritsen's sectoral approach mentions other variables but they are not given adequate weight, and consequently the approach leaves out important factors which explain Iceland's response to European integration. A state's approach to European integration needs a much broader explanation than the leading economic sector. Theoretical frameworks which leave on the sideline important features of states' domestic arenas are in danger of reaching a wrong conclusion.

Notes

1 A quotation from the novel *Salka Valka* by the Icelandic Nobel Prize winner for literature Halldór Laxnes. The scene is a small fishing village in Iceland in the early twentieth century. In the first three decades of the century, saltfish accounted for between a third and nearly 60 per cent of goods exports from Iceland.
2 For example, according to the report by the Competition and Fair Trade Authority, this group owned 47.7 per cent in Útgerðarfélag Akureyringa, the second largest fisheries enterprise in the country, 32.6 per cent in Haraldur Böðvarsson, 18.4 per cent in Skagstrendingur, 12 per cent in the Union of Icelandic Fish Producers (SÍF), 11.2 per cent in SR mjöl, 7.7 per cent in Grandi and 3 per cent in Icelandic Freezing Plants Corporation (SH). (All these companies are vessel operators, fish processors or seafood marketing and exporting enterprises.) Since the report was published, the group's ownership share in the fishing and processing sector has increased considerably. For example, Eimskip currently owns a majority share in Haraldur Böðvarsson.
3 According to the report this group owns, for example, 32.6 per cent in Vinnslustöðin, 17.1 per cent Hraðfrystihús Þórshafnar, 11.5 per cent in Loðnuvinnslan, 8.3 per cent in Guðmundur Runólfsson, 4.9 per cent in Skinney Þinganes and 2.0 per cent in SÍF. (Again, all these are companies in the fisheries sector.)

4 The founder members of the confederation were: the Federation of Icelandic Fishing Vessel Owners (LÍÚ), the Union of Icelandic Fish Producers (SÍF), Icelandic Freezing Plants Corporation (SH), the Federation of Icelandic Fish-Processing Industries (Félag sambands fiskframleiðenda), the Union of Salted Herring Producers in North and East Iceland and the Union of Salted Herring Producers in South and West Iceland.
5 For example, the committee sought comments from fittings and furniture manufacturers, paint manufacturers, tanners, sweet manufacturers, packaging manufacturers, metalworkers, printers, knitwear manufacturers, biscuit producers and bakers.
6 Iceland and the EU traded fishing rights under the EEA Agreement. Iceland yielded to the EU the right to catch 3,000 tons of redfish in Icelandic waters in return for the right to catch 30,000 tons of capelin. The EU has not fully utilized its quota under this arrangement.

Bibliography

Ágústsson, Á. and Júlíusdóttir, K. (2001) 'Sjávarútvegsmál', in E.B. Einarsson (ed.) *Ísland í Evrópu*, Reykjavík: Social Democratic Alliance.
Aldarhvörf [A documentary by the Icelandic Broadcasting Service] (6 November 2000) 'Sjávarútvegur á tímamótum – umheimurinn; Ísland og ESB', cited in Ú. Hauksson (2002) *Gert út frá Brussel?*, Reykjavík: The Icelandic University Press.
Althingi (2002) 'Þingmenn og embætti'. Available online: http://www.althingi.is (accessed 2002).
Arngrímsson, F.J. (16 March 2003) 'Þess vegna ekki Evrópusambandið'. Available online: http://liu.is/news.asp?ID=375&type=one&news_id=221&menuid= (accessed 3 April 2003).
Ásgrímsson, H. (18 January 2002) *Sjávarútvegsstefna Evrópusambandsins*. Available online: http://utanrikisraduneyti.is/interpro/utanr/utanrad.nsf/pages/front (accessed 29 July 2002).
—— (14 March 2002) *Iceland's transatlantic dilemma: Economic ties with Europe – defence ties with the United States*. Available online: http://utanrikisraduneyti.is/interpro/utanr/utanrad.nsf/pages/wpp2026 (accessed 15 March 2002).
—— (15 March 2002) *Samkeppnisstaða Íslands í samfélagi þjóðanna*. Available online: http://utanrikisraduneyti.is/interpro/utanr/utanrad.nsf/pages/wpp2030 (accessed 11 March 2003).
Competition and Fair Trade Authority (2001) *Stjórnunar- og eignatengsl í íslensku atvinnulífi*. Available online: http://www.samkeppnisstofnun.is/utgafa/index.htm (accessed 15 January 2003).
EFTA-nefndin [EFTA Committee] (13 August 1968) 'Fundargerð', unpublished record of a meeting, Ministry of Commerce.
—— (15 August 1968) 'Fundargerð', unpublished record of a meeting, Ministry of Commerce.
—— (20 August 1968) 'Fundargerð', unpublished record of a meeting, Ministry of Commerce.
—— (22 August 1968) 'Fundargerð', unpublished record of a meeting, Ministry of Commerce.
—— (14 October 1968) 'Fundargerð', unpublished record of a meeting, Ministry of Commerce.

—— (16 October 1968) 'Fundargerð', unpublished record of a meeting, Ministry of Commerce.
—— (21 February 1969) 'Fundargerð', unpublished record of a meeting, Ministry of Commerce.
—— (3 March 1969) 'Fundargerð', unpublished record of a meeting, Ministry of Commerce.
—— (4 March 1969) 'Fundargerð', unpublished record of a meeting, Ministry of Commerce.
—— (6 March 1969) 'Fundargerð', unpublished record of a meeting, Ministry of Commerce.
—— (7 March 1969) 'Fundargerð', unpublished record of a meeting, Ministry of Commerce.
European Policy Committee (1990) *Ísland og Evrópa I.–VII.*, Reykjavík: Alþingi.
Evrópunefnd Framsóknarmanna [European Committee of the Progressive Party] (22 January 2001) *Nefndarálit*. Available online: http://framsokn.is (accessed 29 July 2002).
Fréttablaðið [An Icelandic newspaper] (27 June 2001) 'Sláandi hversu mikið hefur farið úr landi', *Fréttablaðið*. Available online: http://www.visir.is (accesssed 27 June 2001).
Fréttastofa útvarpsins [Radio news department of the Icelandic National Broadcasting Service] (November 2002) 'News'.
—— (26 March 2003) 'News'.
GATT nefndin [GATT Committee] (26 April 1965) 'GATT-nefndin', unpublished record of a meeting, Ministry of Commerce.
—— (15 June 1965) 'GATT-nefndin', unpublished record of a meeting, Ministry of Commerce.
—— (24 June 1965) 'EFTA-málin', unpublished memo, Ministry of Commerce.
—— (1 July 1965) 'Rökin með og á móti aðild að EFTA', unpublished report, Ministry of Commerce.
—— (7 July 1965) 'GATT-nefndin', unpublished record of a meeting, Ministry of Commerce.
Geirsson, F. (15 May 2001) *Ísland í fremstu röð*. Available online: http://www.sa.is/frettir/frettir_2001/raeda_finns_geirssonar.asp (accessed 4 April 2003).
Grímsson, Ó.R. (1978) 'Network parties', unpublished research, University of Iceland.
Guðfinnsson, E.K. (5 November 2002) 'Erlendar fjárfestingar í sjávarútvegi – Nei, takk!', *Morgunblaðið*. Available online: http://www.ekg.is/grein.php?id=198&year=2002&fl=1 (accessed 3 April 2003).
Gunnarsson, G.Á. (1989) 'Industrial policy in Iceland 1944–1974: Political conflicts and sectoral interests', unpublished PhD thesis, University of London.
Hannesson, S. (July 2001) 'Erlent lán eða áhættufé', *Íslenskur iðnaður* [A journal by Federation of Icelandic Industries]. Available online: http://www.si.is (accessed 4 April 2003).
Hauksson, Ú. (2002) *Gert út frá Brussel*, Reykjavík: The University of Iceland Press.
Hálfdanarson, G. (1993) 'Íslensk þjóðfélagsþróun á 19. öld', in G. Hálfdanarson and S. Kristjánsson (eds) *Íslensk þjóðfélagsþróun 1880–1990: Ritgerðir*, Reykjavík: University of Iceland Social Science Research Institute and the University of Iceland History Research Institute.

Hjartarson, S.H. (6 October 2000) 'ESB og forræðið yfir fiskimiðunum', *Fiskifréttir*. Available online: http://liu.is/news.asp?ID=375&type=one&news_id=156& menuid= (accessed 30 April 2003).
Hugason, K. (2002) *Markmið og árangur í stjórnun fiskveiða*, Reykjavík: Univeristy of Iceland, Faculty of Social Science, Department of Political Science.
Independence Party (1999) *Kosningayfirlýsing Sjálfstæðisflokksins*, Reykjavík: Independence Party.
—— (October 2001) 'Ályktun um utanríkismál'. Available online: http://www.xd.is (accessed 29 July 2002).
—— (30 March 2003) 'Ályktun um utanríkismál'. Available online: http://www.xd.is/malefnastarf/35landsfundur/grein/138 (accessed 31 March 2003).
Ingebritsen, C. (1998) *Nordic States and European Unity*, Ithaca and London: Cornell University Press.
Jónsdóttir, V., Kemp, B., Bernódusson, H., Halldórsson, J. and Jónsdóttir, S.K. (1996) *Alþingismannatal 1945–1995*, Reykjavík: Skrifstofa Alþingis.
Jónsson, H. (1990) 'Ákvarðanataka í sjávarútvegi', *Samfélagstíðindi*, 10.
Kristinsson, G.H., Jónsson, H. and Sveinsdóttir, H.Th. (1992) *Atvinnustefna á Íslandi 1959–1991*, Reykjavík: University of Iceland Social Science Research Institute.
Kristjánsson, S. (1994) *Frá flokksræði til persónustjórnmála*, Reykjavík: University of Iceland Social Science Research Institute.
Left Green Movement (21 March 2002) *Alþjóðamál*. Available online: http://www.vg.is/kate.php?fmPageID=24&fmExpandTo=00.00.01.05 (accessed 21 March 2002).
Magnússon, G. (1997) 'Hagsveiflan og hagstjórn á Íslandi', in F.H. Jónsson (ed.) *Rannsóknir í félagsvísindum II*, Reykjavík: University of Iceland Social Science Research Institute, Institute of Economic Studies and the University of Iceland Press.
Ministry for Foreign Affairs (April 2000) *Staða Íslands í Evrópusamstarfi: Skýrsla Halldórs Ásgrímssonar utanríkisráðherra til Alþingis*, Reykjavík: Ministry for Foreign Affairs.
Ministries of Industry and Commerce (October 1995) *Tengsl iðnaðar og sjávarútvegs*, Reykjavík: Ministries of Industry and Commerce.
Morgunblaðið [An Icelandic newspaper] (18 August 1961) 'Samtök meginatvinnuveganna styðja inntökubeiðni í Efnahagsbandalagið', *Morgunblaðið*.
—— (31 August 1991) 'Kristín Einarsdóttir kosin formaður Samstöðu um óháð Ísland'. Available online: https://safn.mbl.is (accessed 18 June 2001).
—— (27 May 1995) 'Á annað hundruð manns á stofnfundi Evrópusamtakanna', *Morgunblaðið*. Available online: https://safn.mbl.is (accessed 18 March 2001).
—— (8 May 2002) 'Óheiðarlegt að gefa til kynna að hægt sé að semja sig frá ókostunum', *Morgunblaðið*. Available online: http://safn.mbl.is (accessed 29 July 2002).
—— (3 January 2003) 'Engin flokksformaður útilokar stofnun nefndar', *Morgunblaðið*. Available online: http://safn.mbl.is (accessed 12 March 2003).
—— (10 April 2003a) 'Útflutningur síldarsamflaka hefur fjögurhundurðfaldast', *Morgunblaðið*.
—— (10 April 2003b) 'Greiðslur endurskoðaðar eftir fimm ár', *Morgunblaðið*.
National Economic Institute (14 December 2001) *Historical Statistics 1901–2000*. Available online: http://www.ths.is/rit/sogulegt/english.htm (accessed 25 July 2002).

Oddsson, D. (26 March 2002) *Ræða forsætisráðherra: flutt á ársfundi Seðlabanka Íslands 26 mars 2002.* Available online: http://forsaetisraduneyti.is/interpro/for/for.nsf/pages/raeda0023 (accessed 11 March 2003).

—— (November 2002) 'Interview with Oddsson', the radio news department of the Icelandic Broadcasting Service.

—— (31 December 2002) *Áramótagrein forsætisráðherra í Morgunblaðinu 31. desember 2002.* Available online: http://government.is/interpro/for/for.nsf/pages/raeda0055 (accessed 12 March 2003).

Progressive Party (March 2003) *Ályktunarkafli um stjórnsýslu og umheiminn samþykktur.* Available online: http://www.framsokn.is (accessed 12 March 2003).

—— (12 March 2003) *Utanríkismál.* Available online: http://www.framsokn.is (accessed 31 March 2003).

Ragnarsson, K. (9 November 2000) *Ræða Kristjáns Ragnarsson, formanns L.Í.Ú. á aðalfundi L.Í.Ú. 9 nóvember 2000.* Available online: http://www.liu.is/news.asp?ID=375&type=one&news_id=157&menuid= (accessed 29 July 2000).

—— (11 November 2002) *Ræða formanns LÍÚ á aðalfundi 2002.* Available online: http://liu.is/template1.asp?Id=371&sid=109&topid=338 (accessed 21 March 2003).

Sigfússon, S.J. (7 April 2002) 'Sjávarútvegurinn og aðild að Evrópusambandinu'. Available online: http://safn.mbl.is/ (accessed 29 July 2002).

Skarphéðinsson, Ö. (26 June 2002) *Aðild að ESB og sérstaða sjávarútvegsing.* Available online: http://www.samfylking.is/?i=11&o=1517 (accessed 29 July 2002).

—— (26 March 2003) 'Interview with Skarphéðinsson', the radio news department of the Icelandic National Broadcasting Service.

Snævarr, S. (1993) *Haglýsing Íslands,* Reykjavík: Heimskringla.

Social Democratic Alliance (5 April 2003) *Vorþing Samfylkingarinnar 2003: Nýir tímar kosningastefna Samfylkingarinnar samþykkt á vorþingi 4. til 5. apríl 2003.* Available online: http://www.samfylking.is/?i=3 (accessed 8 April 2003).

Statistics Iceland (2001) *Utanríkisverslun eftir tollskrárnúmerum.* Available online: http://hagstofa.is/toll200/toflur/tafla2.xls (accessed 24 July 2002).

—— (2003) *Útflutningur eftir markaðssvæðum árin 1997–2001.* Available online: http://www.hagstofa.is/template_db_frameset.asp?PageID=554&ifrmsrc=/uploads/files/vorufl2001/vorufl09.xls&Redirect=False (accessed 12 March 2003).

Útvegurinn [An Icelandic journal on fisheries] (December 2000) 'Vona að festa komist á stjórn smábátaveiðimanna með endurskoðun laga um stjórn fiskveiða', *Útvegurinn,* 6.

7 The special relationship between Iceland and the United States of America

Baldur Thorhallsson and Hjalti Thor Vignisson

Introduction

Iceland's location in the centre of the GIUK (Greenland–Iceland–United Kingdom) gap made the country immensely important in the US and Western European defence network during the cold war. Its strategic importance was particularly great from the late 1960s to the end of the cold war period: if armed conflict had broken out, the US military base at Keflavík in Iceland would have played a key role in NATO defences, especially in keeping the North Atlantic area safe and defending the shipping route between America and Europe. The Soviet Union built up its naval base in Murmansk throughout the cold war: the fourth largest Soviet naval base in 1950, it had become the largest by 1960, and continued to grow thereafter (Archer *et al.* 1998: 101). Soviet military aircraft also penetrated Icelandic air space repeatedly, so it is no wonder that the USA stressed the importance of maintaining a credible defence presence in Iceland.

A founder member of NATO (established in 1949), Iceland made a bilateral defence agreement with the USA two years later under which military facilities are provided by Iceland. The defence agreement was made on the basis of the North Atlantic Treaty (Hafstein 1975: 18) and under it, the USA formally undertook responsibility for the defence of Iceland on behalf of NATO. All decisions concerning operations by US forces in Iceland are taken on the basis of bilateral consultation with Iceland. The defence agreement puts Iceland in a special position among the NATO members in terms of its relations with the USA. It contains obligations which go beyond those stated in the terms of Iceland's and the USA's membership of NATO. Iceland's membership of NATO does not commit the country to host military forces: Iceland declared when NATO was formed that forces or bases would not be located in the country during peacetime and that it was the prerogative of the Icelandic government to determine when military facilities would be provided in a time of war (Jónsson 1989: 22–3). This is not the case according to the defence agreement; as is stated above, it provides for a military presence in the country during peacetime. Moreover, should the defence agreement be terminated, Iceland would be committed to make military facilities available to the USA again in the event of an armed attack on one or more of the NATO countries. As a result, Iceland's commitments under the defence agreement are 'significantly greater than those undertaken in the North Atlantic Treaty' (Jónsson 1989: 24).[1]

Iceland has also had close economic and trade ties with the USA ever since the Second World War. These ties exerted a strong influence on Icelandic politics during the cold war period. For example, the defence agreement and the presence of US forces at the military base in Keflavík aroused far more domestic opposition than did the country's membership of NATO. It is unavoidable to ask whether these close ties with the USA influenced the position of the Icelandic political elite towards the integrative process in Europe. Archer and Sogner argue that defence issues have had a crucial influence on the attitude of the Norwegian political elite towards the European Union. It has seen the development of the EU's Common Foreign and Security Policy (CFSP) as an attractive means of strengthening Norway's defences and also a way of making its views felt in the development of European security and defence after the end of the cold war (Archer *et al.* 1998: 128–9,132). By contrast, Iceland's political elite has not shown any tendency towards joining the EU for the sake of security and defence. The aim of this chapter is to analyse the effect of military and economic ties with the USA on the position of the Icelandic political elite regarding participation in European integration. The hypothesis to be tested may be stated as follows: *The close relationship between Iceland and the United States of America in terms of security and economic and trade relations has had a profound influence on Iceland's response to European integration.*

In order to test the hypothesis, attention will be given to three considerations that are important in any discussion of Iceland's policy on European integration. The first of these is how defence interests have influenced Icelandic politics and Icelanders' sense of national identity, and also whether there are any similarities between the rhetoric of the cold war and that used in the debate on membership of the European Union. Second, attention will be given to Iceland's defence interests and the bearing they have had on Iceland's policy on Europe since the end of the cold war. This involves an examination of the changing defence structure in Europe and how it is perceived by the Icelandic political elite. The third consideration is the economic benefit to Iceland of its defence agreement with the USA and whether this, together with the trade between the two nations, has influenced Icelandic government policy.

Political parties and the relationship with the USA: nationalism and the EU debate

Regarding themselves as a Nordic nation, Icelanders have always attached great importance to maintaining good relations with the other Nordic countries. This principle is not disputed in Icelandic politics. The country's relationships with the USA and with other countries in Europe, on the other hand, have been highly controversial. Table 7.1 shows the regions to which Icelanders felt closest in the mid-1980s.

Nine out of every ten Icelanders saw themselves as having the closest ties with the other Nordic countries, and seven out of ten saw themselves as second closest to the countries of Western Europe. The same proportion named North America and Western Europe as their first choice (6 per cent in each case) and 20 per cent ranked North America in second place. Icelanders' attitudes towards other states and peoples depend on many factors, and probably vary according to whether they support particular parties. Disputes over the Keflavík base and the defence agreement with the USA overshadowed other political issues in Iceland and proved to be more divisive than the economic and social issues that originally gave rise to the longest-standing parties in the Icelandic political landscape (Hardarson *et al.* 1987: 220). Figure 7.1 shows the two policy cleavages that were strongest in Icelandic politics: Right–Left orientation and attitudes towards the defence issue.

The conservative Independence Party was, and still is, the furthest to the right and the strongest supporter of the defence agreement with the USA and membership of NATO (Hardarson 1985: 298). Though the Social Democratic Party (SDP) was closest to the Conservatives in terms of foreign policy, some members had reservations about the defence agreement and the military base to begin with, but after the fall of the leftist government in 1958 the SDP adopted a firm policy and supported the agreement and the presence of US forces in the country, notwithstanding criticism by some individual party members. Though the Progressive Party supported Iceland's participation in NATO, it had doubts about the merits of the defence agreement with the USA (Hardarson 1985: 298). In

Table 7.1 'To what region in the world should Icelanders feel closest?' (%) (Respondents were asked to rank the regions in order of preference)

	The Nordic countries	Western Europe*	North America	Small Third World states	Eastern Europe
Closest	90	6	6	0	0
Second	8	70	20	4	3
Third	2	19	57	14	7
Fourth	0	4	14	34	44
Least	0	1	3	48	46
Total	100	100	100	100	100

Source: Hardarson 1985: 310.

Note
*Excluding the Nordic countries.

Pro-NATO/US base

```
                              ■ Independence Party
          ■ Social Democratic Party
                     Progressive Party
                          ■
Left ◄─────────────────────────────────► Right

    ■ People's Alliance
```

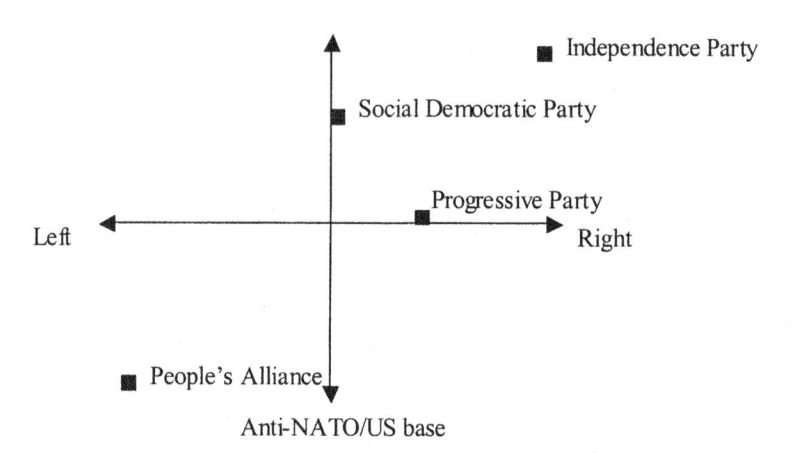

Anti-NATO/US base

Figure 7.1 Location of the four principal parties in Iceland in terms of Left–Right orientation and their position on NATO membership and the US military base at Keflavík.

Source: Grímsson 1982: 168 (adapted).

fact, the party was split in its attitude towards the agreement and the Keflavík base right down to the late 1970s.

The People's Alliance, which took over the mantle of the Socialist Party and the Communist Party, was always the party furthest to the left of centre and the one that most staunchly opposed both the defence agreement and membership of NATO. In its view, the Keflavík base was a threat to Iceland's independence and national identity. An indication of how important defence issues were in the view of the People's Alliance is that right down to the 1970s, it made it a condition for participating in a government coalition that the defence agreement would be terminated. As the Independence Party and the People's Alliance were at opposite ends of the policy cleavages, it was virtually impossible for them to work together. Being more centrally placed, the Social Democrats and the Progressives, on the other hand, could work with parties situated both to their left and their right, and although compromises had to be struck on certain issues, their policies were not so far removed from those of the People's Alliance as were those of the Independence Party.

During the cold war, the People's Alliance and the Progressive Party were prepared to put the political focus on the sensitive issue of foreign policy. At certain times this brought them clear advantages, an example being the increased electoral support gained by the People's Alliance in the 1970s, when foreign affairs were perhaps at their most sensitive (Kristinsson 1991: 350). It was during that decade that Iceland twice came into confrontation with Britain and other European states over fishing rights in the waters off Iceland, and the future of the defence agreement with the USA was also under pressure.

On two occasions it seemed likely that the agreement would be cancelled or reviewed and the Iceland Defense Force at Keflavík sent out of the country. This happened first during the time of the leftist coalition consisting of the Progressives, People's Alliance and Social Democrats in 1956–58 and again in 1971–74 when another leftist coalition was in power, this time including the Union of Liberals and Leftists and not the SDP. On the other hand, these governments did not aim at withdrawing the country from NATO.

It was not only in the political parties themselves that the influence of the defence agreement on Icelandic politics was felt. It gave rise to deep feelings at a grassroots level among both its supporters and its opponents. The strength of this feeling was expressed most clearly when the issue arose of whether or not US forces should be allowed to stay in the country during the time of the leftist government in 1971–74 (Ingimundarson 2001a: 269–328). A movement known as the Campaign against Military Bases, which had long been in existence, underwent a revival during these years with the emergence of a new wave of young supporters and new leadership on the political left wing. Intellectuals were also prominent in the campaign, which gave the movement still greater credibility in public debate on national issues. One of the arguments they adopted at this time regarding the Keflavík base was that foreign influence was harmful for a small nation like Iceland. Although the opponents of the base argued their case with great passion, they encountered monolithic resistance. *Morgunblaðið*, the largest newspaper in the country and a staunch supporter of the American military presence in Iceland, exerted an immense influence on public debate (Ingimundarson 2001a: 290). It worked systematically to bring down the leftist government from the moment it took power until it fell (Sigurðsson 7 May 2002). Supporters of the defence agreement started a nation-wide petition under the slogan 'A Protected Country' in protest against the government's policy on defence. The petition was well organized and produced an impressive result: the 55,522 signatures collected represented about 44 per cent of the electorate at the time (Morgunblaðið 31 March 1999).

Iceland's independence campaign in the nineteenth century had never made use of force, and Iceland's special position as a country without a militia is an important element in the identity and outlook of many Icelanders. This was an element in the attitude of many people towards the Keflavík base, and it was played on to the full by its opponents (Ingimundarson 2001a; Corgan 2002). The existence of the base sharpened Icelandic nationalistic feeling, which was also exploited by the anti-base campaigners (Ingimundarson 2001a). Icelanders regard their campaign for independence as a time when the nation emerged from a sleep that had lasted many centuries and demanded the right to rule itself, as it had done down to the thirteenth century (Hálfdanarson 2001: 179–81). Iceland received sovereignty in 1918, ever since when the fear of losing independence once again and coming under the control of a foreign power has been a conspicuous element in the national consciousness (Hálfdanarson 2001: 144). A large part of public opinion was opposed to the presence of the Keflavík base, largely on nationalistic grounds. The only survey of public attitudes made in the 1950s indicated that 48 per cent were opposed to the base while only 28 per cent supported it (Ingimundarson 1996: 294–5). Surveys made in the 1970s and 1980s indicate a majority in favour of it, but at the same time a strong current (33–48 per cent) opposed it. Only during the 1990s does the level of opposition seem to have declined to less than one quarter of the electorate (Hardarson 1998).

Sovereignty is often referred to in Iceland as the life-blood of the nation. Nationalistic feeling was maintained by references to the time of the Old Icelandic Commonwealth, when the nation was free and its culture flourished. This image was juxtaposed with the assertion that the careless loss of independence had been followed by nothing but centuries of oppression and degradation. This presentation of Iceland's political history was used in the political debate throughout the twentieth century (Hálfdanarson 2001: 179–81).

The dispute over the defence agreement and membership of NATO has receded substantially into the background over the last quarter of a century, during which time the issue of having the military forces at Keflavík leave the country has not really been on the political agenda. The People's Alliance did not make the departure of the forces a condition for participating in the third leftist coalition government in 1978. Its official policy, i.e. demanding the recall of the US Iceland Defense Force from Keflavík and the withdrawal of Iceland from NATO, nevertheless remained unchanged until the party merged with the Social Democrats and the Women's Alliance to form the Social Democratic Alliance (SDA) before the general election of 1999. The Women's Alliance had campaigned against the military presence in Keflavík and membership of NATO ever since its foundation in 1983; nevertheless, the policy adopted by the SDA for its first election campaign was that Iceland should not make any changes regarding its membership of NATO during the coming parliamentary term (Social Democratic Alliance 1999). However, the foreign policy of the Social Democrats has gradually become dominant in the SDA. At its national congress in 2001, the SDA declared its unconditional support for membership of NATO (Social Democratic Alliance 18 November 2001) and its manifesto for the 2003 general election stated that the party supported the defence agreement with the USA (Social Democratic Alliance 5 April 2003). The recently-formed Liberal Party holds the same position (Liberal Party March 2003). The Left Green Movement, by contrast, is completely opposed to NATO membership, the defence agreement with the USA and the presence of American forces in Iceland. The Left Greens' chairman regards NATO as one of the tools used by the USA in its aggressive and expansionist foreign policy. He considers Iceland's membership of a military alliance as incompatible with its status as a small state and out of keeping with the country's non-militarist and pacifist tradition (Einarsson 27 April 2003).

Iceland's governments in the 1990s made efforts to increase the country's participation in the work of NATO and stressed the importance of maintaining close co-operation with the USA, both within NATO and outside it. The Conservative-Progressive coalition that has been in power since 1995 supported the USA's position on enlargement of NATO, both when it opposed the admission of more members in 1999 and in the further expansion of the alliance that is now about to take place. It also supported the USA wholeheartedly in the war in Kosovo and when it attacked Afghanistan and Iraq: Iceland was one of the few Western European countries on the list of 'willing states' supporting the USA in the war on Iraq, the government standing firmly with the USA when military action was taken.

The effect of the defence agreement with the USA on Iceland's policy on Europe fell together, to some extent, with the effect of its NATO membership. Opponents of both the agreement and further involvement in Europe appealed heavily to nationalistic feelings, and consequently the two issues reinforced each another. The reluctance of political leaders to take measures that would bind Iceland more closely to the rest of Europe is therefore understandable, since to put the issue of Europe on the agenda would have run the risk of fuelling the opposition cause: pro-Europeanists, like supporters of the defence agreement with the USA, were accused of undermining Iceland's special position and national character. The discourse on defence issues during the cold war period centred around two main poles. Nationalistic sentiments were aired at the left end of the spectrum, where supporters of the defence agreement were accused of sabotaging Iceland's existence as an independent nation by taking up a position in support of the base at Keflavík. At the other end, supporters of the agreement concentrated on anti-communist arguments and claimed that the left wing, and all opponents of the military base, were simply trying to ingratiate themselves with the Kremlin. *Morgunblaðið* painted the issue in strong colours, arguing mainly that the Keflavík base was necessary not only for Iceland but also for nations that were well-disposed to it in Europe and Scandinavia (Ingimundarson 2001a: 269–329).

When the question of policy on Europe arises in Iceland, supporters of EU membership have no such reliable trump card to play as supporters of the defence agreement with the USA had during the cold war. Membership of the EEA guarantees Iceland access to Europe's internal market while it retains undiminished control over its fishing grounds and at the same time, defence issues are secure as long as the defence agreement is maintained. The anti-European lobby keeps up a vigorous profile in the debate, often resorting to extravagant terms, as in this comment by the prime minister, Davíð Oddsson:

> I think it's sad how people complain so much and think that if only they can get into ... the EU's oxygen tent, where someone will put milk into their bottles and they can stop thinking for themselves, they will start feeling better. This doesn't strike me as an Icelandic attitude. There's no strength, optimism or courage in these people who are so obsessed with telling others how they should behave, and wallowing in their troubles.
>
> (Silfur Egils 24 March 2002)

The pro-European lobby is not able to resort to such emotive arguments as can be found in anti-communist propaganda or invoke defence interests in the debate on Europe as was done when the debate centred on the defence agreement with the USA. When answering opponents of EU membership, supporters tend first and foremost to base their arguments on the danger of exclusion from the integrative process that is taking place in Europe, the fact that Iceland has very limited influence on the legislation of the EU, which nevertheless applies throughout the EEA, and the view that EU membership would bring economic benefits.

The defence link between Iceland and the USA

The US Army had facilities in Iceland during the Second World War, but left the country after the end of the war. As the cold war intensified, Iceland abandoned its policy of neutrality and joined other countries in forming NATO. With a further deterioration of cold war relations and the outbreak of the Korean War, the country abandoned its policy of not permitting armed forces in the country during peacetime and concluded the defence agreement with the USA. The USA set up the Iceland Defense Force; facilities were provided for the force at Keflavík Airport, the country's international airport, which the Americans had been permitted to use since 1946. The Iceland Defense Force then embarked on measures to build up its defences and preparedness in Iceland, including the building of four radar stations, one in each quarter of the country (Iceland Defense Force Public Affairs Office May 2001). In 1951 the US Air Force took over command of the base at Keflavík and one of its representatives was appointed commander of the base. This was done because of Iceland's importance as a landing-place for US military aircraft; in addition, it was seen as a strategically important base for the US aircraft carrying atomic weapons in the event of a war, not least if they were not allowed to use airports in Britain during hostilities.

Changes were made to the structure of the Iceland Defense Force in the early 1960s. In 1961 the ground force units that had been stationed at Keflavík were recalled to the USA, and in July that year the US Navy took over operation of the base from the air force. In addition, two of the radar stations were closed down as an economy measure (Iceland Defense Force Public Affairs Office May 2001). In fact, the Americans never attached much importance to air defence at Keflavík and actually wanted to withdraw their jet fighters in 1960, as will be described below. The 1980s were a special period in this respect, with more combat aircraft stationed at Keflavík and a higher frequency than before of penetrations of Icelandic air space by Soviet military aircraft (bombers and maritime patrol aircraft).

A detailed report on Iceland's strategic significance was prepared by the US State Department in summer 1973. This stated that in peacetime, the Keflavík base was important not only militarily but also politically. It warned that a withdrawal of the US forces from Iceland would seriously weaken NATO's position in Iceland, which would mean that elements favouring neutrality in Iceland would gain support, which could be damaging if armed conflict were to break out because it was absolutely vital for military forces to have facilities in the country. By contrast, the authors of the report did not see the Keflavík base as indispensable in the defences of the USA and NATO during peacetime, highly important though it was. The base was one of the most important links in the warning system for North America and Western Europe, particularly regarding the monitoring of Soviet submarine movements and the sea to the north of the country (Ingimundarson 2001a: 270). The role of the maritime patrol aircraft based at Keflavík was primarily to monitor Soviet submarines, and if necessary to be prepared to attack them, e.g. off the Norwegian coast.

Following the massive Soviet military build-up in the 1970s and 1980s, the defence capacity at Keflavík was enhanced (Iceland Defense Force Public Affairs Office May 2001). Activity by the Soviet fleet in the North Atlantic reached a peak in 1986. Up to that time the number of Soviet ships, submarines and military aircraft monitored by the Iceland Defense Force had been rising gradually. To meet this increased level of activity, considerable work was undertaken at the Keflavík base. For example, the monitoring and command system was strengthened, an oil terminal and storage facility was built, the equipment in two radar stations was replaced, hangars were built for F-15 jet fighters and improvements were made to Keflavík Airport. In addition, the Dutch fleet began operating a maritime patrol aircraft, in collaboration with the Iceland Defense Force (Iceland Defense Force Public Affairs Office May 2001).

As was to be expected, the strategic importance of Iceland declined after the end of the cold war. The US government has responded accordingly and made extensive changes to the operations of the Iceland Defense Force. For example, the number of fighter aircraft was reduced from 18 to 12 in 1991 and the same year the operation of AWACS aircraft was discontinued (Iceland Defense Force Public Affairs Office May 2001). As a result of the withdrawal of the AWACS aircraft, the cut in the number of fighter aircraft and reductions in the numbers of surveillance aircraft and telecommunications personnel, the number of military personnel at Keflavík Airport has been declining steadily since the end of the cold war (Iceland Defense Force Public Affairs Office November 2001). These changes can be attributed, to some extent, to changes in the security environment around Iceland, while technical advances have also played a role (Pálsson et al. 1999). In 1990 there were about 3,300 military personnel at Keflavík; by 1995 the number had fallen by about 1,000 and by 2001 the total was down to about 1,900.

As an example of the enormous changes that have taken place in the level of Soviet, and later Russian, military activity in the North Atlantic since the end of the cold war, only four Russian military jets penetrated Icelandic air space between the beginning of 1992 and May 2003: two in 1999 and another two in April 2003. In the twelve-year period before 1992, by contrast, 1,324 Soviet or Russian aircraft penetrated Icelandic air space. This activity reached a peak in 1985, when 170 Soviet military aircraft entered Icelandic air space (Iceland Defense Force Public Affairs Office September 2001). Another related example, this time of how much military air traffic to and from the Keflavík base has declined, may be cited to illustrate how radically the security situation around Iceland has changed. In 1990, 64 per cent of air traffic via Keflavík Airport, the country's international airport, was in connection with the Iceland Defense Force; by 2000 the proportion had dropped to 30 per cent of the total (Iceland Defense Force Public Affairs Office September 2001); of course it must also be borne in mind that civilian aviation increased substantially during the same period.

The US authorities have had plans to make further reductions in their military presence in Iceland. In October 1993 the newspaper *Morgunblaðið* reported on differences of opinion within the US administration regarding the Keflavík base. It seems that there were a number of viewpoints current at the time: the air force wanted to stop all operations in Keflavík, the defence department wanted to keep the base open, but restructure it, while the US State Department wanted to make the least changes (Morgunblaðið 17 October 1993). In 1994 the US deputy secretary for defence said he saw no threat to any NATO state, including Iceland and the USA, and that there was therefore virtually no defence requirement in the North Atlantic (Morgunblaðið 5 January 1994).

At this point, an agreed minute was added to the defence agreement in 1994 providing for a reduction of the defence capacity at Keflavík, while at the same time the USA reiterated its commitments towards Iceland under the defence agreement (Iceland Defense Force Public Affairs May 2001). In the negotiations leading up to the signing of the agreed minute in 1994, the Icelandic government had pressurized the Americans not to downscale their operations at Keflavík Airport as much as they themselves wanted (Bragadóttir 6 January 1994). The Americans had intended to make fairly drastic cuts in their operations, and it is no exaggeration to say that their proposals caused the Icelandic government dismay. In their original plan, the Americans wanted to withdraw the 57th Fighter Squadron and the 12 F-15 jet fighters still in the country at the beginning of 1994. Second, they planned to dismantle the US naval monitoring and detection system in stages up until 1997, adopting instead a sensing system based on satellite technology. Third, the defence force's helicopter rescue team was to be withdrawn. This had played a valuable role in rescuing Icelandic seamen in emergency situations (Bragadóttir 6 January 1994).[2] Iceland made the counterproposal that credible air defences must be maintained in the country, and this formulation has been advanced ever since when the prospect of cuts in military operations at the Keflavík base has arisen. The Icelandic government also stressed that the defence agreement was bilateral and that for as long as it was still in force it must guarantee a minimum level of defence and security in the country, irrespective of changes in its strategic importance. During these negotiations Iceland's political leaders and negotiators focussed solely on the country's defence interests, never mentioning the economic value of the defence agreement. The outcome was that the defence cuts were not as drastic as the USA had proposed. It was decided that there would never be fewer than four jet fighters stationed in the country and that the defence force's helicopter rescue team would continue in operation, being related to the presence of the jet fighters; the question of dismantling the naval monitoring and detection system in stages was not included in the discussions (Interviews with officials April 2003).

A further agreed minute was added to the defence agreement in 1996, but it entailed little substantial change. It was decided to maintain the defence capacity unchanged but to aim at reducing the cost of operating the base (Morgunblaðið 26 March 1996). This agreed minute was to be valid for five years, following which its terms would be observed until it was superseded by another. Formal discussions on the matter have been delayed due to the change of administration in the USA, the terrorist attacks on 11 September 2001 and the wars in Afghanistan and Iraq (Interviews with officials April 2003).

A report by the ministry for foreign affairs in 1999 stated that Iceland's security and defence policy needed to undergo constant reassessment, emphasizing at the same time the fundamental importance of the defence agreement with the USA and membership of NATO. It proposed that Iceland should become more active in international security co-operation and seek a larger role, alone or with other states, in its own defence (Ministry for Foreign Affairs 1999). These frank assessments indicate that Iceland's policy on security and defence has come a long way in two decades (Corgan 2002: 313–14). A government report in 1993 on Iceland's security and defence in the new international climate was not as outspoken. It emphasized the importance of the transatlantic link, i.e. defence co-operation with the USA. The report stated the government's policy that EU membership was not on the agenda and that if Iceland remained outside the EU, the importance of the defence agreement with the USA would increase. However, it acknowledged that the new international system might make it more difficult for Iceland to make its voice heard or to have other states take account of its wishes (Prime Minister's Office 1993).

Following the terrorist attacks in the USA on 11 September 2001, the US government has begun a restructuring of that country's domestic defence system. The US military actions in Afghanistan and Iraq and tighter security measures within the country have stretched the capacity of its military forces (Morgunblaðið 20 April 2002). Consequently, ever stronger demands are being made to recall forces from areas where there is no urgent need for them, and also for a general restructuring and review of priorities. The US defence secretary, Donald Rumsfeld, is among those who endorse these demands and has called for part of the US forces stationed at Keflavík to be recalled. Neither Rumsfeld nor his deputy, Paul Wolfowitz, see Iceland as being under any security threat that justifies maintaining US air force units in the country (Morgunblaðið 20 April 2002). Officials in the US administration were quoted by *Morgunblaðið* as saying they 'could see no danger threatening Iceland and the security of its people. They said even a search with a fine-toothed comb produced no results' (Sverrisson 18 April 2002).

In autumn 2002, the US military command in Iceland was transferred from Norfolk, Virginia, to the USEUCOM in Stuttgart in Germany. This was done at the initiative of the US government. The Keflavík base is under dual command, one branch of the command structure (SACLANT) being based in Norfolk. NATO's command structure is under review, and it is not unlikely that NATO's senior command at the Keflavík base will also be relocated to Europe, specifically to Mons in Belgium (Interviews with officials April 2003).

The Icelandic government was not in favour of the transfer of the US command of the force at Keflavík from the USA to Europe, and thought it would involve major changes for Iceland. It regarded it as desirable to main the status quo in this respect in the light of the defence agreement (Morgunblaðið 18 April 2002). The foreign minister said a transfer to Europe would mean a major change in Iceland's security (Morgunblaðið 19 April 2002a). Ingimundarson, one of the leading analysts of Icelandic–American relations, described the American proposal as indicating 'a fundamental change in strategic thought' (Morgunblaðið 21 April 2002) and that the USA no longer regarded Iceland as forming part of the USA's own national defences, as it had done ever since the time of President Franklin D. Roosevelt (Morgunblaðið 21 April 2002).

The Icelandic government regards all proposals for a reduction of the defences at Keflavík as unacceptable. In their discussions with the Americans, the Icelandic elite have always emphasized the view that credible defences must be based in Iceland. For example the prime minister, Davíð Oddsson, has said: 'The defence capacity here has come down to an absolute minimum, so if it is cut further it will not be possible to say there are any real defences left' (Morgunblaðið 19 April 2002b). This is at variance with statements by US representatives who say that a credible defence presence can be maintained in Iceland even without a jet fighter squadron being stationed in the country.

The defence agreement with the USA has a clear bearing on Iceland's policy on European integration. Björn Bjarnason, the Independence Party minister of justice and that party's main specialist on defence and security, has said that unlike other countries, such as Finland, Iceland is not motivated by security and defence interests to negotiate to join the EU (Bjarnason 2001: 306). Like other leaders of the party, Bjarnason has been opposed to Union membership. He completely rejects the view that has been advanced in the discussion that as a result of its eastward enlargement, NATO's orientation has shifted from northwest Europe towards the east and south, with an increased danger that Iceland will become isolated with regard to defence and security. He has stated that while the defence agreement with the USA is in force, there is no danger of isolation. But he has also said if the partnership between the USA and Iceland were to break down for any reason, then it would be necessary 'both to take radical measures regarding security and also to formulate a new policy on Europe' (Bjarnason 2001: 316). He considers that the transfer of the command of the Iceland Defense Force to Europe will not affect US-Icelandic collaboration on defence (Morgunblaðið 23 April 2002), a view endorsed by Michael T. Corgan, a specialist in US-Icelandic relations. Nor does Bjarnason see this transfer as weakening Iceland's defences (Morgunblaðið 22 April 2002).

To say that security and defence in Europe are currently in a state of flux is to comment on the obvious. Since the end of the cold war, the focus of attention for NATO and the USA regarding defence has been steadily moving away from northwestern Europe and the strategic importance of Norway and Iceland has therefore declined. Norwegian leaders saw the new situation as having weakened Norway's bargaining position in NATO (Archer *et al.* 1998: 121–2) and embarked on a review of the country's security and defence. Although NATO and the transatlantic link were still seen as the centre of gravity in Norway's defences, already in 1991 the Norwegian defence minister feared that the country would become isolated on the edge of Europe, and his view was that if EU membership were to be decided solely on the basis of foreign and security policy considerations, then Norway should apply for membership immediately (Archer *et al.* 1998: 122). Gro Harlem Brundtland, the prime minister, agreed with this analysis of the situation, saying that if the EU acquired greater weight in Europe's defence balance, then Norway's defences would need to be reviewed. She said it was important that Norway should not be 'a second rank security policy nation in Europe' (Archer *et al.* 1998: 133).

Iceland's political elite has not adopted the same view of the situation as Norway's. Since the end of the cold war, the Icelandic government has never regarded the EU as a defence alliance; it has made every effort to maintain the defence agreement with the USA. Recent developments in the defence landscape in Europe have nevertheless caused the Icelandic political elite some concern. Two points stand out in particular.

First, closer defence co-operation between the EU states could weaken the transatlantic link, with the result that the USA may gradually abandon its defence commitments in Europe (Stephensen 21 March 1997). Halldór Ásgrímsson, the foreign minister, has said that an upgrading of the importance of defence and security issues in the EU must not be allowed to weaken the transatlantic link (Ásgrímsson 7 December 2000). He has also said that Iceland has 'made every effort not to have to choose between Europe and North America in its co-operation on security and defence' (Ásgrímsson 7 December 2000). He regards it as important that the nations of Europe should not go too far in developing a specifically European defence consciousness, so marginalizing the USA in Europe. Fearing that the EU might go too far in this direction, Ásgrímsson has said that Iceland and other nations must avoid being caught up in the process, but should maintain their relationship with the USA (Blöndal 22 October 1999). The prime minister, Davíð Oddsson, has endorsed this view (Oddsson 1 December 2001). The other point in European defence issues that causes the Icelandic government concern is that Iceland is a member of NATO but not of the EU (Stephensen 21 March 1997). This could mean that as a European defence consciousness grows constantly stronger within NATO, decisions would be formulated largely within the EU and not within NATO itself. Thus, Iceland would have less of a say regarding those decisions than it has at present. The EU is growing constantly stronger, so there is a corresponding danger that other institutions in Europe will be weakened. Ásgrímsson has expressed concern at this situation, not merely as regards the transatlantic link but also the Council of Europe and the European Court of Human Rights in Strasbourg (Blöndal 22 October 1999).

Accordingly, the Icelandic government strove harder than any other country in NATO, except Turkey, to be involved in formulating the EU's European Security and Defence Policy (ESDP) when involvement by NATO states in the EU's defence and security issues was discussed in the period 1998–2000. The fact that the Icelandic authorities put far more energy into these efforts than their Norwegian counterparts shows how seriously they regarded these matters. Up to now, the Icelandic government has had representatives involved in the formation of security and defence policy in Europe, i.e. within the Organization for Security and Co-operation in Europe, the Western European Union and NATO. It has been afraid of losing these seats at the decision-making table if decisions on defence and security in Europe were to be transferred increasingly to a greater extent to the EU.

Nevertheless, the outcome of the intense negotiation between NATO and the EU concerning the framework of the relations between the two bodies satisfied the Icelandic government (Interviews with officials). The decision taken by the EU Council in Helsinki in December 1999 was an important step forward for the Icelandic government. The Council ensured the necessary dialogue, consultation and co-operation with European NATO members that are not members of the EU on issues related to ESDP and crisis management. The success of the military and civilian crisis management aspects of the ESDP, which together with conflict prevention are at its core, depends on collaboration with NATO since the EU will have to use NATO resources, including military capabilities, operational planning capabilities, and so on (European Commission 13 February 2002). The close consultation and co-operation process between NATO and the EU has given Iceland the opportunity to follow the development within the ESDP. Since early 2001 NATO and the EU have held regular joint meetings, including some at the level of foreign ministers. The NATO-EU Agreement on Security and Information also contributes to the overall development of the NATO-EU strategic partnership regarding crisis management and conflict prevention (NATO 10 October 2002).

The tension between the governments of the USA and Britain, on the one hand, and those of France and Germany, on the other, over the war on Iraq and its aftermath have weakened NATO. Despite the British government's wholehearted support of US policy on Iraq, the transatlantic link seems to be in trouble. The USA seems to have different ideas and expectations regarding the role NATO should play. The gulf between these two groups of states stems from their different priorities in international affairs, the difference in their scope for exerting influence internationally and their differing evaluation of imminent dangers. Much work therefore remains to be done to harmonize these differing viewpoints within NATO so as to give that organization a new structure that will work well in the interests of all concerned (Arnórsson 8 May 2003: 16).

Furthermore, the declaration by the heads of government of France, Germany, Belgium and Luxembourg in April 2003, calling for the establishment of a separate headquarters for planning EU military operations that would be independent of NATO, has further undermined the transatlantic partnership. The declaration says that those states prepared to take part in establishing the proposed headquarters would contribute arms that could be used in the name of the EU. It is not envisaged that it would make use of NATO's equipment and capabilities. The US secretary of state rejected the idea immediately and said there was no need for a

European control headquarters or a European military force. The British, Spanish, Italian and Dutch leaders also expressed reservations about the idea (Morgunblaðið 30 April 2003).

European states are deeply divided in security terms, and whether they are members of NATO and the EU is immaterial. As the security division in Europe increases, the Icelandic government has opted for the continuation of the special relationship with the USA. The government regards itself as an ally of the USA in its war on terrorism and its effort to stabilize the world. Before the general election in 2003, Oddsson, the prime minister, reminded voters that the government had continued to strengthen Iceland's ties with the USA and that this should be one of the key goals in the foreign policy of the next government (Sigurgeirsson 4 May 2003). The government is particularly keen to strengthen the relationship because it fears that the rift between core members of NATO may damage the transatlantic partnership. As a result, Iceland has adhered to its traditional defence strategy, emphasizing its defence agreement with the USA and the importance of the Keflavík base, its main aim being to guarantee the US presence at Keflavík and resist all attempts by the USA to reduce its activity there.

Like Norway, Iceland has not made co-operation on security and defence issues with other European countries a priority. Norway has always attached more importance to Atlantic co-operation than to co-operation with Europe (Archer *et al.* 1998: 90). As has been described above, Iceland has always made the maintenance of good relations with the USA the cornerstone of its foreign policy, yet it did not take an active role in the work of NATO during the cold war. This is understandable, since the defence agreement between the USA and Iceland was so controversial in Iceland that to have involved the country more deeply in NATO would have risked a furore (Ingimundarson 2001b: 300). The situation has changed greatly, however, since the end of the cold war, and Iceland has played a fuller role in NATO (Ingimundarson 2001b: 300). According to Ingimundarson, there are three main reasons for this change in emphasis in Iceland's foreign policy. First, the bond with the USA has weakened because the security of the North Atlantic is no longer under threat. Second, increased globalisation has pushed Iceland into being more visible and taking a more active part in international co-operation, and third, Iceland's governments have greater room for manoeuvre since the deep divisions and confrontations that characterized Icelandic politics during the cold war are now a thing of the past (Ingimundarson 2001b: 300). Iceland has also become a more active member of NATO in order to strengthen the transatlantic partnership and ensure that NATO will have a voice in decisions that form part of the EU's European Security and Defence Policy, which in turn has an effect, direct or indirect, on the workings of NATO. In addition, changes in the EU's Common Foreign and Security Policy during the 1990s resulted in Iceland playing a more active part in NATO and not seeking closer ties with the EU (Corgan 2002: 216–17).

Economic and trade relations with the USA

Unlike most other European countries, Iceland became considerably richer during the Second World War. American forces, which took over the defence of Iceland from British forces that had occupied the country in 1940, built up much of its infrastructure, which gave a rapid boost to the economy. The US government also undertook to sell Iceland's fisheries products abroad, making loans to Britain and other countries to pay for fish purchases from Iceland, and provided Iceland with all necessities during the war years. Another important economic consequence of Iceland's strategic importance was the assistance the country received under the Marshall Plan. One of the main reasons why the Icelandic government applied for aid under the plan was that it saw immediately how it could exploit the country's strategic importance in the defence of the USA and the other NATO countries (Gunnarsson 1996: 91). The country's need for support was evaluated by specialists of the Economic Co-operation Administration (ECA) in the USA, which was in charge of implementing the Marshall Plan, but every time they questioned the proposals made by Iceland, the US defence department intervened and demanded that Iceland's requests should be met virtually without conditions (Ingimundarson 1996: 163). Iceland received additional funding from the USA in 1953, even though the Marshall Plan was formally supposed to end in 1952 (Ingimundarson 2002: 338). It also benefited from US patronage within the OEEC, where the Americans used their influence to secure Iceland exemption from the requirements on the abolition of trade barriers (Gunnarsson 1996: 89). The US government was concerned at the growth in trade between Iceland and Eastern Europe, and decided to grant Iceland credit in 1957–58 to avoid having it take loans from the Soviet Union. This continued in 1959, and the new Icelandic government was given substantial gifts of money in 1960 (Ingimundarson 2002: 342–4). In fact it would be fair to say that Iceland received a second round of 'Marshall Plan assistance' in 1956–60. This financing from the USA in the form of credit and grants met the cost of most of the major development projects in Iceland between 1948 and 1960 and played an important role in raising the standard of living in the country. The aim of the US authorities was to promote further economic stability in Iceland, so securing their own political and strategic interests while reducing the influence of the Soviet Union and the Socialist Party (Ingimundarson 1996: 405–6).

Although the US government declared in 1960 that it would not make Iceland any direct grants if the country's economy faced difficulties, Iceland continued to benefit from US goodwill during the following years (Ingimundarson 2001a: 11). For example, the US government supported

Iceland during the recession of 1967–69, purchasing a large part of the stockfish that had piled up in Iceland as a result of the war in Biafra: Nigeria was the main market for these exports. The USA also continued to grant Iceland credit at highly attractive terms up until 1970; Iceland was the only western country to receive such treatment at this time. In addition, the effects of the operations of the Iceland Defense Force were felt throughout the Icelandic economy (Ingimundarson 2002: 11).

A survey of the economic effects of the presence of the Iceland Defense Force up to the year 1977 shows that the benefits for Iceland were not confined merely to the services that it provided to the force; it also gained from having access to many of the defence force's structures and facilities without having to pay anything for it (Haarde 1978: 4). First, Iceland has not spent anything on defence, while the other Nordic countries spend 2–3 per cent of their GNP on defence (Morgunblaðið 8 September 1995). Second, the USA built Iceland's international airport at Keflavík and other transport structures in the country at no cost to Iceland (Haarde 1978: 41).

Many Icelanders derive their livelihood from the activities of the Iceland Defense Force. In 2001, about 900 Icelanders were employed by the defence force and about 800 worked for contractors that provided it with various services (Ministry for Foreign Affairs May 2001). The company that has probably profited most from the presence of the defence force is Iceland Prime Contractor, but many other companies derived income from providing services to the force in 1991: about 24 contractors, 15 transport companies, 4 power utilities, 3 oil importing and distribution companies, 10 franchise-holders and car rental companies, 50 operators in the tourist industry and 17 food and catering companies (Helgason 1991: 21). Many other companies in a wide variety of occupations also derived income from the force (Sigurpálsson 1976). Opponents of the defence agreement have accused its supporters of being 'bribed' by the Americans and called them 'whores of the Yanks' (Ingimundarson 2001a: 257). This is clear reference to the economic effects of the presence of the defence force, and also to the fact that the USA has always been willing to assist the Icelandic government when the economy feels the pinch.

An idea of the importance of the operations of the defence force for the national economy can be gained by examining the earnings from work done for the force as a proportion of export earnings and as a proportion of GDP. Measured in terms of export earnings, income from the Iceland Defense Force grew from 5.4 per cent in 1970 to 7.0 per cent in 1990, while they remained more or less the same, measured in terms of GDP during the same period (see Table 7.2). There was clear contraction in the activities of the defence force after the end of the cold war. Iceland also derived a considerable proportion of its foreign currency earnings from the defence force: during the 1950s these rose to 20 per cent of total foreign currency earnings (Snævarr 1993: 364).

Table 7.2 Earnings from work done for the Iceland Defense Force (IDF) (%)

Year	Total export earnings	GDP
1970	5.4	2.6
1975	5.8	2.1
1980	5.7	2.1
1985	6.2	2.6
1990	7.0	2.5
1995	5.4	2.1
2000	4.7	1.6

Source: Central Bank of Iceland 30 April 2002.

Figure 7.2 shows the importance of the US market in Iceland's foreign trade, i.e. merchandise exports to the USA as a proportion of total merchandise exports after 1940. In the first two decades after the war, a peak was reached in 1952 when about a quarter of total merchandise exports went to the USA. This proportion declined in the following years, remaining at a fairly constant level of about 15 per cent from the end of the 1950s throughout the following decade. This was followed by a rise to a maximum of 37 per cent in 1973, remaining largely in the 25–30 per cent range and never under 20 per cent up until 1986. In the last few years, however, the importance of the USA as an export market has declined, due in part to the establishment of the EU's internal market (Eyjólfsson 27 November 1992; DV 23 October 1991): the USA currently purchases 10–15 per cent of Iceland's total merchandise exports.

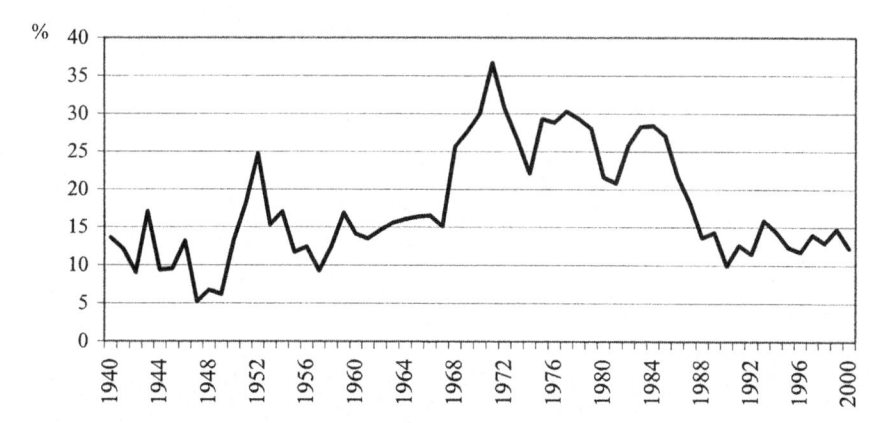

Figure 7.2 Merchandise exports to the USA 1940–2000 as a percentage of total merchandise exports.

Source: National Economic Institute 14 December 2001.

Summary

Considering the close relationship between Iceland and the USA, it is unavoidable to ask whether the existence of a defence agreement between the two is a powerful determinant of the foreign policy of the dependent state, as Moon's consensus model states. Moon's model allows for a network of dependency ties by which the dependent state is bound to the international system, and in particular to the dominant state. The foreign policy of the dependent state will follow from the values, interests and perceptions of the political elite, subject to the constraints imposed on it by domestic and international forces (Moon 1985). Iceland has been bound to the USA by close ties both in the spheres of security and defence and also economy and trade. Trade with the USA was extremely important to Iceland in the postwar period, and remains important at present; its earnings from the presence of the Iceland Defense Force are no less significant. A large number of individuals in Iceland base their livelihood on work for the defence force, and construction projects it has undertaken have played a crucial role, e.g. in the establishment of international airport facilities in the country. The benefits resulting from the presence of the defence force are highly visible in Iceland because of the smallness of the population and economy. It must also be borne in mind that Iceland has not had to bear any costs of maintaining its own national defences. Economic assistance from the USA during the decades immediately following the Second World War was immensely important to the Icelandic government. It could rely on US support when applying for exemptions from the OEEC requirement to abolish trade barriers, and also received aid and credit when faced with economic difficulties.

This support from the USA, particularly in the form of assistance under the Marshall Plan, resulted in a postponement of economic reforms and a delay in lifting barriers to trade, as a result of which Iceland was not ready, in terms of its economic and trade structures, to accept the offer to take part in the moves towards integration in Europe in 1957–59. Though economic reforms instigated by a new government were under way, the country was once again poorly prepared to take part in integration in the early 1960s.

The close trade ties with the USA, added to the fact that the government could turn to the USA when faced with economic problems right up until 1968, meant that it had little motivation to seek closer involvement with the rest of Europe. This situation has changed in the past few decades, however, particularly since the end of the cold war.

The US government no longer gives Iceland the same direct assistance in times of economic difficulty, there have been cuts in construction projects for the Iceland Defense Force and Iceland's export volumes to the USA over the past 15 years have been considerably smaller than during the previous 20 years. It is therefore difficult to say that the attitude of the

Icelandic political elite towards European integration has been directly influenced in recent years by the economic effects of the presence of the Iceland Defense Force or trade connections with the USA.

The part of the hypothesis stated at the beginning of this chapter, stating that the close relationship between Iceland and the USA in terms of economic and trade relations has had a profound influence on Iceland's response to European integration, applies only up to the 1960s insofar as the Icelandic government had no sufficiently strong motivation to cultivate closer ties with Europe because it could always rely on the USA. On the other hand the other element in the hypothesis, regarding the influence of the close US-Icelandic relationship in terms of security, is found to apply, and particularly since the end of the cold war. The European Union has made every effort to press ahead with integration in the areas of defence and security, though with mixed success. Many states have been attracted to the EU for security reasons, including Norway, even though that country's membership of NATO and the translatlantic partnership is the mainstay of its defence and security: Norwegian political leaders have sought to have the country actively involved in defence developments in Europe out of fear that it may otherwise become marginalized as regards security and defence if it has no voice in EU defence policy. Finland, and also the states set to join the EU in 2004, have also seen membership of the Union as a move towards strengthening their security. By contrast, Iceland's political elite has not taken this view because of the defence agreement with the USA.

The defence agreement is a key variable explaining why Iceland has not sought membership of the EU for reasons of defence and security, and as long as the agreement is in force and the USA maintains its present defence capacity at the Keflavík base, a large part of the Icelandic political elite, including most of the Independence Party and a slightly smaller proportion of the Progressive Party, will not be attracted to the EU in terms of security and defence. In the view of this part of the elite, the defence agreement and the presence of the force at Keflavík are sufficient guarantee of the country's security, invalidating the motives that a large part of Norway's political elite had for applying for EU membership at the beginning of the 1990s. The defence link between Iceland and the USA is one of the variables that explain the lack of interest on the part of the Icelandic government to form closer ties with the rest of Europe since the end of the cold war. For example, defence considerations have been the reason behind Iceland's resistance to the USA's moves to reduce its defence capacity in Iceland in recent years: the Icelandic government has stressed the importance of the presence of US forces for the defence and security of the country, and has not referred to the economic interests involved.

Owing to its geographical position, Iceland had immense strategic importance during the cold war. It was the key to security and the defence of shipping routes in the North Atlantic. Geographical position was one element in this strategic importance; another, which was no less important but has changed radically since the collapse of the Soviet Union, was the level of Russian military operations in Murmansk. There is no comparing the level of Russian military operations in the North Atlantic with the level of Soviet operations, particularly when these were at their height in the vicinity of Iceland in the 1980s. Thus, the strategic importance of the country has declined, and is currently extremely small, in the opinion of influential politicians and officials in Washington. It is therefore evident that US and Icelandic politicians take very different views of the security risk around Iceland. The Icelandic government has been forced to respond to these changed international circumstances by playing a more active role in international co-operation and undertaking additional international responsibilities. Iceland now plays a more active role than before in the work of NATO, and has, for example, established a peacekeeping force. The aim of this increased activity has been to demonstrate that Iceland is able to make a contribution to NATO despite its smallness. A more detailed account of Iceland's more active foreign policy will be given in Chapter 10.

The question arises whether there is not a risk that Iceland will lose the audience it has enjoyed up to now with decision makers in Washington. The concerns of the USA, and increasingly of NATO, are becoming more and more focussed towards Eastern and Southern Europe, and also to areas of the world outside Europe. The future of the defence agreement as such is not at risk, but there is some uncertainty as to the level of US defence capability in Iceland that will be maintained in the future. Icelandic political leaders see any reduction in capacity as resulting in a loss of defence credibility, and have made this point strongly in their negotiations with the US government. The opinion has already been expressed within the Independence Party that Iceland might have to review its policy on European integration if Iceland and the USA go their separate ways in the area of defence. The chairman of the Social Democratic Alliance has also pointed out that joining the EU and adopting its security and defence policy would solve the problem of diminishing American military interest in Iceland. This lends further support to the conclusion that the relationship between Iceland and the USA regarding defence and security is a variable that must be taken into account when analysing the position of the Icelandic political elite on European integration.

It is also true to say that the defence agreement with the USA has stimulated nationalistic feeling in Iceland. Supporters of the agreement have often been subjected to verbal attacks by its opponents and denounced as traitors to their people and the cause of national independence. To some extent, the concepts and rhetoric used in the disputes about the defence agreement, with accusations about being prepared to sacrifice sovereignty and independence, have been adopted in the debate on European policy in Iceland, though of course the terms used during the cold war were often even more direct. This factor, i.e. the influence of a sense of national identity and of political discourse on the position of the political elite towards European integration and its importance for Iceland, therefore deserves further attention.

Notes

1 'Iceland appears not to be able to release itself from the obligations in Article VII of the Defence Agreement, except through the termination of the North Atlantic Treaty or by changing the provisions of Article VII of the Defence Agreement' (Hafstein 1975: 18)
2 As most of the defence force's flights are made over the sea, it is essential to have an effective rescue facility to deal with accidents and emergencies. A helicopter rescue team has been in operation at Keflavík since 1952 and Iceland has benefited directly from its presence. The team has saved the lives of about 300 people of various nationalities since 1971 (Iceland Defense Force Public Affairs Office May 2001).

Bibliography

Archer, C. and Sogner, I. (1998) *Norway, European Integration and Atlantic Security*, London: Sage.
Arnórsson, A. (8 May 2003) 'Grafið undan Atlantshafsbandalaginu', *Morgunblaðið*.
Ásgrímsson, H. (7 December 2000) *Ísland og þróun evrópskra öryggis- og varnarmála*. Available online: http://utanrikisraduneyti.is (accessed 30 April 2002).
Bjarnason, B. (2001) *Í hita kalda stríðsins*, Reykjavík: Nýja bókafélagið.
Blöndal, K. (22 October 1999) 'Varast ber að utanríkisstefna ESB veiki NATO', *Morgunblaðið*. Available online: http://www.safn.mbl.is (accessed 3 June 2002).
Bragadóttir, A. (6 January 1994) 'Skeytið sem fékk kerfið til að nötra og skjálfa', *Morgunblaðið*. Available online: http://safn.mbl.is (accessed 25 August 1999).
Central Bank of Iceland (30 April 2002) 'Tekjur af varnarliðinu í Keflavík', unpublished data, The Central Bank of Iceland.
Corgan, M.T. (2002) *Iceland and Its Alliances: Security for a Small State*, New York: The Edwin Mellen Press.
DV (23 October 1991) 'Samningurinn er áfangi að algeru tollfrelsi', *DV*.
Einarsson, G. (27 April 2003) 'Fólkið krefst breytinga', *Morgunblaðið*.
European Commission (13 February 2002) *The common foreign and security policy: introduction*. Available online: http://europa.eu.int/scadplus/printversion/en/lvb/r00001.htm (accessed 16 May 2003).
Eyjólfsson, H.G. (27 November 1992) 'Áhrif EES-samningsins á íslenskan sjávarútveg', *Morgunblaðið*.
Grímsson, Ó.R. (1982) 'Iceland: a multilevel coalition system', in E.C. Browne and J. Dreijmanis (eds) *Government Coalitions in Western Democracies*, New York and London, Longman: 142–86.
Gunnarsson, G. Á. (1996) 'Ísland og Marshallaðstoðin. Atvinnustefna og stjórnmálahagsmunir', *Saga, tímarit sögufélagsins*, XXXIV: 85–130.
Haarde, G.H. (June 1978) *Varnarstöðin í Keflavík í hernaðarlegu og fjárhagslegu tilliti*, Reykjavík: Utanríkismálanefnd og Sambands ungra sjálfstæðismanna.

Hafstein, P.Kr. (1975) 'Um varnarsamning Íslands og Bandaríkjanna á grundvelli Norður-Atlantshafssamningsins', unpublished thesis, University of Iceland.
Hardarson, Ó.Th. (1985) 'Icelandic security and foreign policy: the public attitude', *Cooperation and Conflict*, XX: 297–316.
—— (1998) 'Public Opinion and Iceland's Western Integration', paper presented at Conference on the Nordic Countries and the Cold War: International Perspective and Interpretations, Grand Hotel, Reykjavík, 24 June 1998.
Hardarson Ó.Th. and Kristinsson G.H. (1987) 'The Icelandic Parliamentary Election of 1987', *Electoral Studies*, 6: 219–34.
Hálfdanarson, G. (2001) *Íslenska þjóðaríkið – uppruni og endimörk*, Reykjavík: Hið íslenska bókmenntafélag og ReykjavíkurAkademían.
Helgason, Þ. (1991) 'Ef herinn fer', *Frjáls verslun*, 7: 16–27.
Iceland Defense Force Public Affairs Office (May 2001) 'Varnarliðið á Íslandi 1951–2000', unpublished paper, Iceland Defense Force Public Affairs Office.
—— (November 2001) 'Mannafli og verktaka á vegum varnarliðsins á Keflavíkurflugvelli', unpublished paper, Iceland Defense Force Public Affairs Office.
—— (September 2001) 'Changes in the Iceland Defense Force 1990–2000', unpublished paper, Iceland Defense Force Public Affairs Office.
Ingimundarson, V. (1996) *Í eldlínu kalda stríðsins*, Reykjavík: Vaka-Helgafell.
—— (2001a) *Uppgjör við umheiminn*, Reykjavík: Vaka-Helgafell.
—— (2001b) 'The role of NATO and the U.S. military base in Icelandic domestic politics, 1949–1999', in G. Schmidt (ed.) *A History of NATO – The First Fifty Years*, New York: Palgrave, pp. 285–302.
—— (2002) 'Viðhorf Bandaríkjanna til íslenskrar hagstjórnar á 5. og 6. áratugnum', in J.H. Haralz (ed.) *Frá kreppu til viðreisnar: Þættir um hagstjórn á Íslandi á árunum 1930–1960*, Ísland: Hið íslenska bókmenntafélag, pp. 327–44.
Interviews with officials (November 2000 to May 2003) 'Interviews conducted with civil servants in ministries in Iceland'.
Jónsson, A. (1989) *Iceland, NATO and the Keflavík Base*, Iceland: Icelandic Commission on Security and International Affairs.
Kristinsson, G.H. (1991) 'The Icelandic Parliamentary Election of April 1991: a European periphery at the polls', *Scandinavian Political Studies*, 14: 343–53.
Liberal Party (March 2003) *Málefnaskrá landsþings 7.–8. mars 2003*. Available online: http://www.xf.is/index.php?xf=14&parent=1 (accessed 2 May 2003).
Ministry for Foreign Affairs (1999) *The Security and Defence of Iceland at the Turn of the Century: Report of the Working Group of the Ministry of Foreign Affairs Reykjavík*, Reykjavík: Ministry for Foreign Affairs.
—— (May 2001) *Varnarsamstarf í 50 ár*, Reykjavík: Ministry for Foreign Affairs.
Moon, B.E. (1985) 'The foreign policy of the dependent state', *International Studies Quarterly*, 27: 315–40.
Morgunblaðið [An Icelandic newspaper] (17 October 1993) 'Reykjavíkurbréf', *Morgunblaðið*. Available online: http://www.safn.mbl.is (accessed 30 March 2002).
—— (5 January 1994) 'Sameiginleg bókun Íslands og Bandaríkjanna í varnarmálum', *Morgunblaðið*. Available online: http://www.safn.mbl.is (accessed 30 March 2002).
—— (8 September 1995) 'Líflegar umræður um varnarsveitir', *Morgunblaðið*.
—— (26 March 1996) 'Sami herafli en breytingar á verktöku', *Morgunblaðið*. Available online: http://www.safn.mbl.is (accessed 16 May 2003).

—— (31 March 1999) '„Varið land" og viðhorfið til veru varnarliðsins', *Morgunblaðið*. Available online: http://www.safn.mbl.is (accessed 28 May 2002).
—— (18 April 2002) 'Ráðherra vill yfirstjórn áfram vestanhafs', *Morgunblaðið*.
—— (19 April 2002a) 'Þáttaskil í íslenskum öryggismálum', *Morgunblaðið*.
—— (19 April 2002b) 'Væntir þess að málin leysist farsællega', *Morgunblaðið*.
—— (20 April 2002) 'Við höfum reynt að draga úr viðbúnaði á Íslandi', *Morgunblaðið*.
—— (21 April 2002) 'Lýsir grundvallarbreytingu í hernaðarhugsun', *Morgunblaðið*.
—— (22 April 2002) 'Gæti treyst varnir Íslands', *Morgunblaðið*.
—— (23 April 2002) 'Á ekki að raska samstarfi Íslands og Bandaríkjanna í varnarmálum', *Morgunblaðið*.
—— (30 April 2003) 'Vilja evrópska herstjórn, óháða NATO', *Morgunblaðið*.
National Economic Institute (14 December 2001) *Merchandise exports by countries 1901–2000, percentage breakdown*. Available online: http://www.ths.is/rit/sogulegt/a0709.xls (accessed 2 May 2003).
NATO (10 October 2002) *NATO – EU Relations*. Available online: http://www.nato.int/docu/handbook/2001/hb0403.htm (accessed 16 May 2003).
Oddsson, D. (1 December 2001) *Ávarp Davíðs Oddssonar forsætisráðherra á fundi Samtaka um vestræna samvinnu og Varðbergs*. Available online: http://forsaetisraduneyti.is/interpro/for/for.nsf/pages/raeda0009 (accessed 30 May 2002).
Pálsson, G., Óskarsson, Þ. Æ. and Hannesson, H.W. (1999) *Öryggis- og varnarmál Íslands við aldamót*, Reykjavík: Ministry for Foreign Affairs. Available online: http://utanrikisraduneyti.is (accessed 25 April 2002).
Prime Minister's Office (1993) *Iceland's Security and Defence: Report of a Committee Appointed by the Government*, Reykjavík: Prime Minister's Office.
Sigurðsson, D.L. (7 May 2002) 'Ísland stóð vel að vígi þegar upp var staðið', *Morgunblaðið*. Available online: http://www.safn.mbl.is (accessed 27 May 2002).
Sigurgeirsson, S. (4 May 2003) 'Skattar ekki lækkaðir án Sjálfstæðisflokksins', *Morgunblaðið*.
Sigurpálsson, I. (1976) 'Herinn og hagkerfið: Efnahagsleg áhrif varnarliðsins', *Fjármálatíðindi*, 23/1: 23–48.
Silfur Egils (24 March 2002) 'An interview with Davíð Oddsson the Prime Minister of Iceland', TV programme, Skjár einn [An Icelandic TV station].
Social Democratic Alliance (1999) *Verkefnaskrá Samfylkingar vorið 1999*. Available online: http://www.samfylking.is/?id=3 (accessed 22 May 2001).
—— (18 November 2001) *Ályktun IX – Utanríkismálum*. Available online: http://www.samfylking.is/?i=3&o=1866 (accessed 2 May 2003).
—— (5 April 2003) *Nýir tímar – kosningastefna Samfylkingarinnr*. Available online: http://www.samfylking.is/?i=3&o=1856 (accessed 2 May 2003).
Snævarr, S. (1993) *Haglýsing Íslands*, Reykjavík: Heimskringla.
Stephensen, Ó.Þ. (21 March 1997) 'Tillögur um varnarmál setja Ísland í vanda', *Morgunblaðið*. Available online: http://www.safn.mbl.is (accessed 3 June 2002).
Sverrisson, Á. (18 April 2002) 'Varnarsamstarf á krossgötum?', *Morgunblaðið*. Available online: http://www.safn.mbl.is (accessed 6 May 2002).

8 Discussing Europe: Icelandic nationalism and European integration

Guðmundur Hálfdanarson

'In the same manner as it was unhealthy for us to acquire everything from Denmark, we should not seek everything we need from the new federal state of Europe' declared the prime minister of Iceland, Davíð Oddsson, in a recent new-year's address to the Icelandic nation (Oddsson 4 January 2000: 36–7). With this, he re-emphasized his well-known stand on European integration, and laid to rest any contemplation of Icelandic membership of the European Union – at least for as long as he heads the Icelandic government. Oddsson's words both reflected the dominating policy of his centre-right Independence Party and set the tone for any future development of the party's agenda in this area. While it attaches importance to close co-operation with Iceland's neighbours on both sides of the North Atlantic, the Independence Party has rejected, without reservation, the idea of joining Europe in its process of integration (Independence Party March 1999).

In many ways, this position is both typical of the Icelandic discussion (or, in some people's view, the apparent lack of discussion) on possible Icelandic membership of the European Union, and symptomatic of the fact that the Icelandic political parties seem to lack the discursive traditions to deal with this important issue. To support their position on Europe, the Independence Party and its chairman point out that if Iceland joined the European Union, the EU's common fisheries policy would lead to an immediate transfer of control over Iceland's most important natural resource from Reykjavík to Brussels, which would, in turn, inevitably compromise both Iceland's economic future and its political sovereignty (Oddsson 3 January 1995: 28–9). Another recurrent objection to the Union is, in its opponents' view, its stifling regulatory apparatus. 'Excessive growth plagues its regulatory system', maintained Oddsson in one of his statements on the European Union, 'and the influence of its member states on their own internal affairs has been declining' (Oddsson March 1999).

The Independence Party is not isolated in its political opposition to the European Union, as the party farthest to the left on the Icelandic political spectrum, the socialist-environmentalist Left Green Movement, seems to be in total accord with its counterpart on the right on this subject. In its manifesto on foreign policy, the party 'rejects Icelandic membership of the European Union, because such membership would diminish Icelandic sovereignty and the national control over its resources on land and in the ocean'. To support this stance further, it criticizes the 'undemocratic and corrupt administration of the EU, where bureaucrats and specialists wield great power, although they are not elected public representatives' (Left Green Movement 2003). The party's response to the European challenge is to call for bilateral treaties between Iceland and the European Union on trade and co-operation in fields such as education and research, while all negotiations on Iceland's entrance into the Union are categorically rejected (Tillaga til þingsályktunar um stefnu Íslands í alþjóðasamskiptum 5 October 2000).

Political scientists have frequently commented on the Icelandic *Sonderweg* when it comes to membership of the European Union, at least when the attitudes of the Icelandic political leaders are compared to their colleagues' support for the Union in the other Nordic countries and, in fact, over much of the European continent (Kristinsson 1996: 150–1; Ingebritsen 1998: 129; Thorhallsson 2002: 349–78). Thus, it has been pointed out that although Iceland's economic dependence on fishing and fish processing forces its politicians to take the European fisheries policy very seriously, there is still great uncertainty regarding the actual effects of EU membership on the Icelandic economy. These issues 'can only be answered in the actual negotiation process', maintains one of the leading academic experts on the Icelandic position towards Europe, but there seems to be very slow movement towards such negotiations, in spite of widespread public support for an attempt of this sort (Kristinsson 1996: 154–5; Federation of Icelandic Industries 2002a: 4). When Iceland's view on Europe is considered, the most obvious question to be raised is, therefore, why Iceland is the only Nordic nation never seriously to contemplate joining the EU.

There are, of course, a number of possible answers to this complex question, but the fact is that the political debates on EU membership in Iceland have always been evasive and non-conclusive. It has been suggested, for example, and not without reason, that Icelandic politicians have used the common fisheries policy more 'as an excuse to limit discussion on membership', than as a serious argument in these debates (Thorhallsson 2001: 257–80). The Icelandic minister for foreign affairs and chairman of the centrist Progressive Party, Halldór Ásgrímsson, seems to be of similar opinion, as he has suggested that Iceland could reach a favourable conclusion on the fisheries policy in negotiations with the European Union (Ásgrímsson 14 March 2002). For this reason he has appealed for 'candid debates in society on this issue', regretting that by 'closing their eyes to the development taking place around us, [politicians] fail in their duty toward the nation, and to the coming generations in particular' (Ásgrímsson 5 November 1999). Until now, these debates have not taken place, in part because the minister has not even been able to convince his own party to put the issue on the agenda (Morgunblaðið 22 February 2003).

However, this apparent indifference or hesitation towards the EU makes perfect sense when it is examined in the context of Icelandic political history. Modern Icelandic politics were founded during the struggle for independence in the period from the late nineteenth to the early twentieth centuries, and the nationalistic rhetoric of that era, its myths and ideals, have defined all political debates in the country ever since. Looking at the case of Norway, Neumann argues that 'the power of identity' and the structure of Norwegian political discourse shaped the EU debate and had profound influence on the final outcome (Neumann March 2001: 92). Gstöhl also argues that approaches intending to explain states' responses to European integration have to examine how the constructions of nation and statehood shape the interests of policymakers. Thus, national identity must be taken into account in explaining states' reactions to the European integration process (Gstöhl 2002: 214). This chapter claims therefore, that in order to understand Iceland's response to the 'idea of Europe', or, more appropriately perhaps, the absence of a critical and rigorous debate on European integration in Iceland, it is necessary to examine the logic of the Icelandic political discourse, its history, frames of reference, and ultimate goals. The fourth hypothesis to be tested in this book can be stated as follows: *Icelandic political discourse tends to polarize around nationalist themes, making it difficult for politicians to promote anything that seems to compromise Icelandic sovereignty and independence. For this reason, politicians are reluctant to advocate formal participation in the process of European integration.* It will be argued that while there often seems to be a considerable difference between what Icelandic politicians say and how they act, in the end their approach to European integration will always be formulated in a complex interplay between practical concerns about the economic interests of the Icelandic nation and the traditions that form their political discourse and ideals.

Birth of a nation-state

On 18 June 1944, a large crowd gathered in the centre of Reykjavík, the capital of Iceland, to celebrate the foundation of the Icelandic Republic and full independence from Denmark. This public meeting took place in front of the offices of the Icelandic prime minister, which, symbolically enough, had originally been built in the eighteenth century by the Danish authorities to serve as Iceland's first prison. The meeting was held in continuation of the official ceremonies the previous day at Þingvellir, the meeting place of the country's ancient assembly, the Althingi. At an extraordinary meeting of the Icelandic parliament at Þingvellir, the constitution of the republic had been formally ratified and the first president of the republic elected. At the meeting in Reykjavík, however, the leaders of the four parties that had representatives in parliament expressed their opinions on this important event in the history of Iceland. In his address on this occasion, the chairman of the Independence Party and the first parliamentary prime minister of the republic, Ólafur Thors, compared the foundation of the republic to the end of a long journey: 'Icelanders, we are home. We are a free nation', he announced to his fellow citizens in a language inspired by the nationalistic fervour of the first half of the twentieth century. In his opinion, the new republic was the Promised Land, a place that the Icelandic nation had searched for during almost seven centuries of foreign rule. Ólafur Thors was not alone in this conviction, because for the generation that terminated the union with Denmark, the independent republic was considered to be much more than a political institution: at last the nation 'was home with all its belongings, sovereign and independent', declared the president of the Icelandic parliament in his opening speech at the Þingvellir meeting the day before, applying an analogy that seemed so pertinent at the time (*Lýðveldishátíðin* 1945: 165, 263; Hálfdanarson 2001: 7–9).

Another recurrent theme in the public discourse during those two days in June 1944 was the idea that the republic was not only a home that the nation had desired for centuries, but also an institution with deep roots in Icelandic history. 'We have revived the republic in our country', explained Einar Olgeirsson, chairman of the pro-Soviet Socialist Party, to the crowd in the centre of Reykjavík, 'because the yearning for freedom has never been extinguished in our nation.' His conservative counterpart, Ólafur Thors, was in total accord, claiming that the republic had not really been founded at Þingvellir the day before, but rather resurrected (*Lýðveldishátíðin* 1945: 265, 273). This was the 'restoration of the old Free State, which had created the first golden age in Iceland', wrote still another politician a few years later, comparing the modern, democratic state to the 'Commonwealth' of the tenth to the late thirteenth century (Jónsson 1948: XXI). Thus, the republic was interpreted as an Icelandic institution: the new 'home' of the nation was built on an *Icelandic* idea rather than a European import.

Finally, these 'founding fathers' of the republic viewed the history of the Icelandic nation, from the time it came under the Norwegian crown in the late thirteenth century until it became a fully independent republic in the twentieth, as an unremitting struggle for its freedom. 'Ever since the late thirteenth century', exclaimed one of the veterans of the nationalist movement in his address to the people at Þingvellir on 17 June 1944, 'have our leaders fought with foreign power.' This, 'the most superb day' in Icelandic history, was, in his words, the reward 'for a long and hard battle, centuries of hard work and struggle' (*Lýðveldishátíðin* 1945: 204). This was the essence of Icelandic history, the thread that linked the present with the past, the politicians reiterated again and again, indicating that it was not only a crucial factor in Icelandic history, but also a guide for the future. Hence, it was imperative to 'keep the history of the struggle alive, to make the exertions and battle of past generations for liberty an important part in the life and conscience of coming generations', wrote the socialist Einar Olgeirsson in his description of a historical exhibition set up in Reykjavík on the occasion of the foundation of the republic. 'Culture can only thrive on the basis of freedom', Olgeirsson continued, and if Icelanders realized this, 'the more likely it is that the nation will learn to preserve its liberty' (*Lýðveldishátíðin* 1945: 386).

These statements, marking the birth of the Icelandic nation-state, expressed a very special vision of the history and foundation of the Icelandic republic. First, it is clear that the politicians perceived the freedom and sovereignty of the nation as the indisputable and fundamental objective of all Icelandic political efforts in the past and, by implication, their preservation as its ultimate goal in the future. The republic was the home of the nation, and in the same way as every Icelandic family had to have a roof over its head, the Icelandic nation had also to be sovereign and independent in its homeland. Second, they repeated persistently and with firm conviction that the democratic republic, founded on the principle of popular sovereignty, was an Icelandic creation, harking back to the tribal clan-based society of the Middle Ages, rather than a variation on a common Western political theme. In this manner, they rejected the common European heritage of the Icelandic nation-state, placing its symbolic origins at Þingvellir – the 'Parliament Plains' in literal translation – rather than the Champ de Mars in Paris, where French historians have claimed that 'the first modern nation' was born when the French gathered on 14 July 1790, for the first time as a nation, *une et indivisible*, celebrating the storming of the Bastille the year before (Lavisse 1922: 511).

Seen in the context of European history, however, the formation of the Icelandic nation-state follows a fairly normal pattern, described by theorists such as Ernest Gellner (1983) and Miroslav Hroch (1968). Under the leadership of a small group of intellectuals, nationalists turned a pre-existing culture into a nation, to use Gellner's expression, portraying the nation 'as a natural, God-given way of classifying men, as an inherent though long-delayed political destiny' (Gellner 1983: 42). This nationalist myth still has a hegemonic status in Icelandic society, and therefore Icelandic mainstream politicians have not, so far, expressed the same doubts as their colleagues and opinion makers in Europe about the future of the nation-state system and its capacity to deal with post-modern conditions. For this reason, most Icelandic politicians act as if Iceland were immune from the forces that have driven European integration in the last few decades, because they see them as irrelevant for the periphery in the north, in spite of its vital economic and cultural links with its European neighbours. But, one has to ask, is the common view in Iceland that 'independence is the [country's] most valuable resource', to quote one vocal opponent of the idea of joining the EU (Arnalds 1998: 14), politically tenable in the future?

Is the nation-state dying?

Like so many factors in modern politics, the idea of the sovereign nation took on its final form during the chaotic years of the French Revolution. With the execution of Louis XVI, on 21 January 1793, the French broke the links that bound the Republic to the past, at the same time as they severed the sacred bond that had connected the absolute king with the divinity above. Moreover, regicide completed the transfer of sovereignty from a King-Christ, to use Albert Camus's apposite expression, to the nation.[1] This decisive moment was the result of a political development that had taken place in the preceding years, where the inhabitants of France – or, more correctly, those who acted on their behalf – defined themselves, on the one hand, as an indivisible nation, and claimed, on the other, that the nation was the only true source of authority in the state. Sovereignty was something that the people had in common; something in which no one individual member of the national community could claim a larger share than his fellow countrymen – as women were generally deemed to be unfit for active participation in politics, the gender reference in this formulation is not inappropriate in this context (Godechot 1975: 38; Nora 1992: 339–58; Baker 1992: 483–506; Nicolet 2000: 37–60).

Since the birth of the sovereign nation in the French and American revolutions, in the late eighteenth century, the nation has become the dominating source of political legitimacy in the world. When sociologists study 'societies', maintains Anthony Giddens, 'they think of quite clearly delimited systems, which have their inner unity. Now, understood in this way, "societies" are plainly *nation-states*' (1990: 13). In spite of their apparent success, modern nations are, however, based on an obvious paradox. Thus, their political function is primarily to serve as repositories for sovereignty; they are 'a corpus of citizens equal before the law', to quote the French historian Pierre Nora (1992: 339). In this sense, nations are founded on universal ideals because democratic sovereignty and human rights are individual, and not collective, entitlements, and are supposed to be equally valid all over the globe. For this reason, believers in theories of modernization saw the formation of nation-states as only one stage on the road towards 'an ultimate integration of all societies', as the historian Cyril E. Black argued in the mid-1960s, in a book on the dynamics of modernization (1966: 155, 167; see also Smith 1991: 145). In other words, nations were practical vehicles towards a universal liberal society of free and independent individuals, rather than natural depositories of sovereignty in a fractured world.

In practice, however, modern states have tended to be less extensive in size and tied to a defined territory, a homeland, 'the land of past generations, the land that saw the flowering of the nation's genius', as Anthony D. Smith summarizes the nationalist argument for the bounded, national community (1979: 3). The desire for this land, and the identification with it, served as the basis for national solidarity and definitions of national collectivities. In this historical sense, Nora maintains, nations are 'human collectivities united by continuity, past and future' (1992: 339; Spencer and Wollman 2002: 86–9). This definition of limited communities of citizens, constituted through a lengthy historical process (as in the case of France) or cultural affinity (as in the case of Germany), emerged in the wake of the Revolution and the ensuing Napoleonic expansion. In part, this happened because the idea of a universal state had little support in Europe in the eighteenth and nineteenth centuries, but in part, this was also a natural response to the economic and social realties of the time that often did not allow for larger states than actually emerged in the nineteenth century. Thus, Europe has gradually become divided into nation-states, all espousing the universal principles of citizens' rights, while jealously guarding their national 'characters' and territorial rights.

As time passed, the territorial and cultural definitions of national communities totally overshadowed the universal ideals of democratic liberalism. The reason was, at least partly, functional, since the idea of common destiny has proved to be both a very convincing principle of legitimation of state power, and a potent source of cohesion and identity in modern societies as, with the decline of institutionalized religions, nations have provided people with meaning and purpose in their lives (Giddens 1985: 116–21, 209–21; Schnapper 1994: 186–90). The national community provided people with the sweet sense of belonging or inclusion – 'la douceur d'être inclus', – to use a phrase coined by Michel Morineau (1983: 19–32). Therefore, although most serious students of nationalism reject primordialism or essentialism as an explanation for the emergence of nations (Hutchinson 1994: 3), it is clear that a large part – if not the majority – of Europeans take their nationality more or less for granted and deem it to be a part of their nature.

In spite of its success during the last two centuries, the nation-state – this 'uneasy coexistence of two distinct formations', the nation and the republic, to quote a recent essay by the Polish sociologist Zygmunt Bauman (1999: 162) – has come under increasing pressure in recent years. From above, 'globalization' poses a serious challenge to the ruling political form in the world, both in economic and cultural terms. Thus, with the free movement of capital between countries, and the increased importance of supranational corporations in the global economy, the concept of 'national economy' makes less sense every year (Bauman 1995: 152). Similarly, the advent of satellite television, computerized communications, and the spread of the Internet efface cultural boundaries, making it ever more difficult to sustain belief in the particularity of national cultures.

The collective identity of the nation is also being hollowed from within. Most theorists of nationality, from the French scholar Ernest Renan in the late nineteenth century to Anthony D. Smith in the late twentieth, have stressed the importance of 'collective memories' for the construction and preservation of national communities. 'A nation has no other definition but historical', the French political scientist and diplomat Jean-Marie Guéhenno points out in his book on the end of the nation-state. 'It is the locus of a common history, of common misfortunes, and of common triumphs' (1995: 4). For Renan, the nation is 'a spiritual principle', made of two things, one of which was 'the possession in common of a rich heritage of memories', while the other was the desire to live together 'and the will to continue to make the most of the joint inheritance'. While Renan fully acknowledges that the national remembrance is not at all a truthful rendering of the past, because nations choose only to remember the things that unite them and tend to forget the contested events of the past, he assumes that history is a necessary symbol in the unification of the national community (1947: 887–906). This strategy, which the sociologist Pierre Bourdieu described as 'restructuring retrospectively a past adjusted to the needs of the present' (1987: 160), is hardly as self-evident for most European nations now, at the beginning of the twenty-first century, as it was at the end of the nineteenth. With an increasing flow of immigrants, European nations are becoming increasingly heterogeneous and, therefore, it becomes impossible for individual nations to imagine that they have a unified past. Hence, Anthony D. Smith's description of a nation, which he defines as 'a named human population sharing an historic territory, common myths and historical memories, a mass, public culture, a common economy and common legal rights and duties for all members' (2000: 3) is continuously losing ground in Europe. It remains to be seen how this will affect national identities, but it will certainly change the role of history in the construction and reconstruction of national communities in the future (see Hall 1993: 349–63).

To a certain extent, the European Union can be viewed as a response to these challenges to the modern nation-state system. The original idea behind the integrative process was, of course, to solve the chronic disputes that plagued the continent from the late nineteenth to the mid-twentieth centuries, between France and Germany in particular. The atrocities of the Second World War finally convinced European political leaders that 'the fragmentation of Europe had become an absurd anachronism', as the French politician Robert Schuman, one of the founding fathers of the union, wrote in his memoirs four decades ago. The aim was not to fuse the existing states, or 'to create a superstate', he asserted, stressing the historical role of the national communities. 'Our European states are a historical reality; it would be psychologically impossible to make them disappear' (1963: 24). While many observers, such as the late German sociologist Norbert Elias, have supported this view, arguing that the social habitus of the nation-states is too deeply ingrained in people's minds to be 'eliminated by compromises, by conscious acts, or by what one usually calls ... rational means' (1991: 283–8), the European Union has, all the same, gradually begun to take on the guise of a nation-state. Thus, the Union now flaunts many of the emblems of a normal nation-state, including a flag, and has even begun to develop the institutions that have traditionally been restricted to sovereign democratic states. This has led scholars, such as Zygmunt Bauman, to comment on the immanent divorce of nations and republics, claiming that 'today in Europe, the eminently expandable republics rush into the European Union while the eminently unstretchable nations stay behind and lean over backwards to hold the escaping republics back' (1999: 162–3). It is still too early to predict where this development will lead, but it seems to be difficult for Europeans to perceive the Union as anything but a large nation-state, and therefore the logic tends to direct the integration down that difficult road (Guéhenno 1999). The concerted efforts of the Union to promote an 'idea of Europe' and a 'European dimension' through its educational programmes, appears to support that claim; the goal is to construct a European identity, that could, at least in part, compete with the national identities of the past.

A nation pledges its allegiance to the state

On 17 June 1994, about 60,000 people, or a quarter of the Icelandic nation, assembled at Þingvellir to renew their pledge to the Republic of Iceland on its fiftieth birthday (Hálfdanarson 2000: 5–29). That so large a part of the Icelandic population came to the celebration was a clear demonstration of the fact that the ideals expressed at the time of the foundation of the republic were still very much alive in Iceland half a century later. At the centre of the ceremony was, as it had been at the foundation of the republic in 1944, a public meeting of the Icelandic parliament, to which the entire nation had been invited. The emotional climax of the day came, however, when the nation, i.e. the part of it present at the festival joined in a communal performance of patriotic songs on the slopes at Þingvellir. 'It was at this moment', wrote the semi-official chronicler of the event,

> when these songs sounded from the throats of tens of thousands in the fresh and clear summer air after a shower of rain that a strange and sacred national atmosphere was created at Þingvellir; the spirit and national force left no one untouched. All over one could see tears in people's eyes, which could not be explained in terms of the recently fallen raindrops. The people on the slopes joined in a common song that resounded across the plains. And at this moment something strange happened in the hearts of all those who were present ... Maybe it happened because the tens of thousands of people who stood

on their feet on the slopes ... disarmed by this spirit of unity, suddenly realized how important the Republic and liberty is to us Icelanders. How united we are and close, despite daily quarrels and differences among us.

(Margeirsson 1994: 48–9)

This somewhat hyperbolical account of the public gathering at Þingvellir in 1994 captures perfectly the dominating view of the national community in Iceland. First, the nation, its interests, and its symbols, are still perceived as a living reality in Icelandic public life, in spite of the recurrent doubts about the viability of the nation-state in Europe. Second, the view of the unified nation that, in some magical manner, fuses all its individual members into one metaphorical person, still prevails in Iceland. This idea does not, of course, originate in Iceland, as Herder's theories on the *Volksgeist* and the organic nation laid the foundation for this line of thought already in the eighteenth century (Hálfdanarson 2001: 15–42). In a similar manner, French historians from Jules Michelet in the nineteenth century to Ernest Lavisse in the early twentieth, hailed French national unity in spite of France's racial and cultural diversity, claiming that 'France [was] the country of the world where nationality, or the national personality, was closest to forming an individual personality'.[2] There are few modern nations, however, that still pretend that this unity exists in theory, let alone demonstrate it in action – except, perhaps, during national sporting events or when faced with common danger.

One important effect of this firmly imagined political community in Iceland is the deep-seated conviction that democratic sovereignty is vested in the nation as a collective unit rather than in its individual members, and, therefore, the belief that Icelandic sovereignty cannot be subdivided internally, shared with other countries or partially transferred to international organizations. 'The nation can lose its independence and sovereignty again', maintained the Icelandic newspaper *Vísir* in 1918, in an article on the Act of Union with Denmark, which declared Iceland to be a free and sovereign state in union with Denmark. 'It is, however, the most sacred duty of all Icelanders to be on their guard against this', the journalist concluded his article, 'because if the nation relinquishes its independence again, then it will be lost forever' (Vísir 1 December 1918; Hálfdanarson 1998). Similar arguments have guided Icelandic politics ever since, and are frequently repeated in the public discourse. 'We walk without hesitation into extensive co-operation with both states and international institutions in order to secure our interests', said Prime Minister Davíð Oddsson, for example, in a recent address to the nation,

[but] there are a few fundamental principles for the existence of this nation, which we can never break ... Control over the fishing grounds surrounding the country can never be used as a bargaining counter.

Then, the struggle would have been for nothing, and it would have been best for the nation to stay home on 17 June 1944
(Oddsson 3 January 1995: 10).

This emphasis on indivisible sovereignty, which the nation cannot give up any more than Rousseau's citizen can alienate himself (1762: Book I, Ch. IV), might be taken as an example of how important it is to factor identity into the analysis of attitudes towards the European Union among 'reluctant Europeans' such as Iceland and Norway (Neumann March 2001: 87–94). Comparing the actions of Icelandic politicians to their political statements demonstrates, however, that there is no simple or straightforward connection between identity and policy when it comes to international affairs. Thus, while Icelandic politicians have pledged their unyielding belief in the sanctity of national sovereignty, they have not hesitated to limit the legislative power of the Icelandic parliament through international treaties, but it has been very difficult for them to *admit* that the treaties have had these effects. The European Economic Area (EEA) Agreement with the European Union is a perfect example of this ambivalence, because for the last decade it has compelled Icelanders to accept a great majority of all European Union legislation, without giving them a voice in the decision-making processes, or the right to vote in Union elections. Icelandic politicians have, therefore, willingly accepted the recent fact of European political life, which is that less than half of existing regulations are of national origin (Guéhenno 1995: 50), but they are, at the same time, unable to discuss the implications of their actions, let alone to suggest that the nation should enter the co-operative process as full partners, even though joining the Union in this situation would, as many observers have pointed out, entail a gain of sovereignty rather than a loss (Gstöhl 2002: 216).

This discrepancy between the expressions and actions of the Icelandic political elite might appear as a strange paradox, but it is in perfect accord with Icelandic political traditions in recent decades. A small country like Iceland, with a fairly narrow economic base, cannot survive without extensive foreign co-operation. Hence it became a founding member of NATO in 1949, entrusted the United States of America with its military defence in 1951, entered EFTA in 1970, and accepted the EEA and Schengen agreements in 1993 and 1999 respectively.

Political discourse in Iceland has not, however, evolved in accordance with the policies of the state. Thus, the Icelandic political elite has done little to 'sell' the European idea to the Icelandic public; on the contrary, it has constantly reinforced the nationalist identities of the past, rejecting the idea of surrendering Icelandic sovereignty to the bureaucrats in Brussels. Icelandic international politics have, therefore, always centred on a search for practical solutions to the shortcomings of a small society, without acknowledging that the ideal of national sovereignty has changed radically since Iceland became a sovereign state.

There are two reasons, in my view, for the nationalistic tone of Icelandic political discourse. First, the politicians themselves are formed through the same socialization process as their voters and are therefore heavily influenced by the nationalist rhetoric of the past. The political speeches made on 17 June 1994, at the fiftieth anniversary of the founding of the Republic of Iceland, are a perfect case in point, because they echo all the themes that had characterized the festive days in June 1944. 'The seventeenth of June 1944 had been awaited for almost seven centuries', maintained the prime minister, Davíð Oddsson, repeating the same idea as his predecessor, Ólafur Thors, had expressed in Reykjavík half a century earlier (Oddsson 19 June 1994: 13). 'We possess the most valuable thing for every person and every nation', said Jóna V. Kristjánsdóttir, chairwoman of the Women's Alliance, at the same occasion, 'that is, liberty, the right to control our life and future.... A nation that is not conscious of what is liberty and independence is doomed to perish' (Kristjánsdóttir 19 June 1994: 30). In their parlance, sovereignty and independence were the foundations of Icelandic prosperity, resources that have to be guarded in the same manner as the fishing grounds. Thus, they see the preservation of these resources as their sacred duty and the final goal of Icelandic politics, and to compromise them would be a betrayal of past and future generations of Icelanders (Arnalds 19 June 1994: 29; Pétursson 19 June 1994: 29). Second, the politicians fully realize that nothing galvanizes Icelandic voters in the same manner as nationalism. Therefore, important issues in Icelandic politics, be it Iceland's defence policy or environmental issues, automatically tend to polarize the voters around nationalistic themes (Ingimundarson 2001; Hálfdanarson 2001: 191–216). For this reason, although surveys tend to demonstrate a considerable, albeit fluctuating, support for application for membership of the European Union (Kristinsson 1996: 155–60; Federation of Icelandic Industries 2002b: 4; Thorhallsson 2002: 362–71), it would be a great risk to start the negotiation process. Thus, even the staunch supporters of the European Union fear that it would be difficult to have an agreement with the Union accepted through a referendum, however positive this might be from the Icelandic point of view. Icelandic political leaders have been loath to use public referenda to approve decisions that touch on issues that concern national identity, unless it is absolutely clear that they strengthen Icelandic independence and national sovereignty. The foundation of the republic and its first constitution were, for example, put to the voters in the general elections in 1944, when a huge majority of the voting public came to the polls (Hagstofa Íslands 1945) and voted yes, while the nation was not asked to express its opinion on joining NATO in 1949, the defence treaty with the USA in 1951, or the EEA Agreement of 1993.

Summary

In spite of their ambivalent attitudes towards the European Union, Icelanders have always looked on themselves as a European nation, cherishing their European heritage and culture. In opinion polls, Icelanders appear to view the world around them, and their ties with surrounding countries, in the same way as people in the other Nordic countries: the overwhelming majority of those asked in such polls see Europe, and then their Nordic neighbours in particular, as the region standing closest to them, while only 3 per cent rank the USA at the top of the list (Jónsson *et al.* 1990: 21). Moreover, Icelanders have participated fully and with great enthusiasm in European educational programmes since the early 1990s, in spite of their explicit political purpose, which is to promote a pan-European identity. When it comes to the formal process of European integration, however, Iceland has opted out of, or rather, opted against, finding out whether it could join the European Union on acceptable terms – thus 'risking to be, when faced with immense interests, no more than an operetta nation', to quote Claude Nicolet's argument against the viability of small nations in the modern world (2000: 34).

It is clear, therefore, that although Icelanders have cultivated their economic, cultural and, to a certain extent, political ties with Europe, they have considered Iceland to be immune from the logic that has driven European integration in the past decades. This chapter has emphasized the nationalistic tenor of Icelandic politics as one of the main explanatory factors behind these attitudes, and in particular, the sense that the Icelandic nation forms an organic unity and that the unified nation must not relinquish its sovereignty and independence. Thus, while Iceland remains economically and socially dependent upon its relations with Europe, it seems impossible for Icelandic politicians to accept or promote closer political contacts with the European Union. The strength of the nationalist discourse is, without doubt, based on aspects such as the geographic isolation of the country, the relative homogeneity of its population, and the general economic prosperity that has characterized Iceland for at least the last half-century. Furthermore, living – though reluctantly – under the protective wings of the American eagle, Iceland does not search for security in the European Union. Thus, the finding supports Gstöhl and Neumann's call for national identity and political discourse to be taken into account in explaining states' responses to European integration. The fact that governments in Iceland and Norway have reached different conclusions on EU membership indicates that they do not share the same political discourse on sovereignty and independence and that their perception of their national identity differs. It is thus important to examine in more detail the characteristics of the Icelandic political elite and its domestic arena, as will be done in the following chapter.

It is most unlikely that Iceland will be able to live in its imagined cocoon forever, as it has to deal with the same challenges to the nation-state ideology as other countries in the world. First, globalization is just that – it affects the whole globe, and heeds no national or geographical borders. Second, the homogeneity of the Icelandic nation is also rapidly declining, with growing immigration of foreign workers to fill occupations that Icelanders are not willing to enter. Finally, isolation is only beneficial up to a point; Iceland's strategic position in the North Atlantic secured its access to the international arena during the cold war, and until recently it has been able to find enough European allies outside the Union in order to catch the attention of those inside. As the Union expands to the east and the number of European non-member countries shrinks, Iceland will both receive less attention in Brussels than before, and it will lose its allies in negotiations with the Union. The result of this development could very well be that isolation will change to seclusion, which is a position Iceland can ill afford.

Notes

1 The execution of Louis XVI – or Louis Capet – 'is at the crux of our contemporary history. It symbolizes the secularization of our history and the disincarnation of the Christian God' wrote Albert Camus of this fateful event (Camus 1956: 120–1); see also Walzer 1974: 86–9 and Furet 1988: 128–30.
2 Michelet 1995: 138. In Lavisse's words: 'France, despite her diverse races ... has formed a political entity that most resembles a moral person.... Among the great nations, France is the nation *par excellence*' (Lavisse 1891: 148).

Bibliography

Arnalds, R. (19 June 1994) 'Brýnt að varðveita þann þjóðarauð sem tilvera Íslendinga veltur á', *Morgunblaðið*.
—— (1998) *Sjálfstæðið er sívirk auðlind*, Reykjavík: Háskólaútgáfan, 1998.
Ásgrímsson, H. (5 November 1999) *Stefnuræða Halldórs Ásgrímssonar á aðalfundi miðstjórnar Framsóknarflokksins 5 nóvember 1999*. Available online: http://www.framsokn.is (accessed 28 October 2000).
—— (14 March 2002) *Iceland's transatlantic dilemma: Economic ties with Europe – defence ties with the United States – Europe's neglected north-western flank*. Available online: http://brunnur.stjr.is/interpro/utanr/utanrad.nsf/pages/ (accessed 8 March 2003).
Baker, K.M. (1992) 'Souveraineté', in F. Furet and M. Ozouf (eds) *Dictionnaire critique de la Révolution française. Idées*, 2nd edn, Paris: Flammarion.
Bauman, Z. (1995) 'Searching for a centre that holds', in M. Featherstone, S. Lash and R. Robertson (eds) *Global Modernities*, London: Sage.
—— (1999) *In Search of Politics*, Oxford: Polity Press.
Black, C.E. (1966) *The Dynamics of Modernization: A Study in Comparative History*, New York: Harper and Row.
Bourdieu, P. (1987) 'Espace social et pouvoir symbolique', in P. Bourdieu, *Choses dites*, Paris: Les Éditions de Minuit.

142 Icelandic nationalism and European integration

Camus, A. (1956) *The Rebel. An Essay of Man in Revolt*, trans. A. Bower, New York: Vintage Books.

Elias, N. (1991) 'Les transformations de l'équilibre "nous-je"', in N. Elias, *La société des individus*, Paris: Fayard.

Federation of Icelandic Industries (2002a) *Samtök iðnaðarins. – aðild að ESB – Viðhorfsrannsókn febrúar 2002*. Available online: http://www.si.is/idnthing/idnthing2002/ESB-konnun-Gallup14-26feb2002.pdf (accessed 8 March 2003).

—— (2002b) *Samtök iðnaðarins. – aðild að ESB – Viðhorfsrannsókn júní/júlí 2002*. Available online: http://www.si.is/utgafa/ymis/PDF-skrar/ESB/ESB-Gallupkonnun-26juni-11juli2002.pdf (accessed 8 March 2003).

Furet, F. (1988) *La Révolution 1770–1880*, Paris: Hachette.

Gellner, E. (1983) *Nations and Nationalism*, Ithaca: Cornell University Press.

Giddens, A. (1985) *The Nation-State and Violence*, Berkeley: University of California Press.

—— (1990) *The Consequences of Modernity*, Stanford: Stanford University Press.

Godechot, J. (1975) *Les Constitutions de la France depuis 1789*, Paris: Garnier-Flammarion.

Gstöhl, S. (2002) *Reluctant Europeans. Norway, Sweden and Switzerland in the Process of Integration*, Boulder: Lynne Rienner Publishers.

Guéhenno, J.M. (1995) *The End of the Nation-State*, Minneapolis: University of Minnesota Press.

—— (1999) 'Die neue Machtfrage', *Die Zeit*, 51. Available online: http//www.zeit.de/1999/51/19951_democratie_gueh.html (accessed 10 November 2000).

Hagstofa Íslands [Statistics Iceland] (1945) 'Þjóðaratkvæðagreiðsla um afnám dansk-íslenzka sambandssamningsins frá 1918 og um stjórnarkrá Lýðveldisins Íslands' *Hagskýrslur Íslands*, 118, Reykjavík: Hagstofa Íslands.

Hálfdanarson, G. (1998) 'Fullveldi fagnað', *Ný saga* 10: 57–65.

—— (2000) 'Þingvellir: An Icelandic *"Lieu de Memoire"*', *History and Memory* 12: 5–29.

—— (2001) *Íslenska þjóðríkið – upphaf og endimörk*, Reykjavík: Hið íslenska bókmenntafélag.

Hall, S. (1993) 'Culture, Community, Nation', *Cultural Studies*, 7: 349–63.

Hroch, M. (1968) *Die Vorkämpfer der nationalen Bewegung bei den kleinen Völkern Europas: eine vergleichende Analyse zur gesellschaftlichen Schictung der patriotischen Gruppen*, Prague: Universita Karlova, 1968.

Hutchinson, J. (1994) *Modern Nationalism*, London: Fontana.

Independence Party (March 1999) *Ályktun um utanríkismál*. Available online: http://www.xd.is/landsf/utanrikis.shtml (accessed 28 October 2000).

Ingebritsen, C. (1998) *The Nordic States and European Unity*, Ithaca and London: Cornell University Press

Ingimundarson, V. (2001) *Uppgjör við umheiminn. Íslensk þjóðernishyggja, vestrænt samstarf og landhelgisdeilan*, Reykjavík: Vaka-Helgafell.

Jónsson, F.H. and Ólafsson, S. (1990) *Úr lífsgildakönnun 1990: Lífsskoðun í nútímalegum þjóðfélögum*, Reykjavík: Félagsvísindastofnun.

Jónsson, J. (1948) 'Jón Jónsson Aðils', in J.J. Aðils, *Gullöld Íslendinga. Menning og lífshættir feðra vorra á söguöldinni*, 2nd edn, Reykjavík: Þorleifur Gunnarsson.

Kristinsson, G.H. (1996) 'Iceland and the European Union. Non-Decision on

Membership', in L. Miles (ed.) *The European Union and the Nordic Countries*, London: Routledge.

Kristjánsdóttir, J.V. (19 June 1994) 'Hér megi alltaf búa frjáls og fullvalda þjóð', *Morgunblaðið*.

Lavisse, E. (1891) *General View of the Political History of Europe*, New York: Longmans, Green.

—— (1922) (ed.) *Histoire de France contemporaine depuis la Révolution jusqu'à la paix de 1919*, vol. IX, Paris: Hachette.

Left Green Movement (2003) *Vinstrihreyfingin – grænt framboð – málefnahandbók – alþjóðamál*, Available online: http://www.vg.is (accessed 8 March 2003).

Lýðveldishátíðin 1944 (1945) Reykjavík: Leiftur.

Margeirsson, I. (1994) *Þjóð á Þingvöllum*, Reykjavík: Vaka-Helgafell.

Michelet, J. (1995 [1833]) *Tableau de la France*, Paris: Éditions complexe.

Morgunblaðið [An Icelandic newspaper] (22 February 2003) 'Miðjuflokkur', *Morgunblaðið*.

Morineau, M. (1983) 'La douceur d'être inclus', in F. Thelamon (ed.) *Sociabilité, pouvoirs et société. Actes du Colloque de Rouen Novembre 1983*, Rouen: Université de Rouen.

Neumann, I.B. (March 2001) 'The Nordic States and European Unity', *Cooperation and Conflict*, 36: 86–94.

Nicolet, C. (2000) *Histoire, nation, république*, Paris: Éditions Odile Jacob.

Nora, P. (1992) 'Nation', in F. Furet and M. Ozouf (eds), *Dictionnaire critique de la Révolution française. Idées*, 2nd edn, Paris: Flammarion.

Oddsson, D. (19 June 1994) 'Hamingjudraumur hvers Íslendings tekur svipmót af þessu bjarta landi', *Morgunblaðið*.

—— (3 January 1995) 'Þetta land var sál vorri fengið til fylgdar', *Morgunblaðið*.

—— (March 1999) 'Ræða forsætisráðherra og formanns Sjálfstæðisflokksins á landsfundi 11.–14. mars 1999'. Available online: http://www.xd.is/landsf/utanrikis.shtml (accessed 28 October 2000).

—— (4 January 2000) 'Framkvæmdaviljinn dráttarklár áframhaldandi velmegunar', *Morgunblaðið*.

Pétursson, P. (19 June 1994) 'Tungan gerir Íslendinga að þjóð', *Morgunblaðið*.

Renan, E. (1947) 'Qu'est-ce qu'une nation? Conférence faite en Sorbonne, le 11 mars 1882', in H. Psichari (ed.) *Œuvres complètes de Ernest Renan*, vol. 1, Paris: Chalmann-Lévy.

Rousseau, J.-J. (1762) *Du Contrat Social*.

Schnapper, D. (1994) *La communauté des citoyens. Sur l'idée moderne de nation*, Paris: Gallimard.

Schuman, R. (1963) *Pour l'Europe*, Paris: Les Éditions Nagel.

Smith, A.D. (1979) *Nationalism in the Twentieth Century*, New York: New York University Press.

—— (1991) *National Identity*, Reno: University of Nevada Press.

—— (2000) *The Nation in History. Historiographical Debates about Ethnicity and Nationalism*, Hanover: University Press of New England.

Spencer, P. and Wollman, H. (2002) *Nationalism. A Critical Introduction*, London: Sage.

Thorhallsson, B. (2001) 'The Distinctive Domestic Characteristics of Iceland and the Rejection of Membership of the European Union', *Journal of European Integration* 23: 257–80.

—— (2002) 'The skeptical political elite versus the pro-European public. The case of Iceland', *Scandinavian Studies*, 74: 349–78.

Tillaga til þingsályktunar um stefnu Íslands í alþjóðasamskiptum (5 October 2000) 'A parliamentary resolution'. Available online: http://www.althingi.is/altext/126/s/0004.html (accessed 1 May 2003).

Vísir [An Icelandic newspaper] (1 December 1918) 'Fullveldið: "Vandi fylgir vegsemd hverri"', *Vísir*.

Walzer, M. (1974) *Regicide and Revolution. Speeches at the Trial of Louis XVI*, Cambridge: Cambridge University Press.

9 The Euro-sceptical political elite

Gunnar Helgi Kristinsson and Baldur Thorhallsson

Introduction

What has made the case of Iceland unique in Europe is the attitude of the political elite towards participation in European integration. There are two interesting points of concern here. First, Euro-scepticism of the Icelandic political elite distinguishes the country clearly from the other Western European states, and second, Iceland's political elite has been more sceptical regarding EU membership than has the country's electorate. In surveys from the late 1980s onwards, membership of the EU has been favoured by every second respondent who stated an opinion, and in some cases by a clear majority, even though none of the political parties advocated membership during the greater part of this period.

European integration in many states has elite support but lacks a corresponding popular backing. For instance, the political elites in Norway and Switzerland have pursued EU membership but have been held back by their electorates. The Danish electorate has twice prevented the political elite from deepening Denmark's involvement in European integration. The sceptical view of the electorate in Sweden and Britain towards adopting the euro seems to thwart their governments' intentions. Despite this, the governing political parties in the Nordic states have continued to advocate closer ties with the rest of Europe. They seem to be waiting for a favourable moment to obtain their voters' approval to jump on the European train.

The elitist appeal of European integration is clearly demonstrated in a survey conducted by EOS Gallup Europe for the European Commission in 1996. Ninety-two per cent of politicians, MPs and MEPs in the 15 member states supported membership of the EU while only 48 per cent of voters supported membership. Only 3 per cent of politicians regarded EU membership as a 'bad thing' while 15 per cent of the general public saw it in that light. Twenty-eight per cent of voters regarded membership of the Union as 'neither good nor bad' while the corresponding figure among politicians was only 5 per cent.

There is a similar gap between politicians and voters concerning the opinion on whether EU membership has benefited their country. Ninety per cent of politicians considered that membership had benefited their country. The corresponding figure for the electorate was 43 per cent. Only 8 per cent of politicians considered membership had not benefited their country, while 36 per cent of the population were of the same opinion. The rest were undecided (EOS Gallup Europe 1996).

Political parties in Iceland, with the exception of the SDP and the SDA, have either taken a firm stance against EU membership or adopted a 'wait and see' approach. Governments have only once considered the membership alternative: in 1961–63. The contrast with the other Nordic states is striking. The sister parties of the Icelandic parties in the Nordic states, with the exception of the Left Socialist parties and the Liberals in Norway, have advocated closer involvement in the European project. In the 1990s, governments in all of the other Nordic states were in favour of European integration and 'they had the support of almost the entire political and economic establishment' (Hansen 2002a: 1). The governing parties, the Social Democrats, Conservatives and Liberals, advocated EU membership or closer integration. Opposition in parliament to closer integration was mainly limited to the parties located at the two ends of the political spectrum.

The other striking feature of Icelandic politics is that voters have, on the whole, been more positive towards the question of EU membership than has the political elite. This is contrary to the situation in all the other Nordic states, where a gap has developed between the attitudes of the pro-European elite on the one side and the more Euro-sceptical electorate on the other. The political elite is struggling to have its interpretation of what is in the national interest accepted by its voters (Hansen 2002a: 3 and 5). The first political party in Iceland to advocate membership did so in 1994, more than 30 years after some parties in Norway adopted such a policy, and not a single political party in Iceland spoke out in favour of membership from 1999 to 2002. Moreover, in the 1990s, only a handful of MPs were willing to state publicly that they supported an application, most of them coming from the small Social Democratic Party. In this same period, surveys indicated that a considerable part of the electorate supported an EU application. For instance, in May/June 1999, just after the national election campaign, 38 per cent of voters wanted to apply for EU membership, despite the fact that all political parties running in the election opposed it. Moreover, nearly 35 per cent of voters were undecided and only 27 per cent were against applying for membership. In November the same year, support for membership among the electorate had grown to 42.5 per cent (Hardarson 1999), and in May 2001 a survey indicated almost 54 per cent support for an EU application, while 30 per cent did not support it; 16 per cent were undecided or refused to answer the question (PricewaterhouseCoopers 2001).

Substantial support among voters for an EU application dates back to the late 1980s. From 1988 and throughout the 1990s, surveys indicated that voters could be divided into three roughly equal groups (for, against and undecided) concerning the question of EU membership, each accounting for about one third of the respondents. However, surveys indicate considerable fluctuations in voters' attitudes in different periods (Kristinsson 1996; Thorhallsson 2002). The sceptical attitude of the political elite towards EU membership is even more interesting against this background of support among the electorate.

In order to understand the Euro-scepticism of the political elite in Iceland, an explanation has to be sought elsewhere than in the existing literature. This is particularly the case because in the literature, the Euro-enthusiasm of leading political parties is taken for granted, as will be discussed in the section below. Theoretical frameworks such as neofunctionalism, the sectoral approach and the structuralist approach, identifying how conceptual constellations structure the EU debate (Hansen 2002b: 219), may help us to understand the relationship between the political elite and powerful interest groups, and the elite's ideas concerning European integration. They may also add to our understanding of why the Icelandic political elite has come to the conclusion time and time again that EU membership should not be sought. However, they do not grasp the wider picture, i.e. the background of the elite itself and its characteristics. It is also tempting to address the call by a number of scholars for an explanation couched more in domestic terms of the different positions of states on the question of involvement in European integration, as is mentioned in Chapter 1. To account for the distinctiveness of the Icelandic political elite regarding European integration, i.e. its opposition to membership, it may be useful to consider the outlook and characteristics of the elite itself. What is it in the makeup, position or worldview of the Icelandic political elite that accounts for its reluctance to participate in European integration? This question may be tackled by testing the fifth hypothesis in this study: *The scepticism of the political elite in Iceland towards participation in European integration can be related to its 'realist' concept of foreign policy, its peripheral placement in Europe and its domestic power base in the regions outside Reykjavík.*

Pro-European elites: interests and identity

Theoretical analysts view European integration as an elitist product, but differ when it comes to explaining the pro-European attitude of the elite. There has been considerable debate on whether interests or idealism provide a better understanding of the European integration process.

Jean Monnet and his colleagues emphasized the importance of providing

> a framework through which 'the brightest and the best' could be enabled to pioneer new ideas for collective and supranational policies.

148 *The Euro-sceptical political elite*

It was a strategy designed to permit the shared European policy arena to predominate by producing better-informed policy guidance than the normal process of politics.

(Wallace 1996: 22–3)

Wallace argues that the political space occupied by a form of collusion between the Social and Christian Democrats in the original EU member states 'provided an underpinning consensus of a quasi-ideological (rather than post-ideological) character' (Wallace 1996: 22). This 'cartel' of elites dominated negotiations concerning the European integration process in the early days of integration (Wallace 1996: 33). Wallace continues: 'for many years the EC was the beneficiary of a permissive consensus by which pliant publics allowed economic and political élites a relatively free rein in defining the scope, methods, and functions of European integration' (Franklin *et al.* 1994). Wallace argues that European integration has given policy engineers, such as politicians and bureaucrats advocating policy change, new opportunities for leverage and possibilities to develop policy strategies within the EU framework. Policy engineers have greater freedom to act on their own initiatives within the EU framework since they do not face as much democratic scrutiny there as they do in the member states. This freedom of manoeuvre was particularly evident during the first steps of integration and 'political leaders had many opportunities to "collude"' (Wallace 1996: 33).

Liberal intergovernmentalism and poststructuralism intend to explain countries' reaction to European integration by focussing on national interests and the production of structures of meaning. The approaches analyse the relationship between governments and interest groups and how the political discourse concerning national identity influences the elite's attitudes towards European integration. For instance Moravcsik, advocating liberal intergovernmentalism, argues:

> The difficulties of mobilizing interest groups under conditions of general uncertainty about specific winners and losers permits the position of governments, particularly larger ones, on questions of European institutions and common foreign policy, to reflect the ideologies and personal commitments of leading executive and parliamentary politicians, as well as interest-based conceptions of the national interests.
>
> (Moravcsik 1993: 494)

However, Moravcsik argues that the pro-European elite has difficulties in admitting that European integration is driven primarily by interests rather than idealism (Moravcsik 1999: 374). Thus, according to neofunctionalists, self-interests play an important part in explaining policy on European integration (Moravcsik 1993). Ingebritsen, following the liberal inter-

The Euro-sceptical political elite 149

governmentalist approach, argues that decisions on closer involvement in the European project by the political elite in the Nordic states is 'decided by a partnership between governments and economic interest groups', as is discussed in Chapter 6 (Ingebritsen 1998: 168).

There is considerable debate on how interests are defined and what kind of interests provide the best explanation of European integration (Wallace 1996: 24). For instance, structuralists argue that 'the opposition between ideas and interests is less self-evident' than liberal intergovernmentalists assume (Hansen 2002a: 9). The basic constellation of key collective concepts, such as 'state', 'nation', 'society' and 'the people', structure the debate on Europe (Hansen 2002b: 219). The political elite's perception of these concepts helps to explain its pro-European attitudes and distinguishes it from the attitude of a large part of the population in the Nordic countries. Explaining a detailed analysis on national identity and European integration in the Nordic countries, Hansen argues:

> The conceptual constellations we identify are not to be considered as 'ideas', but as structures which all policies on European integration need to construct themselves within regardless of whether material, economic and strategic interests or ideals of a united Europe are foregrounded.
>
> (Hansen 2002a: 9)

In summarizing the findings she argues:

> while economic arguments matter, it is not that they are made *in opposition* to national identity, but that national identity might entail a specific *economic* dimension. Thus, it is the structure of identity that defines the scope and form of economic rationality – not vice versa.
>
> (Hansen 2002b: 218)

The enthusiasm of the political elite to take part in the European project is seen as reflecting its national identity framework (Hansen 2002b: 219).

The emphasis on a shared ideology or quasi-ideology in explaining the European integration process does not fit the case of Iceland. The Icelandic political elite has never been a part of this 'cartel' of elites advocating European integration. It has had a realist conception of foreign policy, influenced by relatively recent independence and an emphasis on concrete economic advantages. The Icelandic political elite, moreover, has not been closely involved with the elites of the original EU member states. Thus, it has not been exposed to ideological influence from the most enthusiastic pro-European elites in Europe, as will be discussed below.

The emphasis on interests and self-interests by liberal intergovernmentalism and neofunctionalism in explaining states' participation in the European project may provide an explanation of Iceland's partial engagement in the project through membership of the EEA and Schengen, but it falls short of explaining why Iceland has not sought full membership. In order to understand the reluctance of the Icelandic elite to take a full and active part in European integration, we have to examine its background, i.e. its domestic power base. This has to an important degree been located in the more sparsely populated regions, where the fisheries and agriculture play a crucial role. The influence of the regions in the political system is inflated through an electoral system that secures them a disproportionately large share of seats in parliament. This feature of Icelandic politics has to be taken into account in explaining Iceland's approach to the European project.

A 'realist' conception of foreign policy

As is generally recognized, the European integration project is only partly concerned with economic prosperity. Sovereignty, security and culture are integral to the project as well. It involves the sharing of sovereignty to safeguard democratic stability and security in the region, along with economic interests. This broader emphasis sits rather uneasily with the foreign-policy traditions of the Icelandic elite, which have been concerned above all with independence and economic advantage. Part of the explanation for this rather one-sided emphasis lies with the history of Icelandic foreign relations and the mind-frames in which foreign policy is often discussed in Iceland.

During the formative period of the political system in the early twentieth century, Iceland had no official foreign policy and no foreign service of its own. Foreign relations were concerned above all with claims for greater independence from Denmark and the marketing of fish and agricultural products. These remained the primary concerns of Icelandic foreign policy even after sovereignty was obtained in 1918.

With the Union Treaty in 1918 Iceland obtained – along with sovereignty – the power to formulate its own foreign policy. Denmark would, however, continue the administration of this policy so long as the treaty remained in force. This meant that there was, until 1940, no Icelandic foreign service, apart from one ambassador in Copenhagen. A few Icelanders were employed in the Danish foreign service and the Icelandic government had some trade representatives abroad, but there existed no ministry for foreign affairs in Iceland. Foreign policy tasks, such as they were, fell under the responsibility of the prime minister.

Sveinn Björnsson, who later became the first president of the republic, was Iceland's only ambassador in the inter-war period. In his memoirs, he recalls that it was a common attitude in Iceland that his post was too expensive, although in fact he bore part of the cost out of his personal funds. 'Many people were simply of the opinion,' he wrote, 'that Iceland had no foreign affairs and had no need for them' (Björnsson 1957: 125).

Another high-ranking official, Birgir Thorlacius, recalls that before the Second World War, the Icelandic ministries generally had very little foreign contact. As an example he relates the story of a permanent secretary in one of the ministries who took part of his morning mail and said: 'These are foreign, they can be trashed' (Thorlacius 1994: 20).

A foreign ministry was established in 1940 after the occupation of Denmark by German forces. This was undoubtedly a significant step forward in bringing foreign policy matters to the attention of the Icelandic political elite. During the war, of course, the Icelandic government was in close contact with the occupying forces, and after the war it ruled out the option of maintaining the pre-war policy of neutrality. The US military base and NATO membership were probably the most fiercely debated issues in Icelandic politics during the second half of the twentieth century. A large part of public opinion was opposed to the military base, largely on nationalistic grounds.

It is widely believed in Iceland that nationalism is a constant of Icelandic politics which every political party has to make its peace with in one way or another (Grímsson 1978). It may be subject to different interpretations, but it remains the common language of political discourse. While necessity may require participation in international co-operation to some extent, clear and concrete justifications are demanded. Iceland's security arrangements and participation in European economic cooperation only partly met this demand, and consequently the decision to host the military base and to join NATO caused a major stir in Icelandic politics, despite the fact that the economic benefits from both were substantial.

A history of isolation and the security of distance go some way towards explaining the reserve with which many Icelanders consider international relations. Perhaps a general feeling of powerlessness associated with extreme smallness may also explain why they see little point in getting mixed up in the politics of the greater powers. But part of the explanation also lies in the fact that the foreign policy establishment lacked the institutional basis to promote alternative conceptions of foreign policy.

Although Iceland developed a small foreign service in the post-war period, nationalist concepts continued to put a firm stamp on the domestic debate on foreign policy. Iceland has never had any military forces of its own and although security policy was among the most fiercely fought issues of domestic politics, the debate was as much a dispute concerning alternative conceptions of nationalism as of conflicting analyses of the country's military-strategic position. In fact, commentators seem to agree that expertise and independent evaluation of the country's defence interests were largely lacking in the early post-war era (Ingimundarson 1996, Jónsson 1989).

Hardly any research on foreign policy or defence was carried out in Iceland until 1979 when the Icelandic Commission on Security and

Foreign Affairs was established. The commission had one or two specialists in its employment and published a number of reports on foreign policy during the 1980s. It probably played some role in bringing a more balanced atmosphere into the debate on security policy, but it was abolished in 1991 when the government felt it had served its purpose. An Institute for International Affairs was subsequently established at the University of Iceland, but without substantial funding its role has remained limited. A lectureship in international relations has existed at the University of Iceland since the late 1980s.

The continuing grip of nationalism on discussions of foreign policy in Iceland can to some extent be explained by the lack of expert knowledge and research in the area. The political elite had limited access to alternative conceptions of foreign policy that might have resulted from a stronger foreign policy establishment. In the absence of a strong foreign service, a domestic army and strategic research institutes, there was no effective counterweight against the nationalist heritage. In this respect the situation in Iceland differed markedly from that in Norway, where the elite became convinced of the advantages of membership while a majority of the general public remained sceptical or opposed.

The Icelandic elite tends to regard the EU primarily as an economic and legal instrument rather than a political forum and consequently it evaluates membership in economic rather than political terms. Each time the issue has been brought to the surface in Iceland by new developments in Europe, the questions asked in Iceland have primarily centred on access to the European market for fish. Steps to go beyond this rather narrow (though admittedly important) concern have remained unattractive to large parts of the Icelandic elite – at least until the mid-1990s. They lack the concepts and terminology to express Icelandic interests in terms other than those of national self-determination and fish exports. Even those who perceive advantages in broader political co-operation have to admit that there is a substantial political risk involved. No one really doubts that the issue of membership could not only mean the break-up of established coalitions in Icelandic politics but also become a lasting cause of division in its own right.

Towards the end of the twentieth century there were some signs of a different tone in the discussions of membership. The foreign service had been strengthened considerably and the two foreign ministers who have served since 1998 have been markedly more pro-European than their predecessors. Parts of the business and political communities have similarly been affected by the growing pressure from globalization and seem more willing than before to place membership on the agenda.

Peripheral location

One of the reasons why the Icelandic political elite has been less moved by the prospect of a unified Europe is simply its peripheral location in

Europe. Frequent contact facilitates policy transfer from one state to another. During the early decades of the twentieth century, modern ideas and practices reached Iceland to a large extent through Denmark. This changed dramatically during the Second World War when the USA, and in some respects Britain, became Iceland's most important partners. Contacts with the Anglo-Saxon countries was facilitated by language skills, as English came to replace Danish as the preferred foreign language of most Icelanders, with German and French in a distant third and fourth place.

The cold war set its stamp on the foreign contacts of the Icelandic political elite. The bilateral security relationship with the USA opened up a number of other contacts in the areas of business and culture. In fact, for a time during the 1960s the only TV station in Iceland was run by the military force in Keflavík. A great many Icelandic students went to American universities and gradually an increasing part of the administrative elite in Iceland had an experience of living in the USA.

The Second World War marked a watershed by closing old roads to further education while opening up new ones. By 1988 almost a third of senior officials educated abroad had been to the USA, and the joint share of the Anglo-Saxon countries was 59 per cent, as can be seen from Table 9.1. Mainland Europe, on the other hand, including the original six EEC countries, has never attracted Icelandic students to the same extent as the Nordic or Anglo-Saxon countries. To put it differently: those senior Icelandic officials who have been educated abroad have for the most part studied either outside the European Union or else in those member states that are most sceptical of the more ambitious plans for integration.

Commercial relations are, of course, another influential factor in shaping the attitudes of the elite. Of the original six member states of the EEC, only Germany has been one of Iceland's major trading partners. Iceland's most important export countries have been Britain, the USA

Table 9.1 Senior Icelandic officials' education abroad: country of study (%)

Country	Year				
	1905	1917	1949	1965	1988
Denmark	100	96	69	32	14
Other Nordic countries	–	4	13	11	14
Britain	–	–	–	21	28
United States	–	–	6	26	31
Mainland Europe	–	–	12	21	14
Total	100	100	100	100	100
Percentage of senior officials educated abroad	90	96	46	49	69

Source: Kristinsson 1994: 129.

and, at times, the USSR. This pattern was shaped partly by proximity, in the case of Britain, and by the cold war. Both in the USA and the USSR, business opportunities opened up partly due to political events. During the inter-war period, an average of 96 per cent of Icelandic exports went to Europe, mostly to the Nordic countries, Britain and Spain. After the war, the USA became a major market for Icelandic fisheries products, accounting for about one third of exports, by value, in the 1970s. During the cod wars with Britain, considerable markets opened up in the Soviet Union. This trade reached a peak in the 1950s, when one third of Icelandic exports went to Eastern Europe, and continued to be important for Iceland for a long time afterwards.

The pattern of establishment of the first Icelandic embassies abroad illustrates rather well the foreign policy priorities of the Icelandic government. The first, established in Copenhagen in 1920, remained for a long time Iceland's only embassy. The second was established in London in 1940 and the third, after the occupation of Denmark, in Stockholm the same year. The fourth came into existence in Washington in 1941 and the fifth in Moscow in 1944. The first embassy in what was to become the original EEC was established in Paris in 1946. Originally the Icelandic government had intended to serve Paris through its embassy in London, but in view of negative reactions to this from the French government it was decided to have a separate embassy to France in Paris. A German embassy might – in view of Germany's greater importance as a trading partner – have been a more natural choice, but it was not a practical choice until 1952, when an embassy was established in Bonn/Hamburg. An embassy/mission in Brussels to serve the EC and Belgium – ignoring the offices of the permanent secretary in the NATO building – was not established until 1986 (Thorsteinson 1992). In 1967 the permanent mission to NATO was moved from Paris to Brussels and became an embassy/mission to the European Economic Community.

The end of the cold war and the burgeoning of the European Union have changed Iceland's position in the world. A united Europe is, without a doubt, Iceland's most important partner in trade and politics; this is indicted by the fact the Icelandic mission to the EU in Brussels is by far its largest. The USSR no longer exists, and US interest in maintaining the kind of military presence it did in the past is visibly smaller. This new environment may leave an impact on the attitudes of the elite towards membership, but whether it will be sufficient to convince its staunchest opponents seems less likely.

Blocking the issue

The fact that the main export sector in the Icelandic economy, the fisheries sector, is opposed to membership makes it difficult for the Confederation of Icelandic Employers to advocate membership of the EU. Although perhaps not all elements in the fisheries sector are unanimous in the rejection of membership, their main organizations have argued against it with great force. In other sectors of the economy, e.g. manufacturing, the situation is felt to leave room for creativity in the negotiation process, but the key position of the fisheries among the business organizations in Iceland has acted as a brake on any concerted move by them to promote EU membership in Iceland. Thus, although the Federation of Icelandic Industries is strongly pro-Europe, the opposition of the main fisheries organization in effect prevents the joint organization, the Confederation of Icelandic Employers, from taking a stance on the issue. While membership may have considerable following among business leaders in Iceland, they recognize and respect the joint blocking power of the fishing sector. Nearly all interest groups that have taken a stand on the EU question emphasize that Iceland needs to protect its fishing sector and cannot join the EU if it has to allow foreign vessels into Icelandic waters and be subject to the Union's common fisheries policy. For instance, this is the position of the Iceland Chamber of Commerce, despite its rather pro-European stand (Verslunarráð Íslands 1990; Verslunarráð Íslands 2000: 25), the Farmers' Association of Iceland (Freyr April 2001: 30) and the Icelandic Federation of Labour (Thorhallsson 1991: 44).

Opposition from the fishing sector also has wider repercussions throughout the political system because of its strategic political geography. It is a key factor explaining why the regional population in Iceland – outside the urban southwest – remains more sceptical of membership than inhabitants of the Greater Reykjavík area. The regional economy is largely dependent on the fisheries. Already faced with large-scale depopulation in the regions, the rural population feels threatened by the unrestrained rule of market forces and bureaucrats in distant countries that it associates with membership. In the Icelandic political system, by contrast, the regional areas have been well protected. Votes carry considerably more weight in the regional constituencies than in the urban ones: there are fewer voters per seat. For instance, in the 1959 summer election, 71 per cent of MPs came from the regions though only 46 per cent of the electorate lived there, as can be seen from Table 9.2. In 1999, 68 per cent of voters lived in Reykjavík and its surroundings but they elected only 49 per cent of MPs. As a result, the Althingi tends to be rather preoccupied with various aspects of regional policy. Fishing and agriculture – the key sectors of the regional economy – have traditionally enjoyed a privileged status in both the administration and parliament, which they could not be certain of keeping under the conditions of EU membership. Their interests are well represented in the standing committees on agriculture and fisheries in the Althingi, as Chapter 6 demonstrates, and their respective ministries are well known for their intimate relationship with the industries they serve. In fact, the sectoral interest organizations were, until not very long ago, state-run to a certain extent.

156 *The Euro-sceptical political elite*

Table 9.2 Proportions of the electorate living in the regions and the Greater Reykjavík area, and the MPs representing them (%)

Elections (year)	Electorate			MPs		
	Regions	Greater Reykjavík area	Total	Regions	Greater Reykjavík area	Total
1959[a]	46	54	100	71	29	100
1983	39	61	100	58	42	100
1999	32	68	100	51	49	100

Sources: Hagstofa Íslands (Statistics Iceland) 1988, March 2002.

Note
a In each case, the elections referred to above were the last before changes were made to the electoral system to balance the unequal distribution of seats in the Althingi. The changes took place in the second of two elections in 1959 and in 1987 and 2003. The electoral system applying in the first election in 1959 had been unchanged since 1942.

The majority of MPs in Iceland have been elected in the regional constituencies even though a large majority of the population lives in Reykjavík or its surrounding area. This makes it very difficult for the parliamentary parties – the effective policy makers within the Icelandic political parties – to reach a pro-European conclusion. This seems to account for yet another peculiarity of the situation in Iceland: the fact that the major right-wing party is opposed to membership. The conservative Independence Party is the major party on the right in Iceland and also the largest party in electoral terms, usually receiving about 40 per cent of the vote. It has been the most influential party in shaping Icelandic foreign policy, including security policy and NATO membership, and it traditionally takes pride in supporting participation in co-operation between free, democratic nations.

In 1989, when negotiations on the European Economic Area were beginning, the Independence Party seemed willing to consider both the EEA and EC membership as future options. In a report on the future policies of the party, its 'millennium committee' stated:

> We are presently negotiating with the European Community along with the other EFTA states. These negotiations could lead to an agreement which we can accept as a future solution. It may, however, be wise to request immediate negotiations on Icelandic membership of the European Community, although we would have to be prepared to let actual accession depend on whether the terms of entry are considered accessible or not.
>
> (Aldamótanefnd Sjálfstæðisflokksins 1989: 21)

The party left the issue of membership open, maintaining it was not on the immediate political agenda. This continued to be its policy after it formed a coalition government with the Social Democratic Party in 1991. As the other EFTA states applied for membership, one by one, during the early 1990s, there was growing concern among the Icelandic public that this might lead to the isolation of the country, and the foreign minister in the coalition – the SDP chairman Hannibalsson – became more and more concerned with the issue. The Independence Party formally stuck to its 'wait and see' approach towards the question, though its chairman became increasingly outspoken in his rejection of membership. The 'wait and see' approach was a reactive approach to the uncertainty of the EEA Agreement and the outcome of applications for EU membership by the elites in the other Nordic states, which were trying their best to convince their electorates to vote in favour of membership. It was also a convenient policy for the leadership of the party, as some of its members supported EU membership while others, especially the representatives of fishing and agriculture, spoke against any discussion of membership. In 1996, the party formally announced in its party manifesto that it opposed EU membership. This move came when the EEA Agreement had been in force for some time and was thought to guarantee Icelandic economic interests, and when it was clear that Norway would not be joining the EU for the time being. Also, Davíð Oddsson, the Independence Party chairman since 1991, who had faced some hostility in the beginning, had taken firm control of the party.

An interesting point concerning the Independence Party position on membership is that its followers tend to be relatively favourably disposed to membership. During most of the 1990s, only the supporters of the Social Democratic Party were more positive towards membership. Why, then, does the leadership of the Independence Party reject membership of the European Union? The party chairman, Oddsson, was originally favourably disposed to it: 'I have publicly advocated an application for membership,' he maintained in a book published in 1990 (Gissurarson 1990: 69). It is generally acknowledged in Iceland, even among those favourably disposed to membership, that it is a risky issue politically. The experience of two unsuccessful Norwegian applications serves as a constant reminder of what could happen if Iceland were to apply. The Norwegian debates of the 1970s had long-lasting effects on Norwegian politics and dealt a severe blow to some of the established political parties. Opponents of membership in Iceland, including the main newspaper, the conservative *Morgunblaðið*, have emphasized the risk and warned against dividing the nation into two hostile camps on the issue.

The membership issue could easily have exploded in the face of the Independence Party leadership. Even if a large part of the party's following in the urbanized southwest had gone along with a membership policy, it seems likely that the issue would have met with strong resistance from the regions, even to the extent of risking a split in the party. Support for membership is greatest in the urbanized southwest of the country, where the Independence Party is strongest, but the electoral system gives considerable over-representation to the outlying regions in parliament. In 1999, 74 per cent of the Independence Party vote came from the Greater Reykjavík area, but this accounted for only 58 per cent of its parliamentary seats. There is no doubt that the regional part of the party would oppose such a move towards membership strongly, with potentially harmful consequences for the party's standing in Icelandic politics. Taking up the issue of membership could have undermined Oddsson's leadership and proved risky for the Independence Party. Only in the mid-1990s did he establish a firm grip on the party's MPs, by which time his attempts to hold back the Euro-enthusiasts within the party had moved him beyond a point of no return against membership. MPs are very powerful in Icelandic politics and any chairman of the Independence Party taking up the issue of membership would be taking an enormous risk. Thus, the Independence Party leadership would need a very strong motivation to take up the issue – something it has not felt while the EEA has been a viable option.

However, an important change took place in the electoral system in 2003: for the first time, the majority of people in the country, living in Reykjavík and its immediate surroundings and accounting for 63 per cent of the electorate, elected a majority (52 per cent) of the parliament. Though this means a change in the weighting, it must be borne in mind that there is still a considerable imbalance in favour of the rural areas, since the 37 per cent of voters who live in the regions still elect nearly half the MPs.

Conclusion

Three distinctive features of the Icelandic political elite help us to understand its reluctance to participate in European integration. In the first place, for much of the twentieth century, the elite had a 'realist' conception of foreign policy, shaped above all by national self-determination and the search for concrete economic advantages. This attitude shaped the yardsticks against which the possibility of participating in the integration project was measured, and explains in part the general reluctance of the elite in the matter.

Second, the contacts and habits of co-operation formed in Icelandic foreign policy since the Second World War have been centred less on the core states of the European Union than has been the case in many other states in Western Europe. The attraction of the European project has been felt less strongly out in the middle of the Atlantic Ocean, where Iceland lies, than closer to the old battlefields of Europe.

Third, those sections of the elite that are most sceptical of membership occupy controlling positions and have, at least to date, managed to block any moves towards an application for EU membership. This applies above all to the strategically-placed fisheries sector, which along with agriculture dominates the politically important rural regions in Iceland. The unequal distribution of seats in the Althingi in favour of the regions gives the primary sectors, fishing and agriculture, a pivotal role in decision making. Opposition to EU membership is strongest in the regions and plays a significant part in limiting discussion on membership. Parliamentarians from the regions are less likely to challenge the status quo and advocate EU membership. Political leaders taking up the issue face the danger of a political backlash in the regions because of opposition from the fishing and agricultural interest groups with close connections to a disproportionately high percentage of MPs. Connections between the Independence Party's MPs and the fishing sector have been particularly stable, and a considerable proportion of the party's MPs have had connections with the agricultural sector, as is demonstrated in Chapter 6. An internal debate about EU membership within the party could easily rock the calm surface of the party under the present leadership.

Bibliography

Aldamótanefnd Sjálfstæðisflokksins (1989) *Drög að greinargerð um nokkra þætti sjálfstæðisstefnunnar. 28 landsfundur Sjálfstæðisflokksins 5.–8. október 1989*, Reykjavík: The Independence Party.

Björnsson, S. (1957) *Endurminningar Sveins Björnssonar*, Reykjavík: Ísafoldarprentsiðja.

EOS Gallup Europe (1996) *The European Union 'A View from the Top'*. Available online: http://europa.eu.int/comm/public_opinion/archives/top/top.pdf (accessed 9 April 2003).

Franklin, M., Marsh, M. and McLaren, L. (1994) 'Uncorking the bottle: popular opposition to European unification in the wake of Maastricht', *Journal of Common Market Studies*, 137/4: 63–7; cited in Wallace H. (1996) 'The challenge of governance' in H. Wallace and W. Wallace (eds) *Policy Making in the European Union*, Oxford: Oxford University Press.

Freyr (April 2001) Ályktanir búnaðarþings, *Freyr*, 3: 30.

Gissurarson, H.H. (1990) *Island. Arvet från Thingvellir*, Stockholm: Timbro.

Grímsson, Ó.R. (1978) 'Icelandic nationalism: a dissolution force in the Danish kingdom and a fundamental cleavage in Icelandic politics', unpublished paper, University of Iceland.

Hagstofa Íslands [Statistics Iceland] (1988) *Kosningaskýrslur*, Reykjavík: Hagstofa Íslands.

—— (March 2002) *Alþingiskosningarnar 1999*, Reykjavík: Hagstofa Íslands.

Hansen, L. (2002a) 'Introduction', in L. Hansen and O. Wæver (eds) *European Integration and National Identity: The Challenge of the Nordic States*, London and New York: Routledge: 1–19.

—— (2002b) 'Conclusion', in L. Hansen and O. Wæver (eds) *European Integration and National Identity: The Challenge of the Nordic States*, London and New York: Routledge: 214–25.

Hardarson, Ó.Th. (1998) 'Public opinion and Iceland's Western integration', unpublished paper presented at Conference on the Nordic Countries and the Cold War, Grand Hotel, June 24–27 1998, University of Iceland.

—— (1999) 'Icelandic Election Study 1999 Iceland', unpublished paper, University of Iceland.
Ingebritsen, C. (1998) *The Nordic States and European Unity*, Ithaca and London: Cornell University Press.
Ingimundarson, V. (1996) *Í eldlínu kalda stríðsins: Samskipti Íslands og Bandaríkjanna 1945–1960*, Reykjavík: Vaka-Helgafell.
Jónsson, A. (1989) *Iceland, NATO and the Keflavík Base*, Reykjavík: Öryggismálanefnd.
Kristinsson, G.H. (1994) *Embættismenn og stjórnmálamenn*, Reykjavík: Mál og Menning.
—— (1996) 'Iceland and the European Union: non-decision on membership', in L. Miles (ed.) *The European Union and the Nordic Countries*, London: Routledge: 151–65.
Moravcsik, A. (1993) 'Preference and power in the European Community: a liberal governmentalist approach', *Journal of Common Market Studies*, 31: 473–524.
—— (1999) 'The future of European integration studies: social science or social theory?', *Millennium*, 28: 371–91.
PricewaterhouseCoopers (2001) 'News release: Iceland, the EU and the Euro', Reykjavík: PricewaterhouseCoopers.
Thorhallsson, B. (1991) 'Afstaða hagsmunasamtaka til inngöngu í Evrópubandalagið', unpublished thesis, University of Iceland.
—— (2002) 'The skeptical political elite versus the pro-European public: The case of Iceland', *Scandinavian Studies*, 74/3: 349–78.
Thorlacius, B. (1994) *Í þjónustu forseta og ráðherra*, Kópavogur: Almenna bókafélagið.
Thorsteinson, P.J. (1992) *Utanríkisþjónusta Íslands og utanríkismál I–III*, Reykjavík: Hið íslenska bókmenntafélag.
Verslunarráð Íslands [The Iceland Chamber of Commerce] (1990) *Stefnuskrá Verslunarráð Íslands*, Reykjavík: Verslunarráð Íslands.
—— (2000) *Atvinnulíf framtíðarinnar: Ísland meðal tíu bestu*, Reykjavík: Verslunarráð Íslands.
Wallace, H. (1996) 'Politics and policy in the EU: the challenge of governance', in H. Wallace and W. Wallace (1996) *Policy-Making in the European Union*, Oxford, Oxford University Press: 3–36.

10 Shackled by smallness
A weak administration as a determinant of policy choice

Baldur Thorhallsson

Introduction

The effects of Europeanization on national administrations are widely discussed in the literature (Blichner *et al.* 1993; Bulmer *et al.* 1998; Egeberg *et al.* 1999; Trondal 1998; Lægreid 2000). Involvement of countries in European integration is said to influence the day-to-day operations of their national administrations and institutional structures (Lægreid 2000: 29). It is argued that national administrations become Europeanized as European integration becomes more relevant and influences changes in domestic institutions and administrative arrangements (Olsen 1996; Hanf *et al.* 1998; Sverdrup 2000). The main research focus has been on how domestic institutions have adjusted to European integration (Knill 2001). Little attention has been given to the impact national administrations have on states' policy on European integration. National administrations are usually treated as a dependent variable influenced by the process of European integration. This chapter seeks to analyse what influence a small administration may have on a state's response to European integration. The national administration will be seen as an independent variable in order to examine whether its size and characteristics have influenced Iceland's policy on European integration.

Attempts have been made to define the size of states according to the size and capability of their diplomatic corps. For instance, Vayrynen combined different approaches that have been used to define small states in order to come up with a comprehensive definition of what constitutes a small state. Among other things, his analysis takes into account the size of the diplomatic corps. It also includes domestic and foreign governments' perceptions of a state's size and capability (Vayrynen 1971). Population size is the most commonly used criterion for defining the size of a state and is 'seen as being the most relevant in diplomatic and international relations terms' (Archer *et al.* 2002); e.g. population figures are used for calculating states' representation in the European Parliament and their voting weight in the Council of Ministers. Population size, on its own, is a useful tool for indicating the size of states, but it is not a precise index of their capabilities either at the domestic or the international level. A more precise index is needed to examine the capacity of states in international relations. For this purpose, the size, characteristics and capabilities of national administrations provide a useful tool for analysis. It is the national administration of each and every state that conducts the state's business and oversees and handles its international relations.

The size and characteristics of national administrations influence the behaviour of states in decision-making processes within the EU. Small states are forced to prioritize in the EU because of their limited administrative capacity. It has been pointed out that small administrations dealing with EU matters are characterized by informal communication, flexible decision making, manoeuvrability of officials and guidelines, rather than instructions, being given to negotiators when they are dealing with issues that are not regarded as important (Thorhallsson 2000: 106). The smallness of the administrations and the characteristics listed above provide an explanation of the distinctive approach of small states, compared with that of larger states, in the EU's decision-making processes. These administrative characteristics provide an explanation of the different negotiation tactics employed by large and small states in the EU and also help to explain the different approach to the European Commission adopted by small states. This is characterized by a greater willingness to co-operate with the Union, compared to the more confrontational approach of larger states, thus explaining the special relationship between the small states and the European Commission. Consequently, the national administration of each state and its characteristics must be treated as an independent variable explaining the behaviour of small states within the decision-making processes of the EU, and models that fail to take account of the role of the administration in a state's handling of EU affairs will be flawed. Small states' specialized economies and strong corporatist structure, as identified by Katzenstein (1984; 1985), may help to explain their behaviour to a certain extent, but fail to shed light on the difference between their approach and that of larger states in the EU's decision-making processes (Thorhallsson, 2000: 232–40).

It has been established that the size of national administrations and their characteristics influence the behaviour of states within the EU but the following question remains unanswered: Do national administrations and their characteristics influence approaches of states to European integration? In order to answer this question, the following hypothesis is put forward: *The smallness of the Icelandic administration and its limited capability have restricted Iceland's ability to participate in European integration. These factors have also made ministers more reliant on interest groups in their policy on Europe.*

The more limited administrative capacity of small states compared to larger ones has put in doubt their ability to participate effectively in the EU's decision-making processes. But how should a small national administration be defined? To define a small national administration exactly is as difficult as to define exactly what constitutes a small state. The problem becomes more complex when comparison between national administrations is included in the picture, particularly because there can be considerable differences in the criteria that each state uses to define its administration, i.e. what departments and public institutions are seen as constituting the formal administration and how staff numbers within them are counted. For the purpose of the present study, the national administration is defined as consisting of government ministries, together with their institutions and surveillance authorities that deal with domestic and external affairs. However, the responsibilities of ministries and their institutions and departments vary from one state to another, and the number of people working within these bodies does not necessarily give a complete picture of their size. Information on the number of people working in the Icelandic foreign service and the foreign services of all other states in Western Europe and the states set to enter the European Union in 2004 has been gathered for comparative purposes. The responsibilities of foreign ministries may vary from state to state (Iceland, for example, does not have a special defence ministry, so the foreign ministry is in charge of its defence affairs), but in general, the aim of the foreign services is the same, i.e. to co-ordinate and conduct states' business overseas. Foreign ministries have taken over the co-ordination of EU matters in most, if not all, of the EU states; foreign ministry staff account for a higher proportion of the EU's Permanent Representation of Member States in Brussels than the staff of other ministries (Hayes-Renshaw *et al.* 1989: 122 and 135) and they are probably in closer contact with the Council and the Commission than are other domestic bodies. Also, foreign services provide an important backing for national leaders in the European Council. Thus, the number of people working in the foreign services of the states engaged in European integration provides an interesting insight into the scope and capacity of states in EU institutions.

As can be seen from Table 10.1, Iceland's foreign service is very small compared to other foreign services engaged in European integration, with only 150 people in April 2001, excluding locally employed personnel abroad, compared to corresponding figures of 206 for Luxembourg, 1,150 for Norway and 1,663 for Denmark.

Table 10.2 shows the number of people working in the foreign services of the smallest states in Europe as defined in terms of population. Iceland's foreign service is smaller than those of all the other European states except for the micro-states of Liechtenstein, Andorra, Monaco and San Marino. As Table 10.1 shows, it is smaller than the foreign services of the smallest of the new EU member states, Malta, Cyprus and the Baltic states.

Archer and Nugent regard Andorra, Monaco and San Marino, along

Table 10.1 Numbers of people working in the foreign services of the EU member states, EFTA states and seven applicant states,* excluding locally employed personnel abroad, April 2001

State	Number of people
Liechtenstein	29
Iceland	150
Luxembourg	206
Cyprus	231
Malta	256
Lithuania	440
Slovenia	451
Latvia	455
Estonia	479
Ireland**	820
Slovakia	931
Norway	1,150
Austria	1,397
Sweden	1,500
Finland	1,642
Denmark	1,663
Switzerland	1,768
Greece	1,810
Portugal	2,038
Belgium	2,103
Spain	2,619
The Netherlands	3,050
Italy	4,688
The UK	5,500
Germany	6,515
France	9,800

Source: Information obtained from foreign ministries of the respective states in April 2001.

Notes
*Figures for Hungary, the Czech Republic and Poland are not available.
** Approximate figure

with the Vatican City, as micro-states because they not only have very small populations and geographical areas but are also 'heavily dependent on neighbouring states for diplomatic support' (Archer *et al.* 2002: 5). They do not have an independent foreign policy and were not granted membership of the United Nations until 1992, in the case of San Marino, and 1993 in the cases of Monaco and Andorra, because they were not deemed to be sufficiently independent. On the other hand, Archer and Nugent argue that Liechtenstein's increased capacity to engage in international activity and its increased participation in European institutions has moved it to the small-state category (Archer *et al.* 2002: 5).

The question that we are most concerned with is not how the small Icelandic administration copes with all the demands of EEA membership but rather whether it has influenced the policy of Icelandic governments on

Table 10.2 Numbers of people working in the foreign services of the smallest states in Europe, excluding locally employed personnel abroad, April 2001

State	Number of people
Andorra	23
Liechtenstein	29
San Marino	62
Monaco	38
Iceland	150
Luxembourg	206
Malta	256

Source: Information obtained from foreign ministries of the respective states in April 2001.

Note
The Vatican City is excluded.

European integration. This chapter will examine to what extent the smallness of the Icelandic administration and its special historical characteristics, such as limited involvement in policy making, help to explain the approach of the political leadership in Iceland to the European integration process. It will evaluate the impact that EEA membership has had on the administration, i.e. its ability to provide ministers with the information necessary to make a balanced judgement on the issue of European integration. It will also examine the relationship between the administration and interest groups concerning European affairs. The aim is to analyse to what extent the administration relies on interest groups in connection with EU/EEA affairs.

Findings from a comparative survey, which is part of the research project 'National Administration Policy, Europeanization and the Nordic Countries', led by Bengt Jacobsson, Per Lægreid and Ove K. Pedersen, will be used to examine some of the above elements. This chapter will focus mainly on the findings for Iceland but it will compare the Icelandic and Norwegian administrations on a number of occasions since the countries have the same formal relationship with the EU. Findings for Iceland will also be compared to those for Finland and Sweden where appropriate. The survey provides an excellent comparison between two states that are partially engaged in the European project, on the one hand, and two with similar traditions and structures that recently joined the EU, on the other. A standardized questionnaire with fixed response alternatives was used to examine what influence EU/EEA membership has had on the central administration of the Nordic states by asking each individual department about its own experince of EU/EEA matters. The survey was conducted in 1999–2000 in Iceland (Lægreid *et al.* July 2002) and 1998 in the other countries. The questionnaire referred to all aspects of participation and assistance in EU/EEA work and was answered by experts on European

166 *Shackled by smallness*

integration in the relevant departments. Respondents were asked to answer on behalf of their departmental unit and not on behalf of themselves as individuals. A total of 1,060 units in the four countries replied to the questionnaire: 90 in Iceland, 331 in Norway, 381 in Sweden and 258 in Finland. Twenty-five per cent of the units were in ministries and 75 per cent in directorates. The response level was 72 per cent in Iceland, 86 per cent in Norway; 83 per cent in Sweden; and 77 per cent in Finland. The survey provides an important insight into the changes that had taken place within the Icelandic administration and how these changes compare to those in the other states.

An administration in transformation

In the early 1960s and 1970s, when Norway, Denmark and Ireland decided to follow Britain and apply for EC membership, expert knowledge of European integration within the Icelandic administration was restricted to a handful of officials. In 1960, just before the second round of the debate on Iceland's participation in European integration, only 53 personnel worked in the ministry for foreign affairs (the foreign service; all personnel included), as Figure 10.1 shows. In 1965, when officials within the administration started to discuss possible EFTA membership, the number had in fact dropped by two. Five years later, when Iceland joined EFTA, it had risen to 62. Einar Benediktsson, who headed Iceland's permanent mission to EFTA in Geneva in 1970, states: 'Iceland would have to make a considerable effort to implement the accession agreement and, not least, to participate in the daily work of the Association, which was so important for us' (Benediktsson 2003: 135). Describing the smallness of the administration, he continues:

> With me was only my very competent Icelandic secretary, and I was allowed to have a half-time Swiss secretary, employed locally. For the various committee meetings, experts from home would attend ... Admittedly the workload was at times quite onerous but it is only fair to state that we did establish ourselves as a fully creditable partner in EFTA.
>
> (Benediktsson 2003: 136)

Benediktsson was Iceland's sole diplomatic representative in Geneva until 1974. He states that the support from the EFTA Secretariat was indispensable and the other Nordic missions provided important assistance, particularly in the form of reports which were of direct use to Iceland (Benediktsson 2003: 138–40).

The limited capacity of the Icelandic administration is demonstrated by Ingimundarson when he states that in the 1950s, limited knowledge in military affairs both among politicians and bureaucrats was also a hindrance for Iceland in NATO. The country's representatives played little part at the organisation's meetings and seldom spoke. This lack of involvement was so conspicuous that the Americans specially requested the Icelandic government to play a more active role.

(Ingimundarson 1996: 409)

This limited capacity is also demonstrated in a study by the Icelandic Commission on Security and International Affairs where 'small size and lack of expertise of the Foreign Service' (Jónsson 1989: 13) is put forward as one of the explanations of Iceland's limited participation in NATO. The report, written in 1989, concluded that if Iceland's participation in NATO were to be enhanced 'the Ministry of Foreign Affairs and the Icelandic delegation to NATO would need considerably more staff and more expertise than is available now, as well as resources for systematically gathering and processing information' (Jónsson 1989: 15). The constraints of the smallness of the administration were obvious: 'all relations with NATO are handled by one person' (Jónsson 1989: 15) in the ministry for foreign affairs and the Icelandic delegation to NATO consisted of three officials and two staff secretaries. The Norwegian and Danish delegations were much larger at this time, containing 30 and 40 people respectively. Furthermore, they had a considerable number of people working within NATO, which was of great importance to their administrations and governments. At the time of the report, there was only one Icelander on the International Staff in Brussels and an attaché assigned to the International Military Staff in Brussels (Jónsson 1989: 16). According to the report, the consequences of this limited capacity were evident: 'There has been very limited knowledge within the Icelandic government system about military plans for Iceland and the Northern Region' (Jónsson 1989: 17).

The vast majority of experts in the administration were most familiar with law and the legislative processes in the other Nordic countries. It is generally admitted within the administration that Scandinavian legislation provides an important basis for Icelandic legislation. The Icelandic administration did not have the capacity to work on many detailed reports on proposed legislation or external affairs. It already had a huge task on its hands and did not have the resources to look beyond the needs of day-to-day operations and attend to other things. Information gathering was restricted to what was relevant for Iceland's interests in EFTA and gaining access to the EC market by a free trade agreement; monitoring other developments in the EC was not a priority. The administration was not able to build up a database or train any considerable numbers of experts in European integration in order to analyse in detail Iceland's position with regard to the fast-changing EC after the mid-1980s.

The capacity of the administration increased slightly in the late 1980s and the early 1990s but still only a tiny number of experts specialized in

168 *Shackled by smallness*

European integration (Interviews with officials). On the other hand, the foreign ministry has expanded rapidly since the mid-1980s and the number of people working within it nearly doubled in the twelve-year period from 1991 to 2003, as is shown in Figure 10.1.

The comparative survey referred to above, which covered all ministerial departments and those of central agencies and directorates, indicated that the Icelandic administration was more affected by EEA membership than was Norway's. Moreover, on occasion the Icelandic administration has been as much, or even more, affected by European integration than has been the case in the EU member states of Sweden and Finland. For instance, the survey indicates that the overall consequences of EU/EEA membership for the departments' area of competence were greater in Iceland than in the other three states, as is shown in Table 10.3. Sixty-four per cent of respondents in Iceland stated that the consequences of the EEA membership on their department's area of competence were fairly large or very large; the corresponding proportions in Sweden and Finland were close, while that in Norway was 31 per cent. Also, Icelandic respondents regarded the overall consequences of European integration on their departments' areas of competence as more positive than did their counterparts in the other three states. Seventy per cent of respondents in Iceland reported fairly positive or very positive consequences; in Finland the figure was 57 per cent, in Sweden 53 per cent and in Norway 41 per cent.

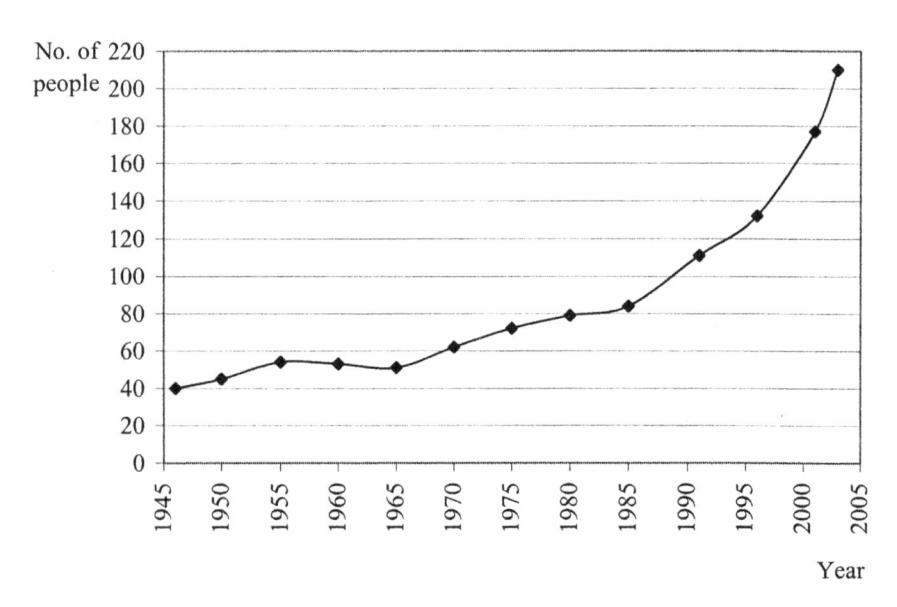

Figure 10.1 The number of people working in the Icelandic foreign service from 1945 to 2003, all personnel included.

Source: Ministry for Foreign Affairs (between 1946–2001); Ministry for Foreign Affairs (May 2003).

Table 10.3 What have been the overall consequences of EU/EEA membership on the departments' area of competence? (%)

	Norway	Iceland	Sweden	Finland
Consequences have been fairly large/ very large	31	64	57	57
Consequences have been fairly positive/ very positive	41	70	53	57

Source: Lægreid *et al.* July 2002: 9.

A possible explanation of the large and positive impact on the Icelandic administration could be that developments in Iceland have been much more dramatic than in the other countries because of the late start in Iceland of adaptation to the EU/EEA. This is further indicated in the survey since a greater number of departments in Iceland than in Norway reported that EEA membership had had a significant effect on their area of competence regarding the three pillars of the EU. These findings may be explained by a combination of factors.

First, the administration had not systematically prepared for greater involvement in European affairs in the late 1980s and early 1990s. No strategic adaptation to EEA membership took place prior to membership. This proved to be particularly problematic since few officials outside the ministry for foreign affairs had a solid knowledge of the decision-making processes of the EU, and for obvious reasons they had no experience of working within them. The burden of the EEA Agreement had been underestimated. For instance, the number of staff working on EEA/EU matters in the ministry's external trade department, which is responsible for the co-ordination of activities related to the EEA Agreement, was cut down after the negotiation process leading to the EEA. As a result, it lacked the staff and expertise to deal with the agreement in the first years of membership and later had to re-engage some of its personnel in order to cope with EEA demands (Thorhallsson November 2001: 44-5).

Considering the figures on the number of people working in the foreign service in Iceland (150) and Norway (1,150) in 2001, it comes as no surprise that Iceland's administration was lagging somewhat behind Norway's in terms of the number of its members skilled in EU affairs and other resources. This was due to the lack of any systematic adaptation of the Icelandic administration to handle potential greater involvement in EU affairs, added to the limited scope that officials had to increase their EU knowledge. The Norwegian administration, by contrast, had already started to prepare for potential EU membership in 1986. (Lægreid *et al.* November 2002).

Second, Iceland has been less active internationally than the other Nordic states. They have taken an active part, and even played a leading

170 *Shackled by smallness*

role, in a number of international organizations, while Iceland has only started to take on appreciably more responsibility in international organizations in the last five to six years. The small size of the Icelandic foreign service and the limited importance that politicians have attached to international activity have restricted its international capacity. As a result, while the Norwegian administration did not face a great challenge from EEA membership due to its previous adaptation and international activity, Iceland's more inexperienced administration had to adapt rapidly to address the wide range of issues covered by the EEA Agreement.

Third, EEA membership seems gradually to be changing particular features of the Icelandic administration as regards the handling of individual cases, such as the lack of regulation of working procedures and the strong influence of politicians. These features have distinguished the Icelandic administration from the administrations in the other Nordic states (Kristinsson *et al.* 1992). Thus, the impact of the EEA Agreement is felt more strongly in the Icelandic administration than in administrations of the other states.

Fourth, something that might explain the greater amount of change reported in the administration in Iceland as compared with Norway's administration is that a number of policy areas in Iceland underwent radical change when the country entered the EEA since they had not followed the policy changes already made in the other Nordic countries. Areas that were radically affected include competition and fair trade, consumer protection, the environment, telecommunications and social policy. Furthermore, the financial sector in Iceland had been bound by restrictions and foreign investment was limited. As a result, EEA membership brought about important changes and increased the workload of the administration in Iceland to a greater extent than in Norway.

Historical development and recent changes

The historical development of the administration provides a background explanation of the limited role of the administration in providing ministers with information on European integration until the mid-1990s. The administration was created late, at the start of the twentieth century in connection with the granting of home rule by Denmark. It developed slowly and has been moulded by a lack of regulation of procedures. Kristinsson argues that politicians have had a strong influence on the handling of individual cases and that working procedures within the administration have been far less cohesive than elsewhere in Western Europe. Civil servants have had to live with direct and indirect interference by politicians in their day-to-day work. The institutional structures of the administration placed little emphasis on long-term policy making since it was not designed as a forum for decisive policy making. This can be explained by the fact that institutions, units and ministerial departments were created according to

Shackled by smallness 171

political priorities at particular times. Also, ministers attached greater importance to maintaining a good working relationship with interest groups rather than general policy making within the administration, and the small number of officials and limited working facilities made ministers very dependent on external assistance (Kristinsson 1993: 349). The smallness of the administration hindered it in gathering necessary information in order to develop cohesive policies, and much-needed information was obtained from interest groups. The relationship with agricultural and fishing interests was particularly close and it was not always possible to see where the role of the state ended and that of interest groups began (Kristjánsson 1979: 349).

Kristinsson explains the development of the administration in terms of its historical context. He argues that the establishment of the legislature before the administration and the executive explains the strong influence of politicians on the administration and its limited autonomy in policy formulation. The national parliament received limited legislative power from the Danish crown in 1874, but executive power was not established in Reykjavík until 1904. At that time the administration consisted of a handful of civil servants with no, or limited, authority to form policies and take initiatives relevant to Icelandic needs. Policy formulation was in the hands of politicians and particular interests. The smallness of the administration and its limited resources prevented it from taking on tasks comparable with those that were dealt with by administrations in the other Nordic states (Kristinsson 1993: 349). Interference by the national parliament and politicians in the everyday work of the administration has continued ever since. For instance, in the 1950s, the share of committees and governmental units appointed by the Althingi in Iceland's administration was greater than the corresponding shares in the administrations of the other Nordic states (Herlitz 1958: 207).

This special historical background and its consequences did not provide civil servants with the autonomy needed to put forward new ideas. Interest groups, political parties and the national parliament formulated policies, and civil servants lacked the autonomy to intervene and put their mark on the outcome (Kristinsson et al. 1992). Thus, the administration was sidelined in policy formulation, particularly on sensitive matters.

The most influential interest groups (consisting of vessel operators, fish-factory owners and farmers) have not felt any motivation to put EU membership on the agenda during the last few decades. They will not take the initiative on EU membership; they fear that full involvement in the European project may damage their interests. They were satisfied with the free trade agreement with the EU in the early 1970s and regard the EEA Agreement as meeting their needs: it secured access for fish to the EU market without opening Iceland's market up to agricultural imports.

In this sensitive policy area, the administration was kept firmly on the sideline. It was not entrusted with the initiative of gathering the considerable volume of information that would have been necessary to evaluate possible closer involvement in European integration. It did not challenge the boundaries set to its role, the interference by interest groups and politicians or the lack of emphasis on long-term policy making. Ministers were left with no immediate domestic pressure to engage in European integration and the administration did nothing to build up a basis on which they could advocate greater involvement in European affairs in the 1980s and the first half of the 1990s.

Previous findings indicate that the Icelandic administration is capable of working within the EEA Agreement (Thorhallsson November 2001; Thorhallsson 2002a). Membership of the EEA has Europeanized the administration, its ministries, institutions and surveillance authorities. European integration has become increasingly more relevant and important for the administration. Politicians and the administration itself have realized that increased participation in EEA affairs serves Icelandic interests. Also, Iceland's membership of Schengen and the EU's increased emphasis on developing a common foreign and security policy have led to an increased participation by Iceland in both the EU and NATO.

The administration has gradually taken measures similar to those taken by its counterparts in the other Nordic states to handle EEA membership. Thirty-one per cent of Iceland's administrative departments reported that they had recruited more staff in order to handle EU/EEA matters in the four or five years before 1999/2000. Interestingly, the figure was almost the same in Sweden, while in Norway, which was in the same position as Iceland, 23 per cent of departments reported an increase in staff sizes (Lægreid *et al.* November 2002). There are now officials in all ministries in Iceland who deal with the EEA Agreement. They tend to have broad responsibilities regarding EEA matters. At the domestic level, they take part in policy making within their ministry, consult institutions and other ministries in order to produce a coherent front towards EFTA and the EEA, and deal with the implementation of the EEA Agreement. At the external level, they may take part in policy formulation in committees of the Commission and co-ordinate polices between the EEA/EFTA states.[1] Furthermore, all ministries, except for the prime minister's office, have officials posted in the Icelandic mission to the EU in Brussels. They attend meetings of the Commission and play an important role in information gathering and adopting a coherent front concerning EEA affairs. The smallness of ministries in Iceland and their institutions makes the position of these officials in Brussels particularly important. This is indicated by the survey quoted above: more of the departments in Iceland contact their national representatives in Brussels than is the case in Norway: 35 per cent compared to 23 per cent (Lægreid *et al.* November 2002).[2]

The EEA Agreement has also strengthened the position of officials and limited the traditional stranglehold of ministers on daily working procedures within the administration. More projects touching on EU/EEA matters have been moved down from the political to the administrative level in Iceland than in Norway (10 per cent and 2 per cent respectively), though some have been moved up from the administrative to the political level (4 per cent in both countries). According to the survey, some officials have greater influence than politicians in EU/EEA matters (18 per cent in Iceland and 10 per cent in Norway). Also, politicians in both countries do not interfere more in EU/EEA matters than in other areas and they have not become more directly involved in the work of the departments since the countries joined the EEA (Lægreid et al. November 2002). This may be explained by the structure of the EEA Agreement, which makes no allowance for the role of politicians in day-to-day decision making: thus, EEA work in Iceland and Norway is left in the hands of civil servants, which gives them greater influence over EEA matters than other matters. A possible explanation for the difference between Iceland and Norway might be the traditionally greater level of interference by politicians in Iceland in the working procedures of the administration, which cannot be fully maintained in the decision-making framework of the EEA. Kristjánsson and Kristjánsson (2000) argue that as a consequence, recruitment of officials to the Icelandic administration is becoming more professional and a number of EU/EEA experts have been employed. The above findings on increased recruitment in the administration confirm this. 'This increases the potential for the development of a more autonomous civil service that serves the citizens rather than the whims of their political masters' (Kristjánsson et al. 2000: 123).

However, the survey indicates that politicians in Iceland interfere more in the day-to-day work of the administration than they do in Norway, so continuing the tradition of political interference to some extent. For instance, 15 per cent of departments in Iceland have contact with their political leadership every week or more. The figure for Norway is only 10 per cent. Furthermore, only 25 per cent of departments in Iceland report that they never have contact with their political leadership in connection with EU/EEA matters, while the corresponding figure for Norway is 47 per cent (Lægreid et al. November 2002). Officials in Iceland are in closer contact with politicians regarding EU/EEA related work than are their counterparts in Norway, though there are clear indications that the traditional interference by politicians in the daily work of the administration is diminishing. The administration is clearly becoming more independent of politicians as fewer departments in Iceland (38 per cent) regard themselves as being bound to submit their decisions to their political superiors for approval than in Norway (46 per cent). This is further indicated by the fact that nearly half of departments in Iceland report that they have largely succeeded in having their views and aspirations on EU/EEA matters accepted by the government and/or the political leadership, compared with fewer than 40 per cent of departments in Norway.

Furthermore, the greater role of the national parliament in the daily operation of the administration (compared to the other Nordic states) identified by Kristinsson and Herlitz may be yielding to the influence of the decision-making framework of the EEA Agreement on the administration, since 42 per cent of departments report that they have succeeded in having their views and aspirations in EU/EEA matters accepted by the parliament. The comparable figure for Norway is only 22 per cent (Lægreid et al. November 2002). The Althingi has not become an active player in EU/EEA matters. It has not challenged the implementation of the EEA Agreement, and its foreign affairs committee has not become active at all in dealing with individual matters under the EEA Agreement or general policy making regarding European integration. Civil servants have the responsibility of solving problems related to the EEA Agreement. The Althingi is not involved, and ministers only become involved when Iceland's vital interests are threatened, e.g. in the fishmeal case discussed below, and when Iceland faces requests concerning increased direct payments to the EU.

The increased autonomy of officials also appears from the guidance signals given to them when they meet in international fora in connection with EU/EEA work. Only 14 per cent of Icelandic officials are bound by precise guidance signals from their departments, compared with 43 per cent in Norway. Furthermore, 4 per cent of officials in Iceland received precise guidance signals from their ministers or cabinet, compared with 10 per cent in Norway. Responses to a question on guidance from a higher-ranking administrative level revealed that the two countries were in a similar position.

The smallness of the Icelandic administration seems to contribute significantly to the manoeuvrability of officials in dealing with EU/EEA matters. Previous findings have indicated that guidance signals to national officials taking part in EU negotiations vary according to the size of the state's administration and the importance of the issue concerned. Officials from the smaller states have greater autonomy if the state regards an issue as not being of vital importance. On the other hand, they receive precise instructions in negotiations concerning direct interests of the state. Instructions to negotiators from the larger states are always fairly strict (Thorhallsson 2000: 91–4). The findings in Iceland and Norway seem to indicate that the mandate to deal with EU/EEA matters is mainly in the hands of officials, not politicians, and that Icelandic officials have considerably more room for manoeuvre than their Norwegian counterparts.

The increased capacity of the foreign service

The Icelandic administration is clearly becoming more Europeanized, and this is particularly evident in the ministry for foreign affairs. The ministry plays the key role in co-ordinating and managing EEA affairs within the administration. Its capacity has increased considerably and it has taken steps to awaken the debate in Iceland about possible EU membership. With its increased resources and expertise on European integration, the ministry has enabled the foreign minister to initiate reports on Iceland's position in Europe since 1999. As a result, the ministry has been in the forefront in the EU debate in Iceland by producing detailed reports which are much referred to in the discussion. In 1994, the foreign minister at that time requested experts at the University of Iceland to conduct a study on the consequences that EU membership would have for Iceland. The report was the first detailed report published by the government on Iceland's position in European integration and what effects EU membership might have on it. It is a sign of the times that five years later, in 1999, the foreign minister initiated a detailed report on Iceland's position in Europe which was conducted within the administration itself. Officials from the foreign ministry and other ministries, stationed in the Icelandic mission to the EU in Brussels, wrote most of the report. Other officials based in their ministries and institutions also took part in writing it; one of them had taken part in writing the previous report when working for the University. Published in 2000, the report examined in detail Iceland's position in the EEA and how it would change if it joined the EU; to some extent, it was an independent account of the country's position and possibilities in a changing Europe. Nevertheless, the report clearly bears the hallmark of political interference. The original draft underwent considerable changes in the prime minister's office. Membership of the EU was made less attractive and the EEA Agreement was said to guarantee Icelandic interests (Interviews with officials). The report gave a balanced view of the possibility of Iceland joining the EU and both supporters and opponents of membership interpreted it as supporting their case. The changes made to the report by the prime minister's office demonstrate the difference in the positions of the prime minister, Davíð Oddsson, and the foreign minister, Halldór Ásgrímsson, on the question of EU membership. The changes may also indicate the strong position of the prime minister and his office within the government and the administration regarding European affairs.

The ministry for foreign affairs published a new detailed report in mid-2001 on the effect of the EU's enlargement on the EEA Agreement. It was produced by the ministry and argued that there were two main issues that concerned Iceland in the enlargement process: first, the country should try to secure the same transition period of five to seven years regarding the free movement of people as the EU member states received,[3] and second, it would need to take measures to safeguard its fish trade, since the free trade agreements it already had with all the new applicant states, except for Malta and Cyprus, concerning fish, would no longer be valid when the applicant states joined the EU (Ministry for Foreign Affairs May 2001: 15). The report concludes its assessment of the EEA

Agreement by stating that though the enlargement would not entail any serious problems for Iceland, it would make it harder for the EFTA/EEA states to guarantee their interests because the functioning of the Agreement would become more difficult (Ministry for Foreign Affairs May 2001: 13).

On the basis of these reports, the foreign minister, Halldór Ásgrímsson, took the initiative in the EU debate in Iceland as from the middle of 2001. He also called for technical amendments to the EEA Agreement and questioned Iceland's ability to defend its interests within the decision-making framework of the EEA (Thorhallsson 2002b: 372). The increased knowledge of European affairs within the ministry provided an important platform from which he could argue his case and hold a number of public lectures in Iceland. Shortly after his call for amendments, the EFTA/EEA states and the EU states began negotiations on technical adaptations to the EEA Agreement, so indicating that Iceland had become a more active player within the EEA. Up to that time it had been a reactive player in the EEA's decision-making processes and not taken the initiative on altering the EEA Agreement. On the other hand, the administration, and particularly the ministry for foreign affairs, has shown that it can defend Iceland's interests within the EEA, as the following example demonstrates.

One of the best examples of the increased capability of the administration is its achievement in raising concern among the EU member states about a proposal by the Commission which would have entailed a ban on fishmeal and fish oil in animal feed and getting some of them to reject it. The proposal was part of the Commission's response to the BSE crisis in Europe in November and December 2000. Fishmeal and fish oil constituted 7 to 10 per cent of Iceland's total export value in goods in the five-year period from 1995 to 1999, and a ban would have caused a major blow to the fishing industry in Iceland. Iceland learned of the proposal only two working days before a final decision was to be reached in the EU's agricultural council. The proposal required a swift response, the success of which was due to the informality and flexibility of the administration. The permanent secretary of state and EU experts at the highest level within the ministry for foreign affairs played a leading role in the crisis. This led to effective decision making involving the use of both formal and informal channels to lobby the EU member states. Officials and ambassadors were given clear instructions on how to handle the lobbying with full backing from home, yet at the same time they had considerable freedom to decide who to contact in the member states. The foreign service managed to put its point of view across in some of the member states that had similar interests. However, the institutional structure of the EEA Agreement was not of much use to it in its attempts to get the EU members to reject the proposal (Thorhallsson *et al.* forthcoming). The foreign ministry used a similar tactic in its response to a demand from the Commission that

Iceland should substantially increase its payment to the EU Structural Funds from the year 2004, i.e. ambassadors and officials were sent on a mission to the member states' capitals to put Iceland's point of view across (Interview with an official).

The Europeanization of the administration, particularly of the ministry for foreign affairs, has made it possible for the administration to engage in such broad lobbying. Increased resources available to the ministry and its increased expertise play the largest part in this. Furthermore, the typically small-state features of the administration, including informal working methods, flexibility in decision making, autonomy of officials, trust between officials since most of them are personal acquaintances and a short distance to ministers, all contribute to an effective response to EU/EEA matters which are regarded as being of importance. This increased capacity of the administration and the successful outcome of the fishmeal case, combined with the discovery that the EEA decision-making framework is not of much use to Iceland when its vital interests have to be defended, have probably encouraged the foreign minister to reopen the possibility of EU membership.

The role of the foreign ministry as the key actor in dealing with the EEA Agreement has not been challenged by the Europeanization of other ministries. The increased awareness of the importance of the EEA Agreement and the increased engagement of the administration in European affairs have given the ministry a greater role within the administration. Europeanization has given the ministry a greater responsibility for co-ordinating the position of individual ministries, their institutions and surveillance authorities on EEA affairs. This has happened despite the gradual internationalization of these bodies both in Iceland and in Norway (Christensen 1996; Egeberg 1980; Sverdrup 1998: 156).

Furthermore, the increased capability of the ministry for foreign affairs, combined with its rapid Europeanization, has enhanced Iceland's role in international relations. In the last five to six years the ministry has been eager to take on wider responsibilities in the international arena. It has cultivated closer contact with states on the European mainland and other states of importance to Iceland. It has also tried to become a more active partner in a number of international organizations in order to project Iceland's interests. Furthermore, it has put more emphasis on development aid; Iceland has spent much less on development aid than the other Nordic countries.

This increased international activity can be explained by the awareness in Iceland of its limited influence within the EEA and the necessity to establish close contact with policy makers in the EEA member states. It can also be linked to the increased willingness of politicians in Iceland to show that their small state has the capacity to participate effectively in international organizations such as NATO and the UN. But it must be kept in mind that this increased international activity has been made possible because of the increased number of experts employed in the ministry for foreign affairs in recent years.

The government has decided to establish a peacekeeping force of fifty personnel which will participate in peacekeeping operations by the EU, NATO, the UN and the OSCE. In the next few years it aims to have up to a hundred people available for peacekeeping at short notice. The peacekeeping force is defined in broad terms and will consist of policemen, doctors, nurses, lawyers, co-ordinators, etc. (Ministry for Foreign Affairs April 2000). The creation of this force can be related to the government's demands for a close formal consultation process between the EU and NATO. The government is worried about independent decisions on European security by the EU, in which it does not have a voice, which might weaken the transatlantic relationship. Also, it is increasingly worried that the USA will further reduce operations at its military base in Iceland, as is discussed in Chapter 7 (Morgunblaðið 19 April 2002). The establishment of the peacekeeping force is supposed to demonstrate that despite Iceland's smallness, it can make a contribution to the new security challenges facing Europe (Interviews with officials), so warranting consideration of its interests within NATO and the EU.

In 1999, Iceland took over the chairmanship of the Council of Europe for the first time, having opened a mission in Strasbourg to serve the Council in preparation for this in 1997. The chair rotates between member states; earlier, the government had always argued that it did not have the administrative capacity to tackle its duties (Interview with an official). Iceland, for the first time, announced its candidature for one of the two rotating seats of the group 'Western Europe and Other States' in the UN Security Council in 2009–10. It is aware of the fact that, like other states, it may well face competition in its bid to enter the Security Council, but is willing to bear the administrative cost of taking part in the election contest. The foreign service has already expanded the staff of Iceland's permanent mission to the UN in New York so as to build up greater knowledge of the work of the Council and prepare for a potential challenge.

The foreign service has also become more active in certain committees of the UN's Food and Agricultural Organization (FAO) and it succeeded in having an Icelander elected to the Executive Board of the UN Educational, Scientific and Cultural Organization (UNESCO) in 2001. Furthermore, Iceland has recently opened embassies in China, Japan, Canada and Finland, and its first embassy in Africa (in Mozambique) to help carry out existing development projects in the region. A permanent mission and an embassy have also been opened in Vienna to serve the Organization on Security and Co-operation in Europe (OSCE) and Austria.

The relationship between interest groups and the administration

It has already been established in Chapter 6 that the interests of the fishing and agricultural sectors are well represented in political parties and in the Althingi. Previous studies have established that the national administration works closely with interest groups and relies on their information and capacity for policy making in areas that are especially relevant for Iceland (Kristinsson *et al.* 1992; Kristjánsson 1979). The question which now arises is to what extent interest groups have continued their close co-operation with the administration concerning EU/EEA affairs since the signing of the EEA Agreement.

The comparative survey of the Nordic countries indicates that interest groups play an important part in the Icelandic administration's policy-making process regarding the EU/EEA. For instance, 42 per cent of departments take account of interest groups' views when executing EU/EEA work; this is considerably higher than the corresponding figure of 19 per cent in Norway, and higher than those of the EU member states Sweden (33 per cent) and Finland (27 per cent). This indicates that organized interests in Iceland have 'a stronger voice and more bargaining power in Iceland than in the other states' concerning EU/EEA matters (Lægreid *et al.* November 2002: 22). On the other hand, 37 per cent of departments in Iceland report that they have succeeded in having their views accepted by interest groups, against figures of 25 to 29 per cent for the other states. This is probably due to the close consultative process between the administration and interest groups in particular sectors in Iceland.

The Nordic countries are known for their close co-operation with interest groups and their corporatist structure, based on close co-operation between the state and the employers' and employees' organizations. The survey shows that as many departments in Iceland and Norway (20 per cent in each case) reported having monthly or more frequent contact with interest groups concerning EU/EEA affairs during the previous year.[4] The survey shows that civil servants in the Nordic countries work closely with interest groups in public committees, public panels and working groups on EU/EEA matters. It is interesting to note that Iceland scored highest as regards participation by interest groups in these bodies. Twenty per cent of departments in Iceland reported that they had worked closely with interest groups within these bodies; the corresponding figure in Norway was 14 per cent. A possible explanation for this may be the close relationship in Iceland between certain interests, particularly those of fisheries and agriculture, and the government.

The relationship between the Icelandic administration and other interest groups is clearly weaker, since nearly half the departments in Iceland do not report any participation by interest groups in public committees, public panels or working groups concerned with EEA matters. This may confirm previous findings which indicate that Iceland is characterized by sectoral corporatism (Guðmundsdóttir 2002; Kristinsson et al. 1992).[5]

The survey indicates that the Icelandic administration works closely with interest groups on EU/EEA matters. It scores highest regarding the influence of interest groups on policy and their participation in administrative bodies. This can be explained by the smallness of the administration, its traditionally limited emphasis on long-term policy and the close ties between politicians and particular interests. The administration still seems to rely to a certain extent on the role of interest groups in its policy formulation.

Summary

The smallness of the Icelandic administration and its lack of expertise have influenced approaches of governments in Iceland to European integration. The administration had difficulty in gathering any appreciable amount of information on developments on the European continent, and consequently it did not develop into a forum in which European affairs could be discussed in detail. It was restricted in its ability to provide ministers with a policy-making forum concerning European integration. In a way it is remarkable how much the handful of officials who dealt with European co-operation at any given time within the administration, mainly in the ministry of foreign affairs, managed to achieve in terms of information gathering, consultation with officials in the other Nordic countries and backing up ministers in their policy on European integration until the mid-1990s. The initiative was in the hands of politicians, and priorities in foreign affairs were chosen by them. On the other hand, the limited capability of the administration made ministers more reliant on interest groups in their policy on Europe. In addition, the administration was weakened by a traditional lack of emphasis on long-term policy making and a close relationship between politicians and particular interests.

Evidence indicates that the Icelandic administration underwent a more rapid change in the mid and late 1990s as a result of EEA membership than did the Norwegian administration, due to its more limited capacity to deal with EEA matters at the beginning. Today, the Icelandic administration, which was probably not ready to join the EU at the time of the entry of Sweden and Finland into the Union, would be able to cope with membership without much difficulty. It would, of course, have to prioritize, as the other small administrations within the EU have done, and leave a considerable number of issues on the sideline, since it only has the manpower and resources to cover its immediate interests. Also, a considerable number of changes would have to take place within the administration for it to deal with membership. The structure is in place to cope with EU affairs but co-ordination between ministries, on the one hand, and between ministries and their institutions, on the other, would have to be strengthened. The administration would have to increase staff levels in the ministries and in their institutions and surveillance bodies. It would also have to increase its expertise in embassies and permanent missions in Europe, particularly in Brussels, and open new embassies, as it currently has embassies in only eight of the fifteen EU member states (Interviews with officials).[6] Outside the ministry for foreign affairs itself, the main staff increases would need to be made in the ministries of finance and fisheries and in the prime minister's office. The ministry of agriculture might also have to expand, depending on the emphasis politicians put on protecting agriculture in Iceland. These ministries do not play as active a role as others in the decision-making processes of the EEA and its implementation because of the scope and framework of the EEA Agreement. However, a number of experts on European affairs already work within them, and as a result it would not be a major task for them to adapt to EU membership. The administration has demonstrated that it can participate in the decision-making processes of the EEA and Schengen. It has also shown that it can implement about 80 per cent of EU legislation without much difficulty.

The capacity of the administration to engage in long-term policy making on European affairs has increased because of the Europeanization of the administration and the expansion of resources to handle the EEA Agreement. The administration, and particularly the foreign ministry, is involved in the acquisition of considerable amounts of information on developments in the EU, the publication of detailed reports on Iceland's choices in a changing Europe and the protection of Icelandic interests within the EU. This increased capability has provided the foreign minister with an essential backup in his attempt to put EU membership on the political agenda in Iceland. In fact, the increased capacity of the ministry has enabled him to become a promoter of the EU debate in Iceland.

The smallness of Iceland's administration limited its ability to participate in European integration until the mid or late 1990s. Its greater capability, especially in the ministry for foreign affairs, in the beginning of the twenty-first century, has equipped Iceland to face the choice of whether or not to join the EU. The national administration cannot be treated merely as a dependent variable influenced by European integration. In Iceland's case the size and characteristics of the national administration are an independent variable that helps to explain the country's approach to European integration.

Notes

1 For a discussion of the broader responsibilities of officials of the smaller EU states, see Thorhallsson 2000.
2 Previous findings have established that small states' permanent representatives

to the EU play a key role in their handling of EU matters, see Thorhallsson 2000.
3 Iceland has a safeguard clause in the EEA Agreement concerning serious disruptions on the labour market.
4 The corresponding figures for Finland and Sweden were 24 and 29 per cent.
5 The survey indicates that interest groups in Sweden tend to work more closely with the administration than those in the other states. Sixty-seven per cent of departments in Sweden report that they have worked to a limited extent, some extent or to a great extent with interest groups. The Swedish administration also works more closely with interest groups at the European level than do the other administrations. These findings support the common claim that Sweden is the clearest example of a corporatist state.
6 Also, an internal report by the foreign ministry concluded after the fishmeal crisis that Iceland needed to consider the establishment of new embassies in order to protect its interests in the EU. Iceland currently has embassies in Denmark, Sweden, Finland, Britain, Germany, France, Belgium and Austria.

Bibliography

Archer, C. and Nugent, N. (2002) 'Introduction: small states and the European Union', *Current Politics and Economics of Europe*, 11/1: 1–10.
Benediktsson, E. (2003) *Iceland and European Development: A Historical Review from a Personal Perspective*, Reykjavík: Almenna bókafélagið.
Blichner, L. and Sangolt, L. (1993) 'Internasjonalisering av offentlig forvaltning', in P. Lægreid and J.P. Olsen (eds) *Organisering af offentlig sector*, Oslo: Tano.
Bulmer, S. and Bruch, M. (1998) 'Organizing for Europe: Whitehall, the British State and European Union', *Public Administration*, 76/4: 601–28.
Christensen, T. (1996) 'Adapting to processes of Europeanization', *ARENA*, 2.
Egeberg, M. (1980) 'The fourth level of government: on the standardisation of public policy within international regions', *Scandinavian Political Studies*, 3: 235–48.
Egeberg, M. and Trondal, J. (1999) 'Innenriksforvaltnings og den offentlige politikkens internasjonalisering' in T. Christensen and M. Egeberg (eds) *Forvaltningskunnskap*, Oslo: Tano Aschehoug.
Guðmundsdóttir, Á.E. (2002) *Íslenskur vinnumarkaður á umbrotatímum, sveigjanleiki fyrirtækja, stjórnun og samskipti aðila vinnumarkaðarins*, Reykjavík: Háskólinn í Reykjavík.
Hanf, K. and Soetendorp, B. (1998) 'Small states and the Europeanization of public policy', in K. Hanf and B. Soetendorp (eds) *Adapting to European Integration*, London: Longman: 1–13.
Hayes-Renshaw, F., Lequesne, C. and Mayor-Lopez, P. (1989) 'The permanent representations of the member states to the European communities', *Journal of Common Market Studies*, 28/2.
Herlitz, N. (1958) *Nordisk offentlig rätt*, 2 bd, Stockholm: Norstedt and Sömmer forlag.
Ingimundarson, V. (1996) *Í eldlínu kalda stríðsins*, Reykjavík: Vaka-Helgafell.
Interviews with officials (November 2000 to May 2003) 'Interviews conducted with civil servants in ministries in Iceland'.
Jónsson, A. (1989) *Iceland, NATO and the Keflavík Base*, Iceland: Icelandic Commission on Security and International Affairs.

Katzenstein, P. (1984) *Corporatism and Change: Austuria, Switzerland and the Politics of Industry*, Ithaca: Cornell University Press.

—— (1985) *Small States in World Markets: Industrial Policy in Europe*, Ithaca: Cornell University Press.

Knill, C. (2001) *The Europeanization of National Administration: Pattern of Institutional Change and Adaptation*, Cambridge: Cambridge University Press.

Kristinsson, G.H. (1993) 'Valdakerfið fram til Viðreisnar 1900–1959' in G. Hálfdanarson and S. Kristjánsson (eds) *Íslensk þjóðfélagspróun 1880–1990. Ritgerðir*, Reykjavík: Félagsvísindastofnun og Sagnfræðistofnun: 321–54.

Kristinsson, G.H., Jónsson, H. and Sveinsdóttir, H.Th. (1992) *Atvinnustefna á Íslandi 1951–1991*, Reykjavík: Félagsvísindastofnun Háskóla Íslands.

Kristjánsson, S. (1979) 'Corporatism in Iceland', unpublished paper, University of Iceland.

Kristjánsson, S. and Kristjánsson, R. (2000) 'Delegation and accountability in an ambiguous system: Iceland and the European Economic Area (EEA)', *The Journal of Legislation Studies*, 6/1: 105–24.

Lægreid, P. (2000) 'Implications of Europeanization on central administration in the Nordic countries', unpublished paper presented at IASIA Annual Conference, Beijing 10–13 July 2000, University of Bergen.

Lægreid, P., Steindórsson, R.S. and Thorhallsson, B. (July 2002) 'Europeanization of Public Administration: Changes and Effects of Europeanization on the Central Administration in the Nordic States', unpublished paper presented at the 18th EGOS Colloquium (European Group for Organizational Studies), Barcelona. July 4–6, 2002.

—— (November 2002) 'Europeanization of public administration: effects of the EU on the central administration in the Nordic states', *Working Paper*, 17, Bergen: Rokkansenteret, Bergen University Research Foundation.

Ministry for Foreign Affairs (January 1946) *Handbók utanríkisráðuneytisins*, Reykjavík: Ministry for Foreign Affairs.

—— (January 1950) *Handbók utanríkisráðuneytisins*, Reykjavík: Ministry for Foreign Affairs.

—— (January 1955) *Handbók utanríkisráðuneytisins*, Reykjavík: Ministry for Foreign Affairs.

—— (August 1960) *Handbók utanríkisráðuneytisins*, Reykjavík: Ministry for Foreign Affairs.

—— (January 1965) *Handbók utanríkisráðuneytisins*, Reykjavík: Ministry for Foreign Affairs.

—— (May 1970) *Handbók utanríkisráðuneytisins*, Reykjavík: Ministry for Foreign Affairs.

—— (January 1975) *Handbók utanríkisráðuneytisins*, Reykjavík: Ministry for Foreign Affairs.

—— (May 1980) *Handbók utanríkisráðuneytisins*, Reykjavík: Ministry for Foreign Affairs.

—— (February 1985) *Handbók utanríkisráðuneytisins*, Reykjavík: Ministry for Foreign Affairs.

—— (December 1991) *Handbók utanríkisráðuneytisins*, Reykjavík: Ministry for Foreign Affairs.

—— (March 1996) *Handbók utanríkisráðuneytisins*, Reykjavík: Ministry for Foreign Affairs.

—— (April 2000) *Skýrsla Halldórs Ásgrímssonar utanríkisráðherra um stöðu Íslands í Evrópusamstarfi*, Reykjavík: Ministry for Foreign Affairs.

—— (March 2001) *Handbók utanríkisráðuneytisins*, Reykjavík: Ministry for Foreign Affairs.

—— (May 2001) *Stækkun Evrópusambandsins: Áhrif á stöðu innan EES*, Reykjavík: Ministry for Foreign Affairs.

—— (May 2003) *Information*, Reykjavík: Ministry for Foreign Affairs.

Morgunblaðið [An Icelandic newspaper] (19 April 2002) 'Þáttaskil í íslenskum öryggismálum', *Morgunblaðið*.

Olsen, J.P. (1996) 'Europeanization and nation-state dynamics', in S. Gustavsson and L. Lewin (eds) *The Future of the Nation State*, London: Routledge: 245–85.

Sverdrup, U. (1998) 'Norway: an adaptive non-member', in K. Hanf and B. Soetendorp (eds) *Adapting to European Integration, Small States and the European Union*, London: Longman: 149–66.

—— (2000) 'Ambiguity and adaptation. Europeanization of administrative institutions as loosely coupled processes', PhD dissertation. Report No. 8, Oslo: Arena.

Thorhallsson, B. (2000) *The Role of Small States in the European Union*, London: Ashgate.

—— (November 2001) 'Stjórnsýslumál', in E.B. Einarsson (ed.) *Ísland í Evrópu*, Reykjavík: Samfylkingin: 29–55.

—— (2002a) 'Consequences of a small administration: the case of Iceland', *Current Politics and Economics of Europe*, 11/1: 61–76.

—— (2002b) 'The sceptical political elite versus the pro-European public: the case of Iceland', *Scandinavian Studies*, 74/3: 349–78.

Thorhallsson, B. and Ellertsdóttir, E. (forthcoming) *The Fishmeal Crisis – Iceland's Response to a Proposal by the European Commission*, Stockholm: Försvarshögskolan.

Trondal, J. (1998) 'Byråkratisk integrasjon. EU-kommisjonens ekspertkomiteer som transformative enheter', *Nordisk Administrativt Tidsskrift*, 79/3.

Vayrynen, R. (1971) 'On the definition and measurement of small power status', *Cooperation and Conflict*, VI: 91–102.

11 Towards a new theoretical approach

Baldur Thorhallsson

The aim of this study has been to examine why the Icelandic political elite has been reluctant to follow its counterparts in Europe and advocate participation in European integration. Seven rounds of debates on whether or not Iceland should participate in European co-operation have taken place in Iceland over the last half century.

Three of these rounds, in 1957–59, 1961–63 and 1994–95, resulted in no formal moves towards closer involvement in European integration. Economically, Iceland was not prepared to participate in the proposed free trade area of the OEEC member states discussed in the first debate, and in the mid-1990s its political parties, with the exception of the SDP, were not willing to consider the membership alternative. In 1961–63 the government seriously considered applying for membership of the EEC but opted instead for an associate agreement after an extensive consultation process domestically and with core EEC member states, the European Commission and its Nordic neighbours. However, an external factor, the French veto of British membership, prevented the government from moving on to formal negotiations with the EEC. External factors also prevented Iceland's participation in the negotiations leading to the foundation of EFTA in 1960: Britain was unwilling to involve Iceland in the preparation process because of the fisheries dispute between the countries.

Three of these seven rounds of debates led to Iceland's participation in European integration in the late 1960s and the early and late 1990s. It took the first step towards closer integration when it joined EFTA and it entered the EEA at the same time as the other Nordic EFTA states. However, with the exception of the Social Democrats, politicians were not very enthusiastic about the negotiation process leading up to the EEA Agreement, and all political parties except for the SDP had considerable reservations about the 'four freedoms'. Moreover, joining EFTA and the EEA were very controversial steps and the debates in the Althingi in the periods leading up to accession were the most intense since Iceland joined NATO. On the other hand, Iceland's membership of Schengen did not arouse much opposition.

The 2003 debate

Whether or not Iceland should apply for EU membership did not become one of the main issues in the general election in 2003. Very limited discussion took place, in fact, about Iceland's approach to European integration: with few exceptions, politicians did not take up the issue, the media rarely put questions concerning European affairs to politicians and did not do any independent analysis of the issue, and judging by their direct input in the election discussion, i.e. articles in newspapers and questions put to politicians at meetings and in the media, voters seemed to have little interest in the European question. The prime minister stated, for example, that he had not received a single question concerning European affairs from voters at the many meetings he attended all around the country in the run-up to the election (Lokaumræða 9 May 2003). This limited focus on whether or not Iceland should apply for membership in the election period is particularly interesting because the issue was extensively discussed by politicians, in the media and by voters from the middle of 2001 onwards and throughout 2002. Newspapers in Norway and Finland that carried reports on Iceland during the election took note of the limited EU debate and wondered why the issue did not receive attention.

The Social Democratic Alliance, the only party advocating an EU application, did not emphasize the issue in the election for fear that it might backfire, a possible reason being that support for EU membership among the electorate had declined considerably in the months leading up to the election because of the EU's demand of a much higher contribution by Iceland to the Structural Funds, the price of extending the EEA to the new EU member states. The SDA was also afraid that its pro-European stand would be used by its opponents as an indicator of the party's willingness to sacrifice Iceland's independence and sovereignty and of its limited emphasis on protecting Icelandic waters from foreign fishing fleets. The SDA is concerned that its EU policy may sideline the party in Icelandic politics. In order to limit this possibility, the party's prime ministerial candidate, Ingibjörg Sólrún Gísladóttir, said when asked why the party had not put more emphasis on its pro-European policy, that it was very difficult to promise anything concerning a government's policy towards the EU after the election because the other parties were not willing to apply for membership and coalition governments are the norm in Iceland, which means compromises on all sides (Ólafsson 3 May 2003: 34; Lokaumræða 9 May 2003). The leader of the party's parliamentary group also stated that a wide consensus would be needed among the electorate in order for a government to apply for EU membership, and it seemed to be some time before this was likely to be obtained (Fréttablaðið 23 April 2003). In the election campaign, the Social Democrats advocated that Iceland should define its objectives for negotiations with the EU on membership, with the retention of sole rights over the nation's fisheries zone as the main objective. It should apply for membership and hold a national referendum if a satisfactory agreement were reached in negotiations. The Social Democrats focussed on the attraction of tangible advantages of membership for the consumer, arguing that food prices and interest rates in Iceland would fall to the same level as those in the rest of Europe if Iceland joined the EU. Membership would also stabilize the exchange rate of the Icelandic krona (Social Democratic Alliance 2003). Furthermore, by joining the EU, Iceland would have some say on the 80 per cent of EU legislation implemented in the EEA (Ólafsson 3 May 2003). The SDA's prime ministerial candidate said she thought it was not a question of whether Iceland should apply for membership but rather when it would do so (Ólafsson 3 May 2003).

The Progressive Party advocated its 'wait and see' approach in the election. The party chairman, the foreign minister Halldór Ásgrímsson, stated repeatedly that he did not rule out EU membership, but that it could only become a reality if certain conditions were met, mainly regarding the fisheries and agricultural sectors. He said the decision on whether or not Iceland should apply for EU membership would be reached sooner than the Conservative leadership anticipated (Jónsdóttir 27 April 2003), and the EU question might even be on the agenda in the forthcoming parliamentary term (Lokaumræða 9 May 2003). He encouraged public interest groups and companies, and in particular the fisheries sector, to examine the EU membership option in more detail (Jónsdóttir 27 April 2003). Ásgrímsson emphasized that it should be up to the nation itself to decide to what extent it agreed to an assignment of its sovereignty. He pointed out that Iceland had very little say in the process of political consultation on the development of the substance of the EEA Agreement. The Althingi had no direct influence on EEA legislation, which Iceland was nevertheless obliged to incorporate in its laws. Ásgrímsson admitted that joining the EU would involve a certain abridgement of national sovereignty, but pointed out that membership of the EEA also involved considerable abridgement: 'And so I think it is obvious that we must do everything we can to see whether there is a better alternative that is more in line with our ideas about sovereignty and independence and gives the best guarantee of Iceland's interests' (Ásgrímsson 11 April 2003).

According to both its chairman and its party manager, the Liberal Party is also willing to consider the membership alternative, despite its scepticism, if Iceland can guarantee sole rights over its fishing grounds. The 'traditional stand' of political parties in Iceland towards the question of membership, the 'wait and see' approach, is manifested in their words. On the eve of the 2003 election, the party chairman stated in a TV debate between party leaders that he wanted to 'wait and see' before a decision were reached on whether or not to apply for EU membership; the party manager had already stated: 'We find it appropriate now to wait and see how the 10 new member states cope with membership' (Fréttablaðið 23 April 2003).

The Independence Party and the Left Green Movement kept up their formal stance against EU application. Their chairmen, together with the chairman of the Liberal Party, said the decision of the British government in mid-April to postpone the much-discussed 'euro referendum' in Britain would reduce the pressure on Iceland to adopt the euro and weaken the arguments of those who advocated EU membership (Morgunblaðið 25 April 2003).

The Left Green Movement spoke out the loudest against EU membership in the election run-up, and its manifesto stated clearly its opposition to membership. It occasionally took up the issue and warned about the possibility of a membership application after the election. The party chairman criticized the lack of discussion on whether or not Iceland should apply for membership (Lokaumræða 9 May 2003), probably because he thought the party might benefit from such a debate.

The Independence Party could be said to have avoided the EU issue in the election run-up. Its chairman, the prime minister, Davíð Oddsson, had spoken firmly against EU membership over the years, and was particularly active on this theme in 2002, but he did not emphasize the party's stance against EU membership in the months leading up to the election, even when given the opportunity to do so, for instance in an interview in the country's largest newspaper, *Morgunblaðið* (Sigurgeirsson 4 May 2003). In a television debate he did, however, say that Iceland would not receive exemption from the EU's common fisheries policy and should therefore not apply for membership (Lokaumræða 9 May 2003). He claimed that the EU was in a crisis, but emphasized at the same time the importance for Iceland of having access to the European market. He maintained that if Iceland wanted to keep its international position, it would have to guarantee this market access and at the same time strengthen its relationship with the USA, which was not less important. He argued that the government had managed to do this (Sigurgeirsson 4 May 2003). Other MPs and leading candidates for the Conservatives did not emphasize the party's policy against EU membership either, a possible reason being that opinion polls had indicated considerable support for EU membership among the party's supporters. On the other hand, the youth movement of the party ran an advertisement on television showing a vision of the future in which fishermen in the EU welcomed Iceland as the twenty-eighth member of the EU, with a shot of a group of vessels setting out from an EU harbour bound for Icelandic waters.

Constraints, sectors and security

This book has applied theoretical approaches that explain responses of states to European integration to the case of Iceland. Katzenstein's model

Towards a new theoretical approach 189

helps us to understand the cautious step-by-step approach of governments in Iceland to the European project, i.e. how they have sought membership of EFTA, the EEA and Schengen in order to alleviate European and international constraints. According to Katzenstein, European constraints are soft, not hard, but they are greater in economic affairs than in the social and security spheres. Governments in Iceland have addressed these constraints by following a policy of partial engagement in the economic aspect of European integration. As small states become more deeply involved in European integration, the softer the European constraints become, according to Katzenstein's thesis; consequently, his thesis lacks explanation value when it comes to the question of why Iceland has not sought membership of the EU in order to alleviate European and international constraints. Full participation in the European project has been seen by most Icelandic politicians as likely to aggravate these constraints.

Ingebritsen's sectoral approach, which accounts for the connections between the fishing industry and politicians, does not tell us the full story either. It omits important variables for explaining Iceland's approach to European integration. Evidence indicates that the fisheries sector is in a good position to influence government policy on European integration. All political parties oppose Iceland's membership of the EU's current common fisheries policy and emphasize the importance of Iceland's maintaining sole control over its fishing grounds. On the other hand, the fisheries sector has not been in a better position to influence successive governments' approaches to Europe than have the agricultural and industrial sectors in government committees on Europe. Furthermore, until the last decade, the agricultural sector had as much chance as the fisheries sector to influence politicians in terms of MPs' sectoral connections, both as regards ordinary MPs and those who sat on the relevant standing committees of the Althingi. Also, none of these three sectors interfere directly in the work of the pro- and anti-European movements. Moreover, the outright opposition of all political parties to allowing foreign vessels to fish in Icelandic waters may have as much to do with nationalism and the newly-gained control over its fishing grounds as it has to do with the interests of the fisheries sector. Thus, it is not correct to conclude that fisheries interests groups are the controlling factor in the response of governments in Iceland to European integration. Other variables can not be sidelined in explaining Iceland's approach to Europe. They have to be taken into consideration in order to obtain the complete picture; otherwise the analysis will reach a sketchy conclusion.

Chapter 7 examined Archer and Sogner's hypothesis that the security element may be a key variable in explaining the approach of states to European integration, the reconsideration of the EU as a source of security by the Norwegian political elite after 1989 being one of the key reasons it had to apply for EU membership. The chapter establishes that security considerations are also of importance regarding the stance of governments in Iceland on European integration, but that the influence in Iceland's case is in a fundamentally different direction compared to Norway. Iceland's special relationship with the USA explains why politicians in Iceland have not viewed the EU as a source of security. This special relationship in terms of security and, in the early days of European integration, in terms of economics and trade as well, limited the pressure on Iceland to seek EEC/EU membership.

Iceland was in a strategically important geographical location during the cold war and dealt with its vulnerability in security terms by making an alliance with the USA. The special relationship with the USA has provided Iceland with security, stability and status. The USA continues to be Iceland's key ally in security terms. At present, stability in economic terms is secure and the North Atlantic region is a stable one. Regional instability is therefore not a factor pressing the Icelandic political elite towards membership of the EU, as is the case of elites in Central and Southern Europe. Security is still provided by the USA without any financial cost to Iceland, and the country can still enjoy an international status, albeit a controversial one, through its alliance with the USA. This is indicated by Iceland's participation in 'the coalition of the willing' in the war with Iraq in 2003. The special relationship with the USA has given Iceland more influence on security matters in the North Atlantic, and in particular more status in the region, than it would otherwise have had, despite its reactive security policy. Membership of the EU is not seen by most of the Icelandic political elite as being likely to enhance this influence and status. Iceland is in no need of bolstering its security by joining the EU. Also, the Icelandic elite has not had any ambition to shape the new security environment in Europe, as has the internationally active elite in Norway.

The political elite and political discourse

Theoretical models often emphasize only one variable or maintain that one variable is of key importance in explaining states' responses to European integration. One factor may be of fundamental importance in explaining the behaviour of states towards the EU, e.g. the end of the cold war, the entrance of a key trading partner into the Union, or a change from a military regime to democracy, as in the cases of Spain, Portugal and Greece. But reality, and particularly the domestic situation of any country, is usually of greater complexity than to allow a single factor to serve as an overall explanation of a state's response to European integration. Approaches need to dig deeper into each individual state's domestic structure in order to explain its reactions to the EU. This is clearly evident from the different responses by the Nordic states to the integration process. Despite their similarity, they have each chosen their own way of participating in European integration. Denmark joined the EC in 1973 but secured a number of important exemptions from the Maastricht

Treaty; Finland joined in 1995 and plays a full part in the European project; Sweden joined at the same time but has hesitated to take a full part; the Norwegian electorate has twice rejected attempts by the country's elite to take it into the EU and Iceland has never applied for membership. The end of the cold war is not a sufficient explanation for the different approaches of the Nordic states to the EU, as three of them were founder members of NATO yet have approached the European project in different ways.

Moreover, the similarities of the Nordic states in terms of Nordic identity, little diversification in exports, corporatism or sectoral corporatism, stable democracy and a strong welfare state lead us nowhere in finding a reason for their distinctive approaches. Differences in terms of security, the nature of the leading economic sector (i.e. primary or secondary) and national identity only provide a part of the explanation for their distinctive approaches. The case of Iceland indicates that there are a number of other variables that have to be examined in order to understand why governments have hesitated to participate in the European project. The complicated domestic features of a state, notwithstanding its smallness and homogeneity, have to be taken into account in order for an approach to grasp the complete picture of the political elite's domestic decision-making process regarding participation in European integration.

Iceland is not only a young republic; it has fought four cod wars since the foundation of the republic. The cod wars have had a profound influence on national pride and nationalism in Iceland. Moreover, the defence agreement with the USA and the US military base in Iceland greatly influenced political discussion during the cold war and increased Icelandic nationalism, as is discussed in Chapter 7. Chapter 8 examines national identity in Iceland and how the political discourse regarding sovereignty and independence has influenced politicians' approach to Europe. National identity is a broad concept and it is difficult to pin down exactly its impact on the elite's attitudes towards the question of closer European integration. Chapter 8 emphasizes the nationalistic tone of Icelandic politics as one of the main explicatory factors behind the reluctance of politicians to consider the membership alternative. It concludes that Icelandic political discourse tends to polarize around nationalist themes, making it difficult for politicians to promote anything that seems to compromise Icelandic sovereignty and independence. Politicians cannot admit that they have transferred power from Reykjavík to Brussels by Iceland's membership of the EEA and Schengen. The fact that EU membership obviously means a transfer of power to the Continent makes it particularly difficult for politicians to advocate EU membership. Politicians even hesitate to find out whether Iceland could enter the EU on satisfactory terms because they fear being charged with wanting to relinquish Iceland's sovereignty and independence. The strength of the nationalist discourse is based on aspects such as the geographical isolation of the country, the relative homogeneity of its population, and the general economic prosperity that has characterized Iceland for at least the last half century.

But what is it in the makeup of the Icelandic political elite that leads it to a different conclusion concerning the question of EU membership compared with its counterparts in the other Nordic states, and in Europe generally? Models intended to explain states' responses to the EU tend to focus on economic interests, security interests or the European vision of their political elites. The political elites in Europe are seen as sharing the same goal of a united Europe, each dragging a hesitant electorate with it to Brussels at a different speed. These models do not focus on the elite itself, i.e. its background and characteristics. Chapter 9 argues that particular features of the Icelandic elite provide an explanation for its scepticism towards closer ties with Europe. An approach intending to explain Iceland's response to European integration cannot ignore the domestic power base of the country's political elite. This has, to a significant extent, been located in the more sparsely populated regions, where the fisheries and agriculture sectors play a very important role. The electorate in these regions tends to be more sceptical towards the question of membership than that in Reykjavík and its surroundings. The influence of the regions is inflated through the electoral system, which is characterized by an unequal distribution of seats in the Althingi in favour of the regions. The majority of MPs have come from the regions, despite the fact that the majority of the population lives in Reykjavík and its immediate surroundings. Thus the electoral system favours the elements that oppose EU membership and has placed them in a good position to block the EU issue. MPs from the regions form a powerful force in the their parties' parliamentary groups and as a result the parties hesitate to embrace a more pro-European conclusion. For instance, the leader of the Progressive Party has had considerable difficulties in convincing the party's MPs to advocate a more pro-European policy. There was also considerable opposition within the parliamentary group of the Social Democratic Alliance in 2001 to adopting a policy advocating EU membership. This opposition had to be overcome before the leadership dared to propose a policy change at a party conference and in a referendum of all party members. This domestic power base structure also helps us to understand the Independence Party's scepticism towards the question of EU membership. Party leaders and the parties themselves, except for the small SDP, tried to avoid an EU debate throughout the 1990s. Political leaders also hesitate to adopt a more pro-European policy because of opposition from their rural-based MPs and supporters.

Furthermore, no model intended to explain Iceland's reaction to European integration can ignore the elite's peripheral placement in Europe and its 'realist' concept of foreign policy. Iceland's elite has had limited contact with elites in the core states of the EU which have advocated closer European integration for more than half a century. The Icelandic elite has not

Towards a new theoretical approach 193

sought ideas on the European continent; rather, it has been influenced by the more Euro-sceptical British elite and the more cautious attitude of the elites in the Nordic states towards European co-operation. The elite's concept of foreign policy is characterized by 'realism', combined with an emphasis on national self-determination. This can be traced to the historical background of recently-gained independence, cod wars fought for concrete economic advantages and heated discussions of national independence concerning the defence agreement with the USA and its military presence in Iceland. To summarize: these particular features of the political elite play an important part in Iceland's reluctance to participate in European integration and partly explain its present status in Europe outside the EU. Any explanation of Iceland's position on European integration must take these features into account if it is not to lead to a flawed conclusion.

The size and characteristics of the national administration

Iceland's smallness must be taken into account in order to understand the country's position on European integration. Chapter 10 identifies the smallness of Iceland's administrative sector, and its characteristics, as one of the factors explaining Iceland's position on Europe. The limited capacity of the administration (in particular, of the ministry for foreign affairs) until the mid-to-late 1990s, prevented it from gathering information on any considerable scale concerning developments on the Continent. The administration faced increased domestic and international demands and had to devote all its capacity to handling its day-to-day business. It could not serve as a decisive forum for forming Iceland's foreign policy. This is demonstrated in its role in European affairs and security affairs, as Chapter 7 indicates. Moreover, the smallness of the administration and its lack of expertise made it reliant on interest groups in its policy on European integration. The close relationship between politicians and particular sectors, as discussed in Chapter 6, further encourages a close relationship between the administration and particular interests. Little emphasis was placed on long-term policy concerning Iceland's reaction to the ongoing European integration process. This was in line with the administration's traditions on little emphasis on long-term policy making. Thus, the smallness of the administration and its limited capability restricted Iceland's ability to participate in European integration. The importance of the size and characteristics of the administration is further indicated by the consequences of the increased capacity of the administration (in particular, of the ministry for foreign affairs) from the mid-to-late 1990s onwards. The rapid transformation of the ministry into a decisive unit that can produce detailed reports on Iceland's position in Europe has been an important basis for the foreign minister to provoke an EU debate in Iceland. The ministry has become a key source of the information on European affairs that is used extensively in the debate. The increase of expertise on Europe and other resources relating to external affairs within all ministries has made a fundamental difference in Iceland's international policy. Iceland has for the first time become proactive within the EEA framework and in international organizations such as the UN, the Council of Europe and NATO. Long-term policy making is now clearly evident in the foreign ministry's response to the changing nature of the EEA Agreement and its attempt to gain a seat in the UN Security Council in 2009–10. It is also demonstrated in its creation of a peacekeeping force and a more sophisticated policy on development aid. The increased capacity of the administration has not only led to more activity internationally; it has given Iceland a choice because the country's administration would be fully capable of participation in the EU if its politicians were to decide to join it. Commenting on Iceland's capacity in this respect, a high-ranking official in the Icelandic administration expressed this as follows:

> It would be a challenge but I think we [the Icelandic administration] can do it. We are precisely on the criteria line. This is the difference between us and Andorra, Liechtenstein and San Marino. They cannot do it. That is the reality. We have got this choice. It is only a choice for us what option we want to take.
>
> (Interview with official December 2000)

Scholars tend to view the national administration as a dependent variable and focus on its Europeanization. The case of Iceland indicates that the size and characteristics of the national administration are an independent variable that helps to explain Iceland's position on European integration.

The national administration: universal applicability?

The question arises whether the case of Iceland is unique or whether this 'new' variable, the size and characteristics of the national administration, has a universal applicability in explaining states' approaches to European integration. Can the national administration's size and characteristics be used to explain the positions of other small states in Europe?

Obviously, small states are not all the same even though they share many similar features. Iceland is obviously characterized by typical Nordic features, but it is probably best compared to Luxembourg and Malta in terms of population and the size of the administration: the numbers employed in the foreign services of these three states in April 2001 ranged from 150 in Iceland to 256 in Malta, leaving Luxembourg exactly in the middle with 206, as is mentioned in Chapter 10. Iceland has also a number of things in common with the smallest states in Europe: Liechtenstein, Andorra, San Marino and Monaco.[1] On the other hand, there is a consid-

Towards a new theoretical approach 195

erable size difference between Liechtenstein, Andorra, San Marino and Monaco on the one hand and Iceland, Malta and Luxembourg on the other. The countries in the former group have fewer inhabitants and their territorial size, gross domestic product and administrations are considerably smaller than those of the latter group. The foreign services of these four small states, for example, are considerably smaller, with staff numbers ranging from 23 in Andorra to 62 in San Marino (see Table 10.2).

Luxembourg's small administration has shown that it can defend that country's interests within the EU. It has preserved its tax privileges and highly competitive banking system. Furthermore, Luxembourg takes an active part in negotiations in the EU where its main interests are at stake, and it implements EU legislation as successfully as other member states. However, it does not have the administrative capacity to participate in all negotiations and committees within the Union. As a direct consequence of this, Luxembourg has opted to have Belgium represent it at a number of meetings where its direct interests are not at stake. Luxembourg is the only member state of the EU that has another member take over its responsibilities within the Union. Its small administration simply does not have the staff and expertise to cover a number of issues. It is forced to prioritize and miss meetings in a number of policy areas in order to be able to concentrate on its most important interests (Thorhallsson 2000).

The smallness of the Maltese administration has had a profound influence on Malta's position on European integration. Pace argues that lack of human resources within the Maltese administration delayed Malta's application to join the EU for three years i.e. until 1990 (Pace 2001: 452–3). For instance, its ministry for foreign affairs had considerable difficulty in setting up an EC directorate because of the shortage of qualified personnel (Pace 2001: 207). Also, lack of administrative resources restricted Malta's effort to canvass support among EU member states in the early stages of the application, particularly because it was slow in employing enough diplomats with an expert knowledge of European affairs. This is related to the fact that Malta took on the presidency of the UN General Assembly in 1990 and the small Maltese administration had difficulties in coping with those tasks at the same time (Pace 2001: 230, 452–3).

The European Commission has published a number of reports on Malta, stating its assessment of the country in response to its application. The Commission's Opinion in 1993 doubted that the Maltese administration could cope with EU membership: 'Malta has only a very few senior public officials with sufficient international experience to play a full part in the decision-making and operational processes of the Community institutions' (Commission of the European Communities 1993: 19). The Commission's Regular Reports in 1999 and 2000 stated that Malta's administrative capacity needed strengthening in a number of areas: it recommended that Malta set up new institutions and regulatory institutions (Commission of the European Communities 13 October 1999). Malta's ability to participate successfully in the EU's common agricultural policy and regional policy was said to be in doubt because its administration lacked systematic control of state aid and the administration had no experience in managing the implementation of funds such as the European Agricultural Guidance and Guarantee Fund (EAGGF) (Commission of the European Communities 2000: 33). Malta responded to this criticism by restructuring its administration and setting up horizontal co-ordination bodies. The Commission's 2000 Regular Report on Malta's progress towards accession stated that various measures had been taken to improve the Maltese administration. However, it argued that it was too early to assess the impact of the reforms and sustained efforts were required for the reform of the public administration aimed at improving its efficiency and effectiveness (Commission of the European Communities 2000: 10). The success of Malta's adjustments to the EU would depend on its administrative reforms. In the year 2000, Malta had made considerable process in adapting the *acquis* in sectors where it had strengthened its administrative capacity. Malta had institutions and expertise to deal with EU membership in those sectors. However, in sectors where administrative reforms had not taken place, it was not able to face the challenges associated with membership. It was not considered to have the necessary institutions and expertise to participate in the decision-making processes of the EU. Nor was it considered to have the capacity to implement the *acquis* in those sectors. As the Commission's 2000 Regular Report concluded: 'While the Maltese administration appears to be adequately staffed, considerable restructuring and staff training is still needed for it to be able to implement the *acquis* in many areas.' (Commission of the European Communities 2000: 67). Furthermore, Malta has not been active internationally and it is questionable whether its ministry for foreign affairs would have an adequate staff with enough expertise to deal with membership of the EU (Cini 27 October 2000: 10). The Maltese administration had to prove that it was able to adopt the *acquis communautaire* before Malta could enter the EU. It also had to demonstrate that it had the expertise to participate in the decision-making processes of the EU before it could join.

Liechtenstein's administration is capable of participating in the EEA Agreement. It has no more difficulty than Iceland and Norway in implementing EU legislation (EFTA Surveillance Authority November 2000). Officials from Liechtenstein have even been invited to Iceland by the ministry for foreign affairs to explain their effective implementation procedure.[2] The smallness of the Liechtenstein administration does, however, make it difficult for it to participate effectively in the decision-making processes of the EEA. The administration simply does not have the staff, experts or other resources to take part in many committees within the Commission, which it has access to through the EEA Agreement. The smallness of the administration makes it reactive in the decision-making processes. On the other hand, the Norwegian administration is an active participant in the processes and is at times over-represented at meetings. The Icelandic administration struggles to cover the most important meetings and leaves out many meetings because of its small staff and limited financial resources. While Iceland could participate without much difficulty as a member state in the EU, by covering the most important meetings, Liechtenstein would hardly manage to do so (Thorhallsson 2001).

Andorra, Monaco and San Marino would be able to adapt to European integration by implementing EU legislation, as Liechtenstein has done. In this sense they could participate in European integration but the smallness of their administrations would prevent them from taking a full part in the European project. Andorra, Monaco, San Marino and Liechtenstein do not have the administrative capacity to participate in meetings where important decisions are made which affect their direct interests. The case of Liechtenstein indicates this. It is not their territorial size, gross domestic product, economic characteristics, military weakness or the number of their inhabitants which directly precludes their membership of the European Union; rather, it is the inability of their small administrations to present and defend their interests within the EU that makes it impractical for them to apply for membership.

The difference in size between the Icelandic administration and the administrations of Liechtenstein, Andorra, San Marino and Monaco is decisive. Iceland does have a choice whether to join the EU or not; the others do not have this option. Luxembourg has already long since exercised this choice but its small administration restricts its activity within the Union. Malta also has a choice. Continuous reform of the Maltese administration has made it capable of participating in the EU.

The cases of other small administrations in Europe further strengthen our claim. The administrative size and characteristics of these states must be taken into account in order to explain their approaches to European integration. The 'national administration' variable is of key importance in explaining their responses.

Domestic characteristics and the political elite

Indicators usually used to define the size of states, such as population size, territorial size and GDP, do not help us to explain the approaches of small states to European integration. Keohane's classification of states may be more helpful. He distinguishes between large and small powers by focusing on whether their leaders think their states have a decisive impact on the international system. According to Keohane, states can be classified into three types: 'system-determining, or system-influencing' i.e. those that can influence the international system through unilateral or multilateral action, 'system-affecting' i.e. those that cannot influence the international system on their own but can do so together with other states, and 'system-ineffectual' i.e. those that adjust to the international system and cannot change it (Keohane 1969: 295–6). Pace, after a detailed analysis of the small-state literature and a case study on Malta's approach to European integration, argues that Keohane's approach is the most useful one in examining Malta's reaction to European integration (Pace 2001: 18). He argues that a substantial section of Maltese society advocates EU membership in order to seek security guarantees and non-economic advantages. Membership is not only sought to gain unrestricted market access to the Union. Moreover, membership is sought to move Malta from the 'system-ineffectual' to the 'system-affecting' category, i.e. by joining the EU, Malta will be able to participate in decision-making processes of the EU 'that can most influence the context in which it (Malta) has to survive' (Pace 2001: 50). The entry of the former EFTA states Finland, Sweden and Austria into the EU can also be seen in this light. They joined the Union in order to gain a seat at the decision-making table. Iceland has been less active internationally, compared with these three states, and leading politicians in Iceland do not share the same perception as their counterparts in the Nordic states and the Maltese National Party of a possible influence on decisions within the EU. Oddsson, Iceland's prime minister, has often said that small states within the EU have very limited influence and that it is declining (Oddsson 7 May 2002). Iceland's fisheries minister has also stated, as has been mentioned earlier, that Iceland would have to fight a new cod war every single year in Brussels if it were to join the Union. An argument commonly used in Iceland against membership is that small states do not exercise any power in the EU and that Iceland would not have any influence there. This perception may stem from Iceland's reactiveness within international organizations over the years: until recently, it was not an active participant in EFTA, NATO, the UN and the decision-making framework of the EEA. Many leading politicians may simply not envisage an active role for Iceland within the EU. They themselves have not been active participants in the international arena and they do not see their role in office as such. Iceland is perceived as a 'system-ineffectual' state in the international system.

It is interesting to note, in this context, that Iceland's last two foreign ministers, Hannibalsson (1988–95) and Ásgrímsson (1995–), who have led Iceland on a more active path internationally, became more and more pro-European in office. Hannibalsson advocated membership from 1994 and Ásgrímsson has stated that Iceland needs to reconsider its position in Europe (Ásgrímsson 11 April 2003). Their emphasis may be interpreted as an attempt to move Iceland from the 'system-ineffectual' to the 'system-affecting' category.

Political elites form states' policy on European integration, though the electorate can sometimes overturn it, as has happened in referenda in Norway, Denmark and Ireland. Decisions on Europe taken by the elite in a small state are shaped by external events, such as the entrance of a key trading partner and the willingness of the EU to accept new members.

Towards a new theoretical approach 199

However, models intended to explain states' responses to European integration must take into account their elites' values, interests and perceptions. Models explaining states' behaviour towards European integration cannot assume, as does the rationalist world of political economy, that 'actor identities are fixed and unproblematic, an intellectually untenable position in the case of the small European states, and perhaps more generally' (Katzenstein March 2003). Scholars of comparative and international political economy 'do not know what to do with ideology as an explanatory construct. With a few notable exceptions, the impermeability of the field of political economy to considerations of identity persists to date' (Katzenstein March 2003).

Pace argues that European integration based on 'pooling of resources' is a 'rejection of classical realism' (Pace 2001: 47). The approach of the political elite in the National Party in Malta to European integration reflects its beliefs in the idea of European unity (Pace 2001: 278) A large part of the Icelandic political elite still views international relations in terms of state-to-state relations, in line with Iceland's special relationship with the USA and Nordic co-operation within the Nordic Council. The Icelandic political elite views pooling of resources as a threat to its independence and newly-won control over its fishing grounds. The elite's political discourse is characterized by phraseology aimed at protecting Iceland's sovereignty and independence from the ongoing process of European integration. The outcome is a very cautious strategy on European integration. Icelandic governments have faced the challenge, as have governments of other small states in Europe, to respond to constraints imposed on the country by European integration. The options available are constrained by international events, but domestic features determine the policy outcome regarding participation in European integration. Strategy has been based on a cautious step-by-step approach towards closer involvement in the European project, the aim being to secure Iceland's immediate economic interests and to serve the clear objective of safeguarding the country's independence and sovereignty. The maintenance of national decision-making powers in areas of key importance, such as the fisheries and agricultural sectors, and also security, is of fundamental value for the political elite. Moreover, the perception that Iceland's sovereignty is still vested in the Althingi, Iceland's parliament for nearly 1,100 years, is a core value in all discussion on closer ties with other states and international institutions.

Iceland does not need what Pace calls a 'security community' that safeguards core values such as democracy, human rights and a market economy, as is being sought by the new member states joining the EU in 2004 (Pace 2001: 110–11). He argues that the dominating concern of small states is security in its wider meaning (Pace 2001: 462). Iceland has already addressed this concern by its membership of the EEA, Schengen and NATO and the defence agreement with the USA. For instance, Iceland's membership of Schengen helps to protect it from 'new' security threats i.e. terrorism and rise of transnational criminal activities. Iceland has solved the problems of economic and security vulnerability, which are the largest concern of small states (Pace 2001: 47). The aim of the cautious step-by-step approach to European integration has been to overcome these vulnerabilities by seeking solutions that lie mainly outside the state, i.e. to gain the economic benefits of European integration by becoming partially engaged in the institutional structure of the EU.

Changes in the domestic arena

The general election of 2003 did not bring about any policy change regarding Iceland's approach to the EU. The coalition government of the Independence and Progressive parties retained its majority and continued in office. The EU question is not on the government's agenda and a policy change regarding European affairs seems unlikely to take place in the current parliamentary term, which ends in 2007. Though the odds are still against membership, the domestic environment surrounding the political elite is nevertheless slowly changing.

In 2003, for the first time, the majority of the electorate (62 per cent), which lives in Reykjavík and the surrounding area, elected the majority of MPs in the Althingi: 33 of the 63 seats. Many of those who have campaigned for a fairer electoral system are optimistic that this change will increase the influence of the urban electorate on issues such as policy on Europe. For instance, 15 of the 22 Independence Party MPs now come from the Greater Reykjavík area. On the other hand, the unequal weight of votes between the regions and the Reykjavík area is still probably the greatest in the whole of Western Europe (Valen et al. 2000; Hardarson et al. 2000; Hardarson 2002). It is doubtful that the new majority in parliament representing the main urban area will have any immediate impact on the government's policy on Europe. For instance, MPs from the regions still form a dominant force in the parliamentary group of the Progressive Party (8 out of its 12 MPs are from the regions), and all the Liberal Party's MPs come from the regions. The 'wait and see' approach is therefore convenient for them and their parties. More radical changes in the direction of an equal distribution of seats may have to take place in order for the electoral system to lead to a more pro-European attitude within parliamentary groups and the government.

The Confederation of Icelandic Employers and the Icelandic Federation of Labour now seem to be more willing to consider EU membership. Having experienced difficulties in their attempts to influence decisions taken within the EEA framework, they are becoming increasingly more critical of the EEA Agreement and concerned that it does not guarantee their interests. As a result, in November 2000 the Icelandic Federation of Labour demanded that the issue of EU membership be placed on the political agenda so that negotiation objectives for a possible membership application could be defined. In May 2001 the Confederation of Icelandic Employers adopted a similar approach to the EU question. Moreover, the Icelandic Federation of Labour has demanded a referendum on the question of an EU membership application. It has said that Iceland must increase its influence within in the EEA framework or join the EU, but it describes the possibility of strengthening the EEA Agreement as a farfetched political utopia (ASÍ November 2000). This policy change moves the federation closer to the position of the Federation of Icelandic Industries and the Iceland Chamber of Commerce (ICC). The Federation of Icelandic Industries has enthusiastically campaigned for EU membership for a decade and has been the unofficial leading force among those advocating membership. For instance, in its 1994 annual report it stated that a serious discussion of the pros and cons of EU membership and the adoption of a clear policy on the membership issue could no longer be avoided (Federation of Icelandic Industries 1994: 17).

It is interesting to review the part played by the ICC in the debate on Europe: it reflects the discussion that took place in the mid-1990s on the question of applying to join the EU and the silence that descended over the matter until it re-emerged as an issue at the beginning of the present century.

The ICC commissioned a detailed report for the Icelandic business forum held in February 1993 under the title 'Joining the EU – Yes or No?', after which it began pressing the government to put the question on its agenda. In June the same year the chairman of the ICC sent a letter to the prime minister, Davíð Oddsson, urging the government to make a special survey of the possibility of Iceland's joining the EU and what implications it would have as compared with membership of the EEA. The ICC recommended that the government appoint a committee of representatives of the major business sectors and all political parties. It expressed its concern that Iceland would become isolated in Europe as a result of the possible entry of other EFTA/EEA states into the EU and saw membership of the EU primarily as a means of ensuring the country's political position among the nations of Europe and strengthening Iceland's status as an independent country (Sveinsson 24 June 1993). The government did not act on this proposal.

A year later, in July 1994, the leaders of the ICC and the Confederation of Icelandic Employers sent the prime minister a joint letter expressing their concern at the future of the EEA Agreement in the light of the forthcoming entry of EFTA/EEA countries into the EU and urging the government to initiate negotiations with the EU so as to produce a clear conclusion regarding the country's future relations with the EU

(Gunnarsson et al. 12 July 1994). At the beginning of December that same year, they again wrote to the prime minister, sending copies of the letter to the chairmen of other political parties, expressing serious concern at the future of the EEA Agreement, both in view of the entry of three EFTA/EEA countries into the EU and of the constitutional position of the agreement in Iceland. They saw Iceland as having less influence on the EU's legislative process than had been expected, in addition to which a larger proportion of issues were under the control of the EU's supervisory institutions than had been foreseen at the outset. Consequently, they feared that the EEA Agreement was incompatible with Iceland's constitution, as had been alleged at the time of its ratification by the Althingi, and urged the government and all the party representatives in the Althingi to amend the constitution so as to remove all doubt as to the constitutionality of international agreements like the EEA Agreement (Gunnarsson et al. 8 December 1994). No such constitutional amendments have yet been made in this direction.

At the end of December 1994 the chairman of the ICC wrote to the prime minister informing him that after detailed examination, it had come to the conclusion that Iceland would have a good chance of securing its interests within the EU and that there were cogent reasons for joining the Union. The government was urged to define goals to be sought in negotiations on entry and to start making these known systematically to the EU states with a view to submitting an application for membership not later than 1996 if these exploratory moves revealed that Iceland would be likely to secure its goals in the course of negotiations. The ICC cited two particular reasons for joining the EU. The first was political: the country had very limited influence on the acts of the EEA and was in danger of becoming politically isolated in Europe. The second was economic: long-term investment in Iceland would become more attractive and the country's legislation on trade, taxation and economic management would be more closely in step with that of its main trading partners (Sveinsson 28 December 1994). This letter was the ICC's last formal attempt to press the government to put the question of Europe on its agenda and apply for EU membership.

As from autumn 1995 the ICC adopted the informal policy of waiting to see what happened to the EEA Agreement while at the same time continuing discussion and examination of the question of EU membership. The ICC's board and management have continued to monitor the integration process in Europe, and the issue has been on the agenda of its annual business forum. These have called for the issue to be put on the political agenda and attention to be given to the possibility of joining the EU. But the ICC has not regarded it as advisable to mount a campaign for a membership application in the way that the Federation of Icelandic Industries has done. Opinions on EU membership within the ICC are divided, the main opposition being voiced by members connected with the fishing industry and those with commercial links with the USA. The financial sector also appears not to be keen on membership. In this context it is interesting to note that the ICC stopped applying direct pressure on the government when the fisheries sector gained a greater number of seats on its board (Vignisson 2001: 34) and the Independence Party became more sceptical of EU membership and adopted a firm position against it.

The Confederation of Icelandic Employers has possibly gone as far as it can in the direction of adopting a pro-European policy, as representatives of the fisheries sector are likely to try to block any further move towards outright support of an EU application. The way the EU issue has been silenced within the ICC shows how opponents of any move towards an EU application manage to prevent pro-Europeans from engaging in an outright campaign. The Icelandic Federation of Labour is more likely to strengthen its call for an EU application but it may have difficulty in getting other unions to support it. They do not have the same amount of expertise and experience in addressing the European issue and most of them have shown little interest in putting an EU application on their agenda. For instance, the leader of the Federation of State and Municipal Employees, an MP and leading figure in the Left Green Movement, is strongly opposed to joining the EU. The Federation of Icelandic Industries will therefore probably continue for some time to be the only substantial interest group campaigning outright for membership of the EU.

Iceland is not characterized by the corporatist structure of the Scandinavian states. The integration of the business sector and labour unions in the corporatist framework in Sweden (Pontusson 1992) helped the government there to pursue EU membership (Ingebritsen 1998: 30). Moreover, in the Nordic states the political process of integration was 'decided by a partnership between governments and economic interest groups' (Ingebritsen 1998: 168). In Iceland, the consultative process between the government and interest groups is characterized by sectoral corporatism. The absence of corporatism, combined with an electoral system favouring the rural areas, contributes to the important role of the fisheries and the agricultural sectors in the policy-making process in Iceland. The smallness of the administration and its lack of expertise, in the past, further contributed to the importance of these sectors. The Icelandic policy-making process does not provide a corporatist structural framework within which the issue of an EU application can be discussed. There is no forum for resolving a conflict of opinion on EU membership where representatives of the main interest groups and the government are present. Committees formed by governments to discuss Iceland's approach to Europe have not provided this forum since representatives of interest groups have not been invited to serve on them.

The government is currently facing a forced policy change in the agricultural sector because of further moves towards free trade in agricultural goods within the World Trade Organization (WTO). Governments in Iceland have always resisted liberalization of trade in agricultural products; the present government has kept up this traditional stance and strongly opposes the current moves by the WTO. Some ministers and leaders of the farmers' unions have even criticized the EU for its 'liberal' position on free trade in agricultural products. However, they have already mentioned the need for farmers and the agrarian sector in general to prepare for this foreseeable liberalization in trade. Restructuring of the agricultural sector in Iceland and a larger influx of agricultural goods will put the sector in a better position to face the challenge of potential EU membership. These factors, combined with a better understanding of the EU's agricultural policy, which is almost totally lacking in Iceland at present, may reduce farmers' opposition to membership even though they might still be far from actively supporting it.

Iceland's importance in the defence of the USA and states in Western Europe is not as fundamental as before. The US focus has shifted away from Europe, and NATO is occupied with eastward enlargement and its changing role in the international system. The Icelandic government is increasingly worried that the USA may further cut down its activity at its military base in Iceland. Ásgrímsson, the foreign minister, stated that soon after the election the prime minister must arrange a meeting with the US president to discuss the defence agreement between the states (Morgunblaðið 29 April 2003). The aim of such a discussion would be to try to prevent the USA from reducing its activity at the Keflavík base to a minimum. Oddsson, the prime minister, also seems to worry about the future of the US commitment to the defence of Iceland and has criticized discussion in Washington about further cuts at the base. He has said that the level of defence capability has been reduced so far as to approach the limit of what is acceptable, and that the question therefore remains whether the intention is to withdraw it completely and have only a monitoring station in Iceland, serving US interests only. 'If so, then this is a new situation which we will have to examine' (Sigurgeirsson 4 May 2003). Other leading politicians have also voiced their concern about possible cuts in US activity in Iceland and stated that such moves might lead to a reconsideration of Iceland's position on Europe, as is discussed in Chapter 7. Furthermore, the tension between the US government and some governments in Europe opposed to the war in Iraq is perceived by the Icelandic government as a threat to the transatlantic link, i.e. the role of the USA in the defence of Europe. Thus, Iceland has stressed its relationship with the USA and demanded a clear link between the EU's increased security role and NATO.

Ásgrímsson, the chairman of the Progressive Party and present foreign minister, will take over as prime minister in September 2004 according to an agreement made between the Progressives and the Conservatives in May 2003. He has been the driving force behind increased discussion on Iceland's position in Europe and the increased activity of the foreign ministry. Moreover, Ásgrímsson is clearly moving away from the traditional nationalistic tone of Icelandic politicians, and has been emphasizing the changing meaning of the concept of sovereignty (Ásgrímsson 18 March 2003; Ásgrímsson 11 April 2003). Whether he will use his position as a prime minister to further emphasize the EU question remains to be seen but at present it looks as if he will be bound by the government's policy statement issued in May 2003. This emphasized the EEA Agreement regarding Iceland's relations with the EU. Discussion of an EU application is not on the government's agenda. For instance, the statement did not mention the committee on Europe proposed by the prime minister in his annual end-of-year article in 2002.

Support for an EU application can be found within all political parties except the Left Green Movement. The Social Democratic Alliance is united in its pro-European approach and leading figures of the Progressive and Liberal parties are willing to consider the membership alternative. Some industrial and business leaders within the Independence Party, and some younger party members, want to examine the possibility of membership, and some of the party's MPs can be seen as potential supporters.

The chairman of the Independence Party, on the other hand, strongly opposes any moves towards possible EU membership, while the chairman of the Progressive Party has moved his party as far as he can, at least at present, towards a pro-European policy. The leaders may therefore be afraid of an internal split: this could happen in the Independence Party if the issue of EU membership were to arise within the party and in the Progressive Party if it were faced with the need to take a decision on whether or not to apply for EU membership. This explains the cautious internal debate within these parties and the Liberal Party: the EU issue is best kept on the sideline. An EU debate within the parties, or a public debate during an election campaign, is to be avoided by all possible means.

The electorate may have the final say in a referendum on whether or not a country joins the EU, but the position of the political elite is decisive when it comes to the question of whether membership should be put on the political agenda and whether the state should submit an application for membership. Detailed discussion on whether or not to apply for membership has only once taken place within the Icelandic government, in 1961–63. Other governments have not considered this alternative. The aim of this book has been to shed light on why governments have been reluctant to participate in European integration. External events have shaped the environment of decisions concerning Iceland's involvement in European integration but domestic features provide the basic explanation for

Iceland's approach to the European project. The individual features of each state have to be taken into account in order for a theoretical framework to account for the reasons behind states' different approaches to Europe. The small decision-making framework within small states may contribute to the importance of domestic features in determining their approaches to international events. Domestic constraints that shape the decision-making framework of the elite, such as the electoral system and the smallness of the administration in Iceland, can have a profound influence on decisions taken by the elite. Moreover, an elite's perceptions of national identity and of the role of states within the international system may have profound influence on its political discourse and the actions it takes. The domestic power base of the elite may also be significant, as may its peripheral or central placement in a grouping of nations.

This study has focussed on the political elite as a whole, particularly the governing elite, i.e. the political elite that has held office when discussions have taken place on whether or not to form closer ties with European states. An interesting follow-up might be to examine particular leaders and how they, on their own, have influenced policy on Europe. This might be particularly important in a small community where the policy-making community is small and each and every individual can play a decisive role. It might also be interesting to analyse in further detail how leaders and the political elite in general in a small state see their role in the international arena. Do leaders in a small community see their states as having no, or very limited, influence on the environment or do they perceive themselves and their states as being able to influence their immediate international environment?

Notes

1 These five states, the smallest in Europe, all have a defence arrangement and a customs union arrangement with their larger neighbours. The USA guarantees the defence of Iceland; Italy is responsible for the defence of San Marino, Switzerland for that of Liechtenstein, France for that of Monaco, and Spain and France guarantee the defence of Andorra. San Marino and Andorra have formed a customs union with the European Union, Monaco has formed one with France and Liechtenstein has formed a customs union with Switzerland and is part of the EEA, as is Iceland. This demonstrates their vulnerability. First, they do not have the military capacity to defend themselves. Second, they cannot produce all necessary products domestically because of the small scale of their economy. They rely on trade with their neighbours to a greater extent than do other states. The Vatican City is left out of this discussion because it is not characterized by the typical features of a nation-state.
2 Iceland's foreign ministry held a one-day conference in 1997 on the EEA implementation process and invited officials from Lichtenstein to learn from their 'successful' experience.

Bibliography

Ásgrímsson, H. (18 March 2003) *Fullveldið og lýðræðishallinn í EES*. Available online: http://www.utanrikisraduneyti.is/interpro/utanr/utanrad.nsf/pages/wpp2329 (accessed 16 May 2003).
—— (11 April 2003) *Hagsmunagæsla innan EES*. Available online: http://www.utanrikisraduneyti.is/interpro/utanr/utanrad.nsf/pages/wpp2348 (accessed 16 May 2003).
ASÍ [The Icelandic Federation of Labour] (November 2000) '*Ísland í dag: Greining og leiðsögn: stefnumörkun 39. þings ASÍ í alþjóðamálum*', Reykjavík: ASÍ.
Cini, M. (27 October 2000) 'The Europeanization of Malta: adaptation, identity and party politics', paper presented at the Malta and the European Union Conference in London, 27 October 2000.
Commission of the European Communities (1993) 'The Challenge of Enlargement. Commission Opinion on Malta's Application for Membership', *Bulletin of the European Communities*, Supplement, No. 4.
—— (13 October 1999) *1999 Regular Report from the Commission on Malta's Progress Towards Accession*. Availble online: http://europa.eu.int/comm/enlargement/report_10_99/pdf/en/malta_en.pdf (accessed 16 May 2003).
—— (2000) *Enlargement Strategy Paper: Report on progress towards accession by each of the candidate countries*. Available online: http://europa.eu.int/comm/enlargement/report_11_00/pdf/strat_en.pdf (accessed 16 May 2003).
EFTA Surveillance Authority (November 2000) 'Single Market Scoreboard – EFTA States No. 7'. Available online: http://www.eftasurv.int/information/pressreleases/2000pr/dbaFile1703.html (accessed 16 May 2003).
Federation of Icelandic Industries (1994) *Ársskýrsla Samtaka iðnaðarins 1994*, Reykavík: Federation of Icelandic Industries.
Fréttablaðið (23 April 2003) 'Umsókn að ESB ólíkleg', *Fréttablaðið*.
Gunnarsson, M. and Sveinsson, E. (8 December 1994) 'no title', an unpublished letter from the chairman of the Iceland Chamber of Commerce and the chairman of the Confederation of Icelandic Employers to the prime minister of Iceland, Chamber of Commerce.
—— (12 July 1994) 'no title', an unpublished letter from the chairman of the Iceland Chamber of Commerce and the chairman of the Confederation of Icelandic Employers to the prime minister of Iceland, Chamber of Commerce.
Hardarson, Ó.Th. (2002) 'The Icelandic electoral system 1844–1999', in A. Lijphart and B. Grofman (eds) *The Evolution of Electoral and Party Systems in the Nordic Countries*, New York: Agathon Press.
Hardarson, Ó.Th. and Kristinsson, G.H. (2000) 'Iceland', *European Journal of Political Research*, 38: 408–19.
Ingebritsen, C. (1998) *The Nordic States and European Unity*, Ithaca and London: Cornell University Press.
Interview with an official (December 2000) 'Interview conducted with a civil servant in a ministry in Iceland'.
Jónsdóttir, R.S. (27 April 2003) 'Setjum stöðugleikann á oddinn', *Morgunblaðið*.
Katzenstein P.J. (March 2003) 'Small states and small states revisited', *New Political Economy*, 8/1.
Keohane, R.O. (1969) 'Lilliputians' dilemmas: small states in international politics', *International Organization*, 23/2: 291–310.

Lokaumræða (9 May 2003) TV program, Icelandic National Broadcasting Service.
Morgunblaðið [An Icelandic newspaper] (25 April 2003) 'Skiptar skoðanir um áhrif á Evrópuumræðu hér', *Morgunblaðið*.
—— (29 April 2003) 'Sakar Samfylkinguna um tækifærismennsku'. Available online: http://safn.mbl.is/ (accessed 16 May 2003).
Oddsson, D. (7 May 2002) *Ávarp forsætisráðherra á aðalfundi Samtaka atvinnulífsins*. Available online: http://forsaetisraduneyti.is/interpro/for/for.nsf/printview/raeda0025 (accessed 5 May 2003).
Ólafsson, E. (3 May 2003) 'Aðalatriðið er að fella ríkisstjórnina', *Morgunblaðið*.
Pace, R. (2001) *Microstate Security in the Global System: EU-Malta Relations*, Valletta: Midesa Books.
Pontusson, J. (1992) *The Limits of Social Democracy*, Ithaca, Cornell University Press.
Sigurgeirsson, S. (4 May 2003) 'Skattar ekki lækkaðir án Sjálfstæðisflokksins', *Morgunblaðið*.
Social Democratic Alliance (2003) *Samfylkingin*, Reykjavík: Social Democratic Alliance.
Sveinsson, E. (24 June 1993) 'no title', an unpublished letter from the chairman of the Iceland Chamber of Commerce to the prime minister of Iceland, Iceland Chamber of Commerce.
—— (28 December 1994) 'Efni: Ísland og ESB', an unpublished letter from the chairman of the Iceland Chamber of Commerce to the prime minister of Iceland, Iceland Chamber of Commerce.
Thorhallsson, B. (2000) *The Role of Small States in the European Union*, London: Ashgate.
—— (2001) 'Stjórnsýslumál', in E.B. Einarsson (ed.) *Ísland í Evrópu*, Reykjavík: Social Democratic Alliance.
Valen, H., Narud, H.M. and Hardarson, Ó.Th. (2000) 'Geography and political representation', in P. Esaiasson and K. Heidar (eds) *Beyond Congress and Westminster*, Ohio State University Press.
Vignisson, H.Th. (2001) 'The influence of economic sectors on the policy-making of governments in Iceland', unpublished study sponsored by the Icelandic Students' Innovative Fund.

Index

Page numbers in *italics* refer to tables and figures.

Act of Union 137, 150
administration, national (Iceland) *see also* foreign service: autonomy 174, 177; compared with Norway 173; definition 163; expansion 172; flexibility 174, 177; history 170–4; Iceland *vs.* other small states 194–7; Iceland's limited capacity 166–8; impact of EU/EEA membership 168–70; influence at EU/EEA 173; and interest groups 179–80; interference by politicians 170–1, 173; lack of expertise and staff 169; size and characteristics 13–14, 162, 193–4; trust 177
Afghanistan 109, 113, 114
Africa 120, 178
Agricultural Production Council 27, 76
agriculture 23, 42, 45, 69, 79; connections to political parties 80–3, 204
air space, Icelandic 112
Althingi 1, 4, 6, 15, 23, 24, 30, 32, 38, 43, 47, 68, 69, 75, 130, 155, 159, 171, 174, 179, 186, 187, 189, 192, 199, 200, 202; debate on EEA membership 3; debates on Schengen and EU 55; and EEA Agreement 64; and interest groups 79–86
Amsterdam Treaty 46, 51, 52–3
Andorra 163–4, *165*, 194–5, 197
anti-European: lobby 110; movements 189
Archer, C. 1, 11, 104, 163–4, 189
Ásgrímsson, Halldór (Foreign Minister): abstention on EEA 42; call for EEA Agreement amendments 176; changing concept of sovereignty 205; on the common fisheries policy 90–1, 129–30; on defence 116; on defence agreement with US 204; on EU membership 187; on the euro 73
Association of Icelandic Canning Factories 30
Association of Icelandic Importers, Exporters and Wholesalers 27
Atlantic Ocean 103, 111, 118
Austria 12, *164*, 198
autonomy, civil service 171–2, 173–4

Baltic states *164*
Bauman, Zygmunt 134, 136
Belgium 50, 114, 117, 154, *164*, 195
Benediktsson, Bjarni (Prime Minister, Iceland) 27, 31
Benediktsson, Einar 166
Benelux countries *see* Belgium; Luxembourg; Netherlands, The
Biafra 120
Bjarnason, Björn (Minister of Justice) 115
Björnsson, Sveinn (President of Iceland) 150
Black, Cyril E. 133
borders, control of *see* Schengen Convention
Bourdieu, Pierre 135
Britain 26, 32, *164*; and EFTA 28, 31; exports from Iceland 72, 153; on fish quotas 31; fishing dispute *see under* fisheries and fishing; measures on quota jumping 95; refused entry to EEC 3, 63; and Schengen 4
Brundtland, Gro Harlem (Prime Minister, Norway) 115–16
Brussels 95, 172, 191; International Military Staff (NATO) 167
Bulmer, S. 9

Campaign against Military Bases 107
Camus, Albert 133
Canada 39
capital, free movement of *see* 'four freedoms'
Checchini Report 39
China 178
civil service *see* administration, national
classes, social 69
coalitions 7, 24–5, 30, 33, 41, 107
'cod wars' 2–3, 24, 191
cold war 103, 106–7, 109, 110–11, 153
collective memories 135
Commission, European *see* European Commission
Committee on Europe 77–8, 91, 205
committees, government 75–8
Common Fisheries Policy 10, 89, 90–1, 92–3, 94–5, 96, 128, 129–30
Common Foreign and Security Policy (CFSP) (EU) 11, 104, 116–17, 118–19
Competition and Fair Trade Authority 70
competitiveness: and European free trade areas 23–4
Confederation of Fisheries Employers 73–4
Confederation of Icelandic Employers 27, 44–5, 73, 77, 79, 87, 154–5, 201–2, 203
consensus model (Moon) 122
Conservatives *see* Independence Party
constraints 9, 62–3, 63–4, 65, 188–90
Corgan, M.T. 115
corporatism 14, 203
Council of Europe 116, 178, 194
Council of Ministers 95, 161, 163
currencies: common currency *see* euro, adoption of; fluctuations 73
Cyprus 163, *164*, 175

de Gaulle, Charles (French President) 3, 28, 63
defence 151, 204; agreement with USA 11, 103–4, 105–18; and attitudes to EU 104, 115–17, 189–90; EU co-operation 46; European perspective 115–19; evolution of policy 113–14; Iceland's strategic location 103, 111; peacekeeping force 178; position of parties 105–7; and Schengen membership 200
Delors, Jacques (President of the European Commission) 40
Denmark 5, 26, 32, 46, 61, *164*; Act of Union 137, 150; national administration 14; at NATO 167; and Schengen 51–2, 54; views on EU membership 5
discourse, political 13, 138–9, 190–3

EAGGF (European Agricultural Guidance and Guarantee Fund) 196
Eastern Europe 27, 29, 31, 105, 119 *see also* Russia; Soviet Union
EC (European Community) *see* EU (European Union, formerly EC, EEC)
ECA (Econonic Cooperation Administration) 119
economic zone 23, 24, 33
Economic Cooperation Administration (ECA) 119
ECSC (European Coal and Steel Community) 22, 62
education: European programmes 140; political elite 153
EEA (European Economic Area) 3, 194; alleviating constraints 9, 63–4; amendments to Agreement 176; attitudes of political parties 41–3; consequences of membership *169*; debate in Althingi 42–3; EEA Agreement *vs.* Schengen 53–4; effects of EEA Agreement 45–7, 172–3; importance for exports 71–2; obligations of membership 38; opposition to joining 86–7; and sectoral groups 44–5; and sovereignty 138
EEC (European Economic Community) *see* EU (European Union, formerly EC, EEC)
EFTA Committee (Iceland) 75, 76–7
EFTA (European Free Trade Association) 2–3, 24; 1961 report on possible membership 25–6; and EU 25, 39–41; export to *71*; negotiations on membership 30–1; obstacles to membership 26; opposition to membership 30, 32; permanent mission in Geneva 166; pros and cons 28–30, 63; relationship with EU 25
elections, general *see* general elections
electoral system *see* elections, general; party system
electorate 5, *156*; discussion on EEA membership 3; lack of interest in Europe 186; support for EU membership 5–6, 146–7
Elias, Norman 135–6

elite, political: domestic power base 192; against EU membership 146; fear of European constraints 65; foreign contacts 152–4; nationalism 138–9, 191–2; other countries 145–6; pro-European 147–50; realist conception of foreign policy 13, 150–2, 192–3
Embassies of Iceland 154, 178
employment, policy on 78
enlargement *see under* EU (European Union, formerly EC, EEC)
equality, principle of 27, 29
Estonia *164*
EU (European Union, formerly EC, EEC) *see also* CFP (Common Fisheries Policy, EU): attitude of fishing industry 73–4; attitudes of political elites 145–7; co-operation of member states 46; Common Foreign and Security Policy 104; consequences of membership *169*, 175; debate on membership 3, 26–8, 87–9, 128–30; defence co-operation 116; Delors initiative, 1989 40; and EEA Agreement 46; and EFTA 25, 39–41; enlargement 175–6; export to *71*; free trade agreement 32–3; lack of democratic scrutiny 148; as nation-state 135–6; and NATO 117–18; not relevant to defence 109–10, 123, 189–90; opposition based on fishing interests 89–93, 154–5; proposed ban on fishmeal and oil in animal feeds 176; and Schengen scheme 51–6; and security policy 11; seen as imposing constraints 9, 62; and small member states 162–3, 198; tariffs on fish 26–7, 40, 72–3
euro, adoption of 46, 73, 90
Euro-scepticism xii, 145, 147
European Agricultural Guidance and Guarantee Fund (EAGGF) 196
European Coal and Steel Community *see* ECSC
European Commission 40, 162, 176–7, 195–6
European Community (EC) *see* EU (European Union, formerly EC, EEC)
European Council 116, 163, 178, 194
European Court of Human Rights 116
European Economic Area *see* EEA
European Economic Community (EEC) *see* EU (European Union, formerly EC, EEC)
European Foreign and Security Policy 18
European Free Trade Association *see* EFTA

European Parliament 161
European Policy Committee 75, 77
European Security and Defence Policy (ESDP) 18, 116–17, 118–19
Europeanization 161, 165, 174–5, 177, 181, 194
EUROPOL 46
Evrópusamtökin (pro-EU) 87–8, 89
exports 22, 29–31, 71–2, 153–4 *see also* tariffs; fishing industry *70*, *71*; to USA 121

FAO (Food and Agricultural Organization) 178
farmers 32, 42, 45; Farmers' Association of Iceland 27
Federation of Crafts and Industries 27
Federation of Icelandic Cooperative Societies (*Samband íslenskra samvinnufélaga*) 27, 76
Federation of Icelandic Fishing Vessel Owners 27, 74, 76, 79, 95, 96
Federation of Icelandic Industries 44, 73, 87, 89, 155, 201, 202
Finland 5, 10, 46, 52, 54, 64, 74, 91, 115, 123, *164*, 165, 166, 168, 178, 179, 180, 186, 191, 198; consequences of membership *169*; security 11; views on EU membership 5
Finnbogadóttir, Vigdís (President, Iceland) 43
fisheries and fishing *see also* Common Fisheries Policy: and anti-European feeling 155; attitude of industry to EEA 44; and Common Fisheries Policy 94–5; disputes 2–3, 24, 191; dominance within economy 69–71; EU ban on fishmeal and oil in animal feeds 176; EU tariffs on seafood 26–7, 39, 40; extension of economic zone 23, 24, 33; foreign investment 9 5; help from USA 119; implications of EEC 23; implications of EFTA 25; industry attitude to EU 73–4; largest obstacle to joining EU 89–93; management system 85–6; most important sector 10; political influence 85–6; and political parties 79, 80–2, 83–4; quota jumping 95; source of prosperity 67; symbol of sovereignty 137–8
Fisheries Congress 85
Foreign Ministers (Iceland) *see* Ásgrímsson, Halldór; Hannibalsson, Jón Baldvin
foreign policy 13, 150–2, 192–3

212 Index

Foreign Service (Iceland) *see also* administration, national: increased capabilities 177–8; increasing Europeanization 174–5; limited capacity 166–8; peacekeeping force 178; size 161, 163, *164*, *165*, 168–70
'four freedoms' 3, 40, 43, 63
France 23, 24, 50, 117, 133, 134, 135, 137, 154, *164*
free trade: agreement with EU 32–3; agriculture 204; government committee 76; and Iceland's competitiveness 23–4; Iceland's special position 26; OEEC negotiations 23–4; unwillingness to accept in postwar period 22–3
French Revolution 133

GATT Committee (Iceland) 76
GATT (General Agreement on Tariffs and Trade) 22, 63; 'Kennedy round' 28
Gellner, Ernest 132
general elections: 1999 6–7; 2003 5, 6, 186–8, 200; overrepresentation of rural regions 69
geography: Iceland's location 111–12, 123–4, 152–4
Germany 12, 23, 50, 61, 72, 114, 117, 134, 135, 153, 154, *164*
Gestsson, Svavar (MP of the People's Alliance) 43
Giddens, Anthony 133
Gísladóttir, Ingibjörg Sólrún (MP and prime minister candidate of the SDA) 43, 186
Gíslason, Gylfi P. (Social Democrat minister) 23, 25, 27, 30; criticisms of 32
globalization 134
goods, free movement of *see* 'four freedoms'
Government of Reconstruction 24–5, 30
Greece 23, *164*, 190
Gstöhl, S. 1, 12, 13, 130, 138, 140
Guéhenno, Jean-Marie 135, 138

Hannibalsson, Jón Baldvin (Minister for Foreign Affairs) 40, 41, 55
Hansen, L. 149
Hauksson, Úlfar 94–5
Heimssýn (anti-EU) 88, 89
Hermannsson, Steingrímur (Prime Minister) 40, 42
'herring boom' 28, 63
history 131–2, 135

Hroch, Miroslav 132
Hugason, Kristinn 85–6
hypothesis(es) 1–2, 8–14, 15, 62, 67, 97, 104, 123, 130, 147, 162, 189

Iceland *164*, *165*; birth of nation-state 130–3; campaign for home rule 107–8; compared with other small states 194–7; consequences of membership *169*; feelings towards world regions 104–5, 140; framework of case study 1–2; government committees 75–8; historical development 68–9; history of national administration 170–4; national unity 136–7; parliament *see* Althingi; party system 6–7; peripheral location 152–4; special position of 2; strategic significance 111–12, 123–4; uniqueness 8–9, 56–7
Iceland Chamber of Commerce 27, 44–5, 76, 79, 87, 89, 115, 155, 201–3
Iceland Defense Force 107, 110–13, 114–15; economic benefits 120, *121*, 122–3
Iceland Prime Contractor 120
Icelandic Commission on Security and Foreign Affairs 151–2, 167
Icelandic Federation of Labour 27, 45, 76, 77, 155, 200–1, 203
Icelandic Freezing Plants Corporation 27, 29
Icelandic Republic: foundation 130–3
identity, national *see* national identity
ideology 148, 149
Independence (Iceland) 107, 130–3
Independence Party: 2003 election 188; and agriculture 42, 82; attitude to EEA 41, 42; attitudes to Schengen 55; coalition with Progressive Party 7, 109; coalition with SDP 7, 24–5, 30, 41; connections with commerce and fishing 79; connections to sectors *81–3*; debate on EEC 27; and defence 105, 115; and fishing 79, 83; and fishing industry 42, 81; and free trade areas 24; no consensus on EU 205; opposition to EU 4, 89–90, 128, 156–8, 205; position of parties *106*; unity of 7
Ingebritsen, C. 9–11, 67–8, 74–5, 77, 86, 97–8, 148–9, 189; critics 12–13
Ingimundarson, V. 107–8, 109, 111, 119–20, 139, 166–7
Institute for International Affairs, University of Iceland 152
interest groups 26, 27, 41–5, 96, 179–80;

Index 213

occupational sectors and social movements 85–9; occupational sectors and the parties 78–85
interests, sectoral 179–80 *see also* agriculture; fisheries and fishing; manufacturing industry
intergovernmentalism 148–9
International Monetary Fund 22
investment: foreign 95
Iraq 109, 113, 114, 117, 190, 204
Ireland 3, 21, 23, 26, 28, 32, 56, 62, 72, *164*, 166, 198; and Schengen 4
Ísland í Evrópu (SDA report, 2001) 92–3
Italy 23, *164*

Jacobsson, Bengt 165–6
Japan 178
Jónsson, Eysteinn (Chairman of the Progressive Party) 32
Jónsson, Halldór 85–6

Katzenstein, P. 1, 8–9, 61–5, 188–9
Keflavík military base 103, 104, 105, *106*, 110–15, 123; contribution to Icelandic economy 12; public opposition 107–8
Keohane, R.O. 197–8
Kosovo 109
Kristinsson, G.H. 170–1
Kristjánsdóttir, Jóna V. (MP of the Women's Alliance) 139

languages, knowledge of 153
Latvia *164*
leadership xiii, 4, 6, 16, 23, 44, 95, 97, 107, 132, 157, 158, 159, 165, 172, 187, 192
Left Green Movement 5; 2003 election 188; and agriculture 82; and Committee on Europe 78; connections to sectors *81–3*; and defence 108–9; no connections with fishing industry 81, 82; opposition to EU 6, 93, 128–9, 205; opposition to NATO and agreement with USA 6; opposition to Schengen 55–6
legislation: EU and EEA Agreement 46; Iceland's based on Scandinavian 167
liberal intergovernmentalism 148–9
Liberal Party 7, 78, 108, 187–8, 205
Liechtenstein 72, 163–4, *164*, *165*, 195
Lithuania *164*
LÍU *see* Federation of Icelandic Fishing Vessel Owners
Luxembourg 50, 52, 117, 163, *164*, *165*, 194, 195, 197
Luxembourg Declaration 38–9

Lægreid, Per 161, 165–6

Maastricht Treaty 51
Malta 163, *164*, *165*, 175, 195–7, 198
manufacturing industry: attitude to EEA 44; attitude to EFTA 32; and fisheries sector 70; Iceland's competitiveness 23–4; lack of representation 85; and political parties 79, 80, 82–3
Marshall Plan 11, 22, 119, 122
member states (EU) 5, 46, 145–6, 175–6 *see also under* individual entries
memories, collective 135
MEPs 145–6
micro-states 163–4
military base *see* Keflavík military base
Ministers for Foreign Affairs (Iceland) *see* Hannibalsson, Jón Baldvin (Foreign Minister)
Ministry for Foreign Affairs (Iceland) *see* Ásgrímsson, Halldór; Hannibalsson, Jón Baldvin
Ministry of Commerce (Iceland) 29, 30
Mixed Committee (Schengen) 53
Monaco 163–4, *165*, 194
Monnet, Jean 147
Moon, B.E. 122
Moravcsik, A. 148
Morgunblaðið (newspaper) 5, 107, 109, 112, 114, 157
Morineau, Michel 134
Mozambique 178
MPs: EU member states 145–6, *156*; Iceland 80–6, 146 *see also* Althingi; entries for individual parties
Murmansk naval base 103

nation-state: foundation 130–3; viability 133–6
national administration *see* administration, national (Iceland)
national identity 12–13, 130, 149, 191
nationalism: in debate on EU membership 28; and defence 109; fundamental to Icelandic politics 151; grip on foreign policy 152; and the nation-state 132; of political elite 138–9, 191–2; public manifestation 136–7; and US military presence 107–8
NATO 11; opposition to 6
NATO (North Atlantic Treaty Organization): change in Iceland's policy 118–19; and Iceland's defence agreement with USA 103–4; limited capacity of representatives 166–7;

NATO (North Atlantic Treaty Organization) *contd.*
  position of parties *106*, 108–9; relationship with EU 117–18
Nej till EG (Norway) 87
neofunctionalism 148, 149–50
Netherlands, The 50, 111, *164*
Neumann, I. 1, 12–13, 130, 140
'new variables' 2, 194–7
Nigeria 120
Nora, Pierre 133
Nordic Council 199; and fish quotas 31
Nordic Passport Union 50, 51–2, 54, 55
Nordic states 46–7, 179, 192; attitudes of political elites 145, 146; co-operation with interest groups 179; comparative survey 165–6, 168–70; consultations about free trade 26; and EU membership 190–1; Icelandic collaboration 28; importance of good relations 104–5; industrial development fund 31; mutual co-operation 46–7; and Schengen scheme 51–3, 54–5; sectoral approach 74–5; views on EU membership 5
North America 105 *see also* Canada; United States
North Atlantic 103, 111, 118
Norway 4, 5, 12, 26, 32, 39, 61, *164*, 196–7; administration in EU/EEA 172–4; anti-EU movement 87; consequences of membership *169*; debates on EU membership 157; defence 104, 115–16, 118; EU as source of security 11; national administration 14; national identity 12–13; and NATO 115–16; at NATO 167; rejection of EU membership 4; and Schengen 52–4, 56–7; views on EU membership 5
Nugent, N. 163–4

Oddsson, Davíð (Prime Minister, Iceland) 157; 2003 election 188; on defence 115, 118; on the economy 73; on independence from Europe 128; limited influence of small states 198; and nationalism 139; outspoken critic of joining EU 7, 110; proposed Committee on Europe 77–8; on sovereignty 137–8
OEEC (Organization for European Economic Co-operation): benefits did not outweigh costs 62; debate on free trade area 2; exceptions from conditions 11; and Iceland's restrictive policy 22; negotiations on free trade area 23–4; US patronage of Iceland 22, 119
Old Icelandic Commonwealth 108
Olgeirsson, Einar (MP) 24, 131, 132
Organization for European Economic Co-operation *see* OEEC
OSCE (Organization of Security and Co-operation in Europe) 178

Pace, R. 198, 199
Parliament *see* Althingi
party system 6–7
peacekeeping 124, 178, 194
Pedersen, Ove K. 165–6
people, free movement of *see* 'four freedoms'; Nordic Passport Union; Schengen (Convention, Agreement, Acquis etc.)
People's Alliance 87; and agriculture 82; appeal to nationalism 28; coalition with Progressive Party 41, 107; coalition with Social Democratic Party 41, 107; connections to sectors *81–3*; and defence 106, 108; and fishing industry 82; formerly Socialist Party, Communist Party 6; and free trade areas 24; and manufacturing 83; opposition to EEA 41, 42, 43; opposition to EFTA 32; position of parties, 106
peripheral: or central placement 206; location 152; placement 13, 16, 147, 192
petition against defence policy 107
policy, foreign 150–2
political discourse 13, 138–9, 190–3
political elite *see* elite, political
political parties *see* party system
politicians *see* Althingi; elite, political; party system
population: defining size of a state 161–2
Portugal 24, 72, 39, 50, *164*, 190
poststructuralism 148
Presidents *see* Björnsson, Sveinn (President of Iceland); de Gaulle, Charles (President of France); Delors, Jacques (President of the European Commission); Finnbogadóttir, Vigdís (President of Iceland); Roosevelt, Franklin D. (President of the USA)
pressure groups 179–80
Prime Ministers: Benediktsson, Bjarni (Iceland); Brundtland, Gro Harlem

(Norway); Hermannsson, Steingrímur (Iceland); Oddsson, Davíð (Iceland); Thors, Ólafur (Iceland); Nordic 52
pro-European positions 87, 88–9, 110, 146–7, 147–50, 157–8; reluctance to adopt 5
producer subsidy equivalents 45
Progressive Party: 2003 election 187; and agriculture 82; coalition with Independence Party 7, 109; coalition with People's Alliance 41, 107; coalition with Social Democratic Party 41, 107; and Committee on Europe 78; connections with agriculture 79; connections to sectors *81–3*; and defence 105–6; dispute with government parties 28; and EFTA 30, 32; EU membership as option 4–5; and fishing industry 81; and free trade areas 24; and manufacturing 82; no consensus on EU 205; opposition to EEA 41, 42–3; opposition to EU 90–2; policy on fisheries 91; position of parties *106*; vote on EEA Agreement 42–3
'Protected Country' (petition slogan) 107
public opinion 105, 151

quota jumping 95

Ragnarsson, Kristján 74
realism 13, 150–2, 192–3
Reconstruction Government 24–5, 30
referenda 92, 139
regions, influence of 69, 155–6, 192
Renan, Ernest 135
Retailers' Association 27
Reykjavík 130–2, *156*, 171, 191
Roosevelt, Franklin D. 114
Rumsfeld, Donald (US defence secretary) 114
Russia 112

Samstaða um óháð Ísland (Stance on an Independent Iceland) 86–7
San Marino 163–4, *165*, 197
Scandinavia *see* Nordic states
scepticism about Europe 5, 6, 8, 13, 16, 41, 88, 128–30, 145–7, 156–9, 187–8, 192; Left Green Movement 6
Schengen (Convention, Agreement, Acquis etc.): background to Iceland's entry 51–3; Iceland's active participation 4; mixed committee 53; and national security 199–200; nature

of scheme 50–1; reasons for participation 54–6; unique situation of Iceland and Norway 56–7; voting system 53; *vs.* EEA Agreement 53–4
SDA (Social Democratic Alliance): 2003 election 186–7; and Committee on Europe 78; connection to sectors *81–3*; and defence 108; and fishing industry 82, 92–3; no connections with agricultural sector 82; policy on EU 6–7, 92–3, 205; referendum on EU entry 5; support for EU 205
SDP (Social Democratic Party): coalition with Independence Party 7, 24–5, 30, 41; coalition with People's Alliance 41, 107; coalition with Progressive Party 41, 107; connection to sectors *81–3*; debate on EEC 27; and defence 105; on EEA Agreement 63–4; and fishing industry 81–2; and free trade areas 24; and manufacturing 83; no connections with agricultural sector 82; policy 4; position of parties *106*; and Social Democratic Alliance (SDA) 4; support of EEA 41, 42
seafood *see* fisheries and fishing
Second World War 22, 69, 119, 153
sectoral approach 9–11, 67–8, 74–5, 77, 86, 97–8, 148–9, 189; critics 12–13
sectoral interests 41–5, 179–80
sectors *see* agriculture; fisheries and fishing; manufacturing industry
security *see* defence: aviation 46
Security Council (UN) 178, 194
services, free movement of *see* 'four freedoms'
Sigfússon, Steingrímur J. (Chairman of the Left Green Movement) 93
Single European Act, 1986 39
SÍS *see* Federation of Icelandic Cooperative Societies (*Samband íslenskra samvinnufélaga*)
size 13–14, 162, 193–4
Skarphéðinsson, Össur (Chairman of the SDA) 92
Slovakia *164*
Slovenia *164*
small states 1, 2, 63, 188–9, 194–7, 199, 206; administrative procedures 13–14; behaviour within EU 162–3; case of Iceland 64–5; characteristics 2; definition 161–2, 197–8; and Germany 61–2; micro-states 163–4; response to European integration 8–9; in the third world 105

Smith, Anthony D. 134, 135
Social Democratic Alliance *see* SDA
Social Democrats *see* SDA and SDP
Social Democratic Party *see* SDP
Sogner, I. 1, 11, 104, 189
Southern Europe 124, 190
sovereignty 132, 137–8, 199; life-blood of the nation 108
Soviet Union *see also* cold war; USSR
Spain 39, 50, 72, 154, *164*, 190
'special relationship' Iceland and USA *see* United States: defence agreement with Iceland; United States: economic relationship with Iceland
states: definitions of size 161–2, 163; Nordic *see* Nordic states; small states *see* small states
structuralism 149
supranationalism 135–6
Sweden 5, 10, 12, 24, 26, 39, 46, 52, 54, 61, 64, 73, 74, 75, 145, *164*, 165, 166, 168, 172, 179, 180, 191, 298, 203; consequences of membership *169*; views on EU membership 5
Switzerland 24, 145, *164*

tariffs: EFTA 31; EU 39, 72–3; Icelandic 26, 29
terrorism 114
The Netherlands *see* Netherlands, The
theoretical considerations 8–14; the 2003 debate 186–8; constraints, sectors, security 188–90; domestic changes 200–6; domestic characteristics 194–7; national administration: size and characteristics 193–4; 'new variable' 194–7; political discourse 190–3; political elite 190–3, 194–7; security 188–90; theories underpinning the study 1–2
Third World 105
Thorlacius, Birgir (high-ranking official, Iceland) 151
Thors, Ólafur (Prime Minister) 24, 27, 131
Treaty of Amsterdam 46, 51, 52–3

Treaty of Maastricht (Treaty of the European Union) 51
Treaty of Rome 27, 51
Turkey 23

UNESCO (UN Educational, Scientific and Cultural Organization) 178
Union of Fishery Workers 76
Union of Icelandic Fish Producers 44
Union of Liberals and Leftists 33, 107
Union of Stockfish Producers 27
United Kingdom *see* Britain
United Nations 164, 178, 194
United States of America: defence agreement with Iceland 6, 11, 103–4, 105–18, 190, 204; economic relationship with Iceland 11–12, 104, 119–21; export 71; exports from Iceland 72, 153; future of agreements 124; government policy 11–12, 111–12, 119–20; Iceland's support of policies 109; State Department 111
University of Iceland 152
US government *see under* United States
US military base *see* Keflavík military base
USSR 103, 111, 112, 119 *see also* cold war; trade 24, 31

Varynen, R. 161
Vatican City 164
voters *see* electorate
vulnerability 114–15, 190

'wait and see' policy (Iceland) 4, 25, 42, 146, 187–8
Wallace, H. 148, 149
Wallace, W. 9, 61
Western Europe 105
Western European Union 117
Wolfowitz, P. 114
Women's Alliance 5, 6, 7, 43, 47, 87; and defence 108; and Social Democratic Alliance (SDA) 4
World Bank 22
World Trade Organization 47, 204

Made in the USA
Coppell, TX
15 March 2021